D0990610

DISCARDED

THE
UNIVERSITY OF WINNIPEG
PORTAGE & BALMORAL
WINNIPEG 2. MAN.   CANADA

The Nature of Democracy

JC
423
.H744
1974

The Nature of Democracy

BARRY HOLDEN

Nelson

Thomas Nelson and Sons Ltd
36 Park Street London W1Y 4DE

Nelson (Africa) Ltd
PO Box 18123 Nairobi Kenya

Thomas Nelson (Australia) Ltd
597 Little Collins Street Melbourne 3000

Thomas Nelson and Sons (Canada) Ltd
81 Curlew Drive Don Mills Ontario

Thomas Nelson (Nigeria) Ltd
PO Box 336 Apapa Lagos

First published in Great Britain by Thomas Nelson and Sons Ltd., 1974

Copyright © Barry Holden 1974

All Rights Reserved. No part of this publication may be reproduced,
stored in a retrieval system, or transmitted, in any form or by
any means, electronic, mechanical, photocopying, recording or otherwise,
without the prior permission of the publishers.

ISBN 0 17 711074 0 (boards)
 0 17 712074 6 (paper)

Printed in Great Britain by A. Wheaton & Co., Exeter.

Contents

To the Memory of my Mother

Preface

The idea of writing a general book on democracy developed from a more specific interest in the relationship between democratic theory and the findings of studies of voting behaviour. A consideration of this relationship inevitably raised general issues concerning the nature of democracy. And this, together with a conviction that there were few discussions of democracy that covered the right ground, led to a desire to attempt a general analysis of democracy. Moreover, an attempt at an analysis of this kind is connected with an interest in a more general issue lying behind the original concern with voting behaviour and democratic theory : the question of the relationship between political philosophy and the empirical analysis of politics.

There are many to whom I am grateful for help, although I am, of course, entirely responsible for shortcomings, deficiencies or errors. In particular I should like to thank the following. Dr J. C. Rees of Swansea University for first suggesting that I should look at the implications of voting behaviour studies for democratic theory. Professor A. H. Birch of Exeter University, Professor D. M. Emmett, and Professor W. J. M. Mackenzie of Glasgow University (all formerly at Manchester University) for their help with, and comments upon, my first inadequate attempts at analysing these implications. Professor P. W. Campbell and Mr A. J. Coates, both colleagues of mine at Reading University, for their assistance with the book itself. Professor Campbell read most of the draft manuscript and made many helpful comments. Mr Coates read part of the manuscript and similarly provided helpful comments. In addition he has helped me to develop both my general ideas and those specific to this book; in both respects I have benefited much from discussions with him. I should like also to thank the general editor of this series, Dr K. W. Watkins of Sheffield University. He read the whole book in draft and made numerous helpful comments and suggestions.

Last, but not least, I would like to thank my family. My wife not only put up with the disruption of family life that the writing of this book involved, but she also typed most of the manuscript as well as suggesting improvements to it. My children likewise uncomplainingly accepted the suspension of ordinary family life. To Barbara, Karen and Robert my grateful thanks.

Reading 1973

Introduction

The aim of this book is to provide a concise overall view of the subject of democracy. It is not, of course, possible to cover every aspect of the subject. Rather, there is an attempt to indicate and clarify some of the key points concerning the nature of the concept of democracy and its relationship to the political systems with which it is associated. It is an attempt worth making, not only because democracy is important, but also because considerations of the concept of democracy and its relationship with political reality tend to be fraught with difficulty and confusion. This is in part due to the inherent difficulties—but only in part. It is also due to certain (often unnecessary) confusions engendered by modern political analysis. This is not to deny that modern analysis has been of great importance for democracy and has in significant ways increased our understanding of it. But it is to say that, in some ways, modern anlaysis has posed difficulties for, and confused our perception of, the theory and practice of democracy. This introduction will indicate briefly how and why this has happened. The body of the book will be concerned (among other things) with the attempt to bring some clarity to these areas of difficulty and confusion.

An important characteristic of modern political analysis has been the development of the 'positivist' approach to the study of politics.[1] By this is meant the desire and the attempt to study politics scientifically. More specifically, the guiding idea is that politics should be studied by means of what are believed to be the methods and techniques of the natural sciences, particularly physics. The basis for this idea is the view that scientific analysis of this kind is the only reliable way to obtain knowledge. Hence the application of what is conceived as the epistemology and methodology of the natural sciences to the study of politics—and to other spheres of social inquiry as well.

There are also many students of politics who are critical of the positivist approach. The present author would agree that this approach involves some fundamental mistakes and confusions—although not accepting everything said by some 'anti-positivists'.[2] However, the point to be made here is the more restricted one of showing that the positivist approach has, in some important respects, brought confusion to the subject of democracy. It has done so in four main ways. First, it has by-passed or misconstrued the nature of important conceptual problems, and thereby made them more problematical. Secondly, empirical work (a central feature of the positivist approach) on democracy has been, in important ways, vitiated by this conceptual confusion. Thirdly, empirical studies have apparently produced findings that pose crucial problems of substance for democratic theory. Fourthly, the positivist approach has involved, or been involved with, a view of the nature of moral judgements and their role in academic analysis that has removed from political analysis a vital element of democratic theorizing—the justification of democracy. These issues will be discussed in the body of the book, but it will be helpful to provide a conspectus at this point.

First, then, the misperception of conceptual problems. What has happened is that some crucial problems concerning the concept of democracy and its application have often been ignored or misperceived. Consequently, they have either been inadequately dealt with, or they have been made more difficult by not being dealt with at all. Problems do not go away when ignored, but become more difficult by manifesting themselves in unperceived ways.

This partial blindness to the conceptual problems of democracy is connected with the positivist approach in two interrelated ways. First, the emphasis on empirical work has often involved what is seen as a direct approach to the analysis of political reality without the intervention of 'woolly abstractions' and 'ivory tower theorizing'. The idea has been that knowledge of democracy should be obtained by direct and 'uncluttered' inspection of actual democracies. But not only is this to forget that all inspection and observation is conceptually structured,[3] it is also to ignore, and thereby further obscure, such questions as whether, and by virtue of what, these 'actual democracies' are democracies. There has, indeed, often been a fundamental confusion over the definition of democracy. There has been a tendency to 'by-pass' the question of definition, in the interests of undelayed and 'unsullied' empirical work, and to assume—illegitimately—that political systems are democracies simply because they are commonly called democracies. This 'definitional fallacy' is discussed in Chapter I.

The empirical work of most positivist analysts is, however, supplemented and organized by theories and conceptual frameworks. But this often only serves to further complicate and confuse the issue. This is the other way in which the obscuring of the conceptual problems of democracy is connected with the positivist approach to political analysis. What tends to happen is that the concepts of the analysts' 'empirical theories' structure the subject-matter rather than the concepts of democratic theory. And this tends to mean that conceptual problems of *democracy* are ignored (and thereby further obscured) in favour of the conceptual problems of the 'scientific theory'. Such scientific theory is concerned with aspects of political systems called democracies, but does not necessarily constitute a theory of democracy any more than a theory of linguistics constitutes a theory of literature. This kind of theorizing, then, not only often commits the 'definitional fallacy', but tends also to obscure other crucial conceptual issues, including questions of how the definition of 'democracy' is to be interpreted. Simple answers are assumed to such questions as those concerning the notion of the 'will of the people', rather than being reasoned out of the complex issues involved. Of course, not all 'scientific theory' ignores the conceptual problems of democracy in this way. Indeed, some varieties explicitly set out to deal with some of these problems—most notably those theories that seek to deal 'rigorously' with questions concerning the summation of individual preferences (see Chapter 4). But there is much 'empirical democratic theory' that by-passes these problems. Even the rigorous conceptual theory just mentioned fastens on only one aspect of the conceptual questions and thereby ignores the others and confuses the overall issues.

The substantive issues with which empirical democratic theory is usually concerned centre on attempts to explain the existence and workings of political systems called democracies.[4] Again, because the focus is on this rather than on the crucial conceptual problems, the latter tend to be ignored and/or drastically oversimplified.

Scientific empirical democratic theory, then, tends to obscure central conceptual problems of democracy, both because its subject is something other than these and because it involves and generates conceptual problems of its own. The latter are concerned with the nature of the scientific theory rather than with the nature of democracy.

Confusion of this kind has meant not only that the conceptual issues have been obscured, but also that the empirical work itself has suffered. Positivists exclude the concepts most helpful (because most relevant) in organizing their empirical work when they lose sight of the traditional central concepts of democracy. Moreover, they are also diverted into problems, of method and approach, that further vitiate their work—besides having little to do with the subject of democracy. For example, studies of the necessary conditions of democracy tend to become exercises in statistical correlations (with their attendant methodological problems) of various factors with insufficiently analysed features of the political systems called democracies. They lose sight of the extent to which such studies demand analysis of the various features to determine how far they *are* constituents of democracy.

The empirical analysis then loses much of its depth and insight—as well as putting its relevance at risk.

The third main way in which positivist political analysis has produced difficulties in thinking about democracy arises from some of the findings and analyses it has come up with. Traditional democratic theory has been confronted by a portrayal of actual political systems seriously at odds with its own models of them. Studies of pressure groups, elites and voting behaviour have yielded a picture of the Western 'democracies' very different from the kind of political system outlined in traditional democratic theory. The difficulties and issues raised by this discrepancy are taken up in Chapters 5 and 6. These problems—some of them complex—have added further to the general confusion surrounding the subject of democracy.

The fourth of the ways in which confusion has been engendered stems from the positivist view of the nature and role of moral judgements. A hallmark of positivist political analysis has been the notion of value freedom. Scientific political analysis, it is held, is value-free —political analysis that is free of all value judgements, including (and especially) moral judgements. Value judgements are seen as subjective, arbitrary and non-rational : perhaps expressions of emotion, perhaps calls to action.[5] As such they are not the concern of science, since they cannot be shown to be true or false—indeed, statements conveying value judgements are not statements of which it makes sense to ask whether they are true or false. Scientific analysis, then, should not contain, and cannot 'validate', value judgements. In this way the positivist approach has excluded from academic political analysis the question of the justification of democracy. Value judgements concerning democracy are to be excluded along with all other value judgements.

This banning of the evaluation of democracy from political analysis has produced yet further confusion. It is bewildering for the citizens of democracies to be told not to turn to political analysts for help in dealing with such important questions as whether and why democracy is a good system of government. Nor is it any comfort to be referred to political philosophers for help, since, according to the positivists' account of value judgements, the 'answers' to such questions are subjective and arbitrary. What the political philosopher tells us is just as subjective and arbitrary as anyone else's view. One is forced to the sad and puzzling conclusion that there are to these questions no answers as such, and that political philosophy is an intellectual game with no apparent purpose other than that of intellectual amusement.[6] In so far as it is anything more than this, we have been told that it consists in the clarification of concepts.[7] This view of the irrelevance of political philosophy to the answering of questions about the value of democracy is often—somewhat paradoxically—reinforced by another and very different current of thought : that which sees political philosophy (and, indeed, all ideas about politics) as the outcome of the thinkers' position in society rather than as the expression of detached and objective reasoning. Such 'outcomes' are often viewed as expressions of group—usually class—interest : evolution then becomes rationalization rather than objectively valid justification. If the justifications of democracy are explained away as ideas that were bound to arise from a certain sort of social structure and situation, they will lose their point and their effectiveness. When all political thought becomes ideology,[8] 'evaluations'—including those contained in political philosophy—become but part of a socially determined outlook and lose their central feature of making a case for or against something.

The undermining of justification not only causes confusion in the way just indicated, but also calls in question the whole status and validity of traditional democratic theory. A central feature of such theory was the evolution of democracy and its characteristics—and it is exactly this kind of enterprise that is apparently being disposed of. Democratic theory is destroyed along with the rest of political philosophy in the way we have just seen. This destruction of traditional democratic theory adds yet more confusion to all thought about democracy! Our view of democracy is derived from traditional democratic theory. With the demise of the theory, our thinking is thrown into confusion as the crucial concepts and the rationale are dispensed with or called into question.

Value freedom has, then, had a powerful and dislocating effect upon thinking about democracy—an effect that has also arisen in a very different way from ideas about the social determination of political thinking. Some of these issues are discussed in Chapter 8, where the 'debunking' of academic evaluation is critically assessed.

Democracy—the idea and its application—has always needed careful analysis. Too often, instead of providing this, modern political science has—for the reasons just outlined—brought obscurity. The aim of this book will be to attempt to introduce some clarity. Clarification will be attempted of a number of matters besides those already mentioned. Different sorts of democracy will be analysed and related to the general definition of democracy—and it will be explained that the main concern of this book is with 'Western' or liberal-democracy (Chapter 2). The relationship between the concepts of 'liberal' and 'democratic' will also be briefly considered. Traditional theories of democracy will be outlined in Chapter 3, while modern theories, and their relationship to traditional theories, will be discussed in Chapter 6. This latter discussion will form part of the general analysis of the implications of the findings of political science for democratic theory that was referred to above

(p. x). Before this—in Chapter 4—some 'internal difficulties' of democratic theory will be discussed : difficulties and issues raised by the
translating of differing individual decisions into *a* collective decision
by the whole people. The question of the necessary conditions for
democracy is taken up in Chapter 7. Besides an indication of some of
the main theories involved, the concept of 'necessary conditions' is itself
analysed. Particular attention is paid to some distinctions that are
commonly blurred, in particular the relationship between the necessary
conditions and the defining features of democracy. Finally, in Chapter
9, there is a brief discussion of some contemporary critiques of liberal-
democracy.

The effort to clarify will inevitably involve some compression and
simplification, but it is hoped that this will be kept within permissible
limits. In what follows the aim will be to provide the reader with an
introduction and a guide to the many themes, ideas and issues that are
raised by a consideration of democracy and what it involves.

NOTES AND REFERENCES

1 The full flowering of the positivist approach was represented in 'behaviouralism'. Indeed, for some, behaviouralism—or the behaviouralist approach
—seems to be synonymous with the positivist approach to political analysis.
On behaviouralism (or, more accurately, 'behavioralism'—as it is predominantly an American word and activity), see, for example, the first
three contributions (and the references cited therein) to J. C. Charlesworth,
Contemporary Political Analysis, New York, The Free Press, 1967; and H.
Eulau, *Behavioralism in Political Science*, New York, Atherton Press, 1969.

2 A comprehensive and excellent treatment of many of the central issues can
be found in H. Stretton, *The Political Sciences*, London, Routledge & Kegan
Paul, 1969. Stretton argues an 'anti-positivist' case—but not in a dogmatic
manner, and with a full appreciation of all the complexities involved.

3 This is now very widely acknowledged, and it is (as indicated in the text)
only the more 'naïve' positivists who would overlook this. There are, however, different varieties of this recognition of conceptual structuring. These
vary from the acknowledgement that selection of problems and data is
guided by concepts (especially of value—as mentioned below), through the
view that 'raw data' are unmanageable unless we arrange and classify them
with concepts, to the notion that our whole perception of reality is structured
for us by concepts. Positivism would normally be understood to include
positions up to an area somewhere between the second and third conceptions. It may be objected that the third notion is also involved in natural
science. However, the point here is that the positivist approach to the study
of politics involves a *conception of* natural science—which may or may not
correspond with actual scientific activity.

4 See, for example, C. F. Cnudde and D. E. Neubauer, *Empirical Democratic
Theory*, Chicago, Markham Publishing Co., 1969.

5 See Chapter 7 for further discussion of the nature of value judgements, and of the conception of value freedom. The present discussion refers to only one aspect of this conception—although it is the one most affecting thought about democracy. This aspect has been summed up by A. Brecht by the term 'Scientific Value Relativism'—A. Brecht, *Political Theory*, Princeton, Princeton University Press, 1967 (first published 1959).

6 This is, perhaps, an exaggeration. Nonetheless, it is true that the positivist approach has apparently undermined the whole enterprise of political philosophy, and consequently that there is considerable puzzlement about the nature and purpose of political philosophy. For a discussion of political philosophy and modern trends in political analysis, see, for example, D. Germino, *Beyond Ideology: The Revival of Political Theory*, New York, Harper & Row, 1967; articles in, and the introductions to, the four series of *Philosophy, Politics and Society* (first edited by P. Laslett, second and third by P. Laslett and W. G. Runciman, and fourth by P. Laslett, W. G. Runciman and Q. Skinner), Oxford, Basil Blackwell, 1956, 1962 1967, and 1972; and Chapter 27 ('Political Theory and the Science of Politics') of L. C. McDonald, *Western Political Theory*, New York, Harcourt, Brace, 1968.

7 See T. D. Weldon, *The Vocabulary of Politics*, Harmondsworth, Middlesex, Penguin Books, 1953.

8 In this sense of that slippery and complex term. This notion of the social determination of ideas is fairly central to the concept of ideology, and one which is associated with the best-known exponents of the concept and its validity—Marx and Mannheim. For a lucid discussion of these points, and an excellent short introduction to the whole subject of ideology, see J. Plamenatz, *Ideology*, London, Pall Mall, 1970.

CHAPTER I

The Definition of Democracy

In order to analyse democracy it is first necessary to define it. This would be true even if a full definition were to be left until after the analysis. Without a working definition of 'democracy' the analysis of democracy could not begin, for we would not know what to begin analysing. Those writers who say, or imply, that initial definition is unnecessary are merely deceiving themselves and their readers. The area of their investigation is delimited by an unexamined and ill-formed implicit conception rather an an explicit definition. The initial demarcation is—as it must be—always there, but it can become unnecessarily vague and confused if it is not brought to light in some sort of a definition,[1] even when the formulation of a full definition is left until after the analysis.

It is, then, necessary at this stage to define democracy. However, the definition of democracy is a notoriously difficult and controversial business. It will be argued shortly that the difficulties and disagreements involved are not nearly so great as is commonly supposed—or, at least, that many of them pertain to something other than the question of the *definition* of democracy. Nonetheless, there are certain difficulties; and it will also be necessary to look at some of the reasons why it is so often supposed that many more exist. So, before we construct a definition —and before we look at a prevalent fundamental confusion concerning the definition of democracy—some of these complications will be outlined.

To begin with, there is a genuine difficulty in defining any word used in widely varying circumstances and often with little thought for the way in which it is being used. Moreover, 'democracy' is used with regard to political systems—complex phenomena about which thinking is notoriously vague and confused. In short, 'democracy' *is* a slippery term and its meaning *is* vague and confused.

It is, however, fairly commonly held that there is vagueness and confusion to such a degree that the term 'democracy' has become virtually meaningless. Such a view arises from the observation that, on occasion, virtually everything political (and not only things political) has been called 'democracy' or 'democratic'. The position appears to be that one can label anything one wishes a 'democracy'. When a term is applied to everything and anything, it simply ceases to have any meaning at all—it ceases to have any distinguishing features.

It is also quite often argued that this intolerable vagueness is associated with—and reinforced by—another feature of modern conceptions of democracy : the universal approval given to democracy. This, it is argued, often results in people labelling as a 'democracy' any political system of which they approve. This can mean that definitions of democracy vary as moral judgements vary : each will define 'democracy' as whatever type of political system he judges as morally best. This, of course, is to confuse moral judgements with questions of meaning. One's ideal political system may or may not be a democracy, and to characterize it as a democracy *merely* because one judges it the best is to cause, and be the victim of, a fundamental confusion. Moreover, the corollary of this is that one cannot define 'democracy' without implying that one approves of that which appears in the definition. As one writer put it : 'The problem [regarding the definition of "democracy"] . . . which might appear to be a purely semantic one, is complicated by the fact that democracy today is regarded as an ideal régime symbolizing a positive value, for which men will fight. By giving "democracy" a certain definition, the positive value is transferred to the meaning defined, so that discussion on the meaning of "democracy" centres, not on the question of language, but on the ideal political régime.'[2] It is sometimes felt that this sort of confusion has become so bad that the term 'democracy' has been emptied of all descriptive meaning. 'Democracy', it is said, has become a 'hurrah ! word'. The idea is that the use of the word 'democracy' merely shows that the speaker approves of that to which the word is being applied, but that nothing is conveyed about its nature : in other words, 'This political system is a democracy', could be rephrased as, 'Hurrah for this political system'.

It is quite true that this kind of confusion about the meaning of 'democracy' does exist—in the sense that, when people come to define the word, these sorts of muddle do occur. This is, however, largely an instance of people becoming muddled in their definitions rather than the actual meaning of the word exhibiting these characteristics. Words are used and understood with much greater ease than they are defined. 'People understand each other rather better than they understand each other's definitions.'[3] In other words, characteristics of definitions do not necessarily reflect characteristics of meanings. And it seems to the present writer that moral approval is not actually part of the very meaning of 'democracy'. It is logically quite possible—although unusual —to say, 'This political system is a democracy and I disapprove of it.'

It is true that democracy now attracts almost universal approval. There-fore there is always a danger that the approval—and anything that is approved—will get mixed up with the meaning, particularly when definitions are being formed. But this *is* a question of separate items being confounded.[3a]

The meaning of 'democracy', then, has not become emptied of descriptive content because of the widespread approval of democracy. But we are still left with the argument that the term is applied to a wide variety of political systems (whether or not because of approval of the systems in question). There is no denying that, because of this, there is a certain vagueness about the meaning. However, this is not nearly so great as is often supposed. Very often, where 'democracy' is applied to very different political systems—to the American or the Russian, say—this reflects not a difference in meanings so much as a difference in conceptions that are held to fall within an agreed meaning and a difference in interpretation of the nature of the political systems in question. Such differing conceptions and interpretations go together with different theoretical outlooks which crucially affect (and therefore yield differing interpretations of) components of the common meaning; this is an aspect of the notion of 'logically necessary conditions' (see below). In other words, I am suggesting that an American and a Russian could agree that 'democracy' meant, say, 'government by the people',[4] but that they would disagree about whether the American and Russian political systems were ones in which government by the people was a fact—and that part of the reason for this disagreement would be differing conceptions of how the people could be said to govern. Dis-agreements about whether Britain, America, Russia, etc., are democ-racies are, after all, rather more important and substantial than assertions of different linguistic usages. Such disagreements are *not* in fact resolved by calling attention to different meanings of the word 'democracy'. It is true that the apparently different meanings are often reflected in actually different definitions—but we have already recog-nized that definitions can vary in a way that meanings do not.

It can be seen, then, that questions of meaning become confused with other questions. In particular, there are five different questions that frequently become hopelessly muddled together : (1) What is the mean-ing of the term 'democracy'? (2) What are the logically necessary conditions for democracy? (3) What are the empirically necessary con-ditions for democracy? (4) What are the features associated with or promoted by democracy? and (5) What are the desirable features associated with or promoted by democracy? Disagreements about answers to the last four of these question often become mistaken for dis-agreements about anwers to the first (as well as becoming confused with each other). But only if there is some agreement about the meaning of democracy can there be intelligible and significant disagreement about the answers to the other questions.

Before illustrating the muddle that may be caused by a failure to attend to these distinctions, it is necessary to explain the difference between empirically and logically necessary conditions. An empirically necessary condition is one which has to be present before a democracy can come into—or remain long in—existence. It would be *logically* possible for a democracy to exist without the presence of this condition —indeed, it might in fact exist for a short time. However, empirical study would have led to the conclusion that, in fact, it could not exist— or exist for long—without the presence of this factor. Further empirical study might reveal this to be a mistaken conclusion. Similarly, the presence of air in a form that was absorbable by human lungs might be thought to be an empirically necessary condition for the existence of a man. Yet future development might conceivably show that a man could be provided with artificial gills and thereby enabled to exist underwater. But it might also be said that the existence of a brain is a *logically* necessary condition for the existence of a man. The assertion here would be that even if a being—otherwise like a man—could exist without a brain, we would not call him a man.[5]

An example may help to make the point clearer (further examples and discussion will be found in Chapter 7, which is devoted to the subject of the necessary conditions of democracy). Freedom of speech is something that frequently manages to obscure the differences between our five questions. Very often it is not clear whether an author sees freedom of speech as one of the defining characteristics of democracy, as one of the conditions logically necessary for its existence, as one of the conditions empirically necessary for its existence, as one of the features that accompanies democracy, or as one of the things that are desirable about democracy—or as some combination of these.[6] That is to say, it is not often made clear whether it is being said that freedom of speech enters into the meaning of the term 'democracy' or whether, without saying this, it is nonetheless asserted that it has to exist if a political system is to be called a democracy; or whether the assertion is that a political system called a democracy will not, as a matter of fact, be able to exist—or to continue long in existence—unless freedom of speech is present. Or the assertion might simply be that freedom of speech is usually found in democracies, although such an assertion is usually accompanied by the judgement that this is one of the desirable features of democracy (such a judgement also usually accompanies the first three views of the relationship between freedom of speech and democracy). The present writer's view is that freedom of speech is not a defining feature. It is true that it is often listed as such, but this is more correctly to be regarded as spelling out a view of what is necessary to bring about 'government by the people'—in other words, the assertion of a necessary condition. It is not always too clear, however, whether it is being seen as an empirically or a logically necessary condition. The reasoning would usually be of the form : government by the people is government in accordance with the will of the people; if the true will of the people is to exist and to assert itself, then all points of view must be allowed expression. This is held to be necessary both to allow a proper flow of information for the formulation of the popular will, and to allow the proper expression—and therefore assertion—of the popular will once it is formulated.

A further complication about the meaning of democracy to be cleared out of the way concerns a historical change. The meaning of democracy is now broader than it was in the eighteenth century :[7] consequently some of the fountainheads of democratic theory—Tom Paine, for example—at times proclaim themselves to be advocating something other than democracy. It appears that, at least up until near the end of the eighteenth century, the meaning of the term 'democracy' was restricted to what would now be called direct democracy—a political system in which the people governed directly rather than through the medium of elections and representative institutions. 'It seems to be a rule without any exceptions at all that "democracy" was not used to express . . . a concept where "representative rule" or "representative or direct rule" were conceptual characteristics, or were properties implied by conceptual characteristics. Further it may be said that all actual governments labelled "democracies" (that is, taken as denotata of a concept labelled "democracy") were direct. This holds good at least up to the time of the Constitutional Convention (1787).'[8] Today, however, the term 'democracy' quite clearly includes within its meaning both direct *and* indirect (representative) democracy—as the very term 'indirect democracy' indicates. Some of the issues involved here are further discussed in Chapter 2.

We have now seen various ways in which misconceptions and muddles about the meaning of democracy can arise—and how these can often suggest a degree of vagueness in the meaning which does not in fact exist. But there is one fundamental confusion concerning the meaning of democracy which has not yet been discussed. This confusion is fairly common, and often arises precisely because of the vagueness and uncertainty felt to be involved in the meaning of democracy. It is, perhaps, convenient to label this confusion the 'definitional fallacy' : it involves a fallacious view of the way in which words are defined and have meaning.

The definitional fallacy is widespread in democratic theory and in thinking about democracy generally, but it is particularly prevalent in modern writing about democracy. As was indicated in the Introduction, this modern prevalence of the fallacy is largely due to the type of emphasis on empirical work typical of modern political science. It is the urge to come directly to grips with empirical reality which gives rise to the temptation to 'by-pass' the 'woolly', abstract, unempirical process of definition and to start straight in on analysing democracies—it being assumed that democracies can simply be identified as those political systems commonly called democracies. This is the definitional fallacy—the view (more often implicit than explicit) that a democracy is simply any political system to which the term 'democracy' is commonly attached.[9] This 'hard' or 'realistic' view about the meaning of democracy is thought to dispense with woolly-minded abstractions and utopian conceptions. It is exemplified in Schattschneider's reference to 'the reluctance of intellectuals to develop a definition that describes what really happens in a democracy'.[10] According to this view, then, the term 'democracy' 'means' the political systems that are commonly called democracies. Britain and the USA are regarded as democracies because they are called democracies. But this view of the meaning of 'democracy' is surely mistaken. It is forgotten that they are called democracies because their political systems exhibit—or are held to exhibit—certain characteristics. Certain political systems do not themselves constitute the meaning. Rather, certain political systems are called democracies because they are held to have certain characteristics. The meaning of a term is one thing; that which is denoted by a term because it has a certain meaning is another (this distinction is sometimes referred to as the distinction between connotation and denotation).[11] If the political systems denoted as democracies themselves constituted the meaning of 'democracy', then no future—or postulated—political system could correctly be called a democracy (without the meaning of the term being changed). This is obviously absurd.

A possible rejoinder here is that, while it is admittedly true that 'democracy' does not mean particular political systems, it is still the case that the meaning is not determined by unempirical reference to abstract characteristics. The meaning may not be particular political systems, but—it might be urged—the meaning of 'democracy' is constituted by that which these systems have in common—and which other systems do not have. Dahl, for example, refers to what he calls a descriptive theory of democracy, 'one that in effect states something like this : Here is a set of social organizations that have this and that characteristic in common'.[12] According to this view, then, the meaning of 'democracy' will be determined by empirical study of the various systems called democracies. Such study will show what they have in common. The meaning is firmly tied down to empirical reality : as Bachrach says, those who hold this view are left 'in the position of saying that democracy is that political system which actually exists in [those features common to the political systems which exist in] various countries such as the United States, Britain, Canada, and the like'.[13]

However, even this modified version of the belief in the 'direct empirical determination' of the meaning of 'democracy' must be fallacious. If it was not so there would be no adequate standard of correct and incorrect application of the term. According to the 'direct empirical' view, the meaning is simply contained in the systems to which the term is applied. But this implies no rule governing those political systems to which it is *correct* to apply the term. Any application—any calling of any system a democracy—would, *ipso facto*, be correct. It would necessarily be a correct application (and therefore would adequately convey the meaning of the word) precisely because the meaning is held to be determined by application—and this would constitute an application. Again, this is an obvious absurdity. There *are* correct and incorrect applications of 'democracy': anyone who called, say, Tsarist Russia a democracy would, quite simply, be applying the term incorrectly. Even though the meaning of 'democracy' is problematical and vague to some extent, and there are no very precise indications of correct and incorrect use, there are *some* uses that are definitely correct or incorrect. The same is true of many other words. For example, 'mountain' has a somewhat vague meaning; nonetheless anyone who called, say, Hampstead Heath a mountain, and anyone who refused to apply the term to Everest, would quite simply be using it incorrectly.

There can be correct and incorrect applications only if meaning determines application, and not if application determines meaning. It is true that there is an extent to which meaning is given by application: there is a chicken-and-egg relationship between meaning and preponderance of applications, even if not between meaning and particular applications. If and when most applications of a word change, then the meaning changes. Nonetheless, the important factor is the reasons for the applications, whether these change or not. In a sense, the meaning and correct use of 'democracy' are given by majority use—by the majority of applications of the word. But majority use is what it is for certain reasons. These reasons are, as it were, enshrined in the rules for the use of the word. Correct use and meaning are then established by reference to these rules, not by an exhaustive survey of all actual applications of the word.

The meaning of 'democracy' is therefore not determined simply by the application of the word. Rather, the meaning is delineated by the characteristics it connotes. Such characteristics are, of course, necessarily possessed by all systems denoted by the term—but they are (as we have just seen) established independently of a study of those systems. Study of political systems denoted by 'democracy' gives us more knowledge about democracy, how it works, etc., but it does not tell us what it is. In short, democracies are not democracies *because* they, and they alone, possess certain features *in common*, but simply because they possess those features. This is illustrated by remembering that, if this were not so, we would have to be familiar with all possible political systems before we could know the meaning of democracy. This would be because only in this way could we know the features which are shared by the systems called democracies but which are not possessed by other systems.

In summary, the definitional fallacy is the belief that the meaning of 'democracy' is found simply by examining the systems commonly called democracies. As we shall see later (Chapters 3 and 6), this fallacy has led to some theories being unquestioningly considered as democratic when, in fact, whether they are democratic or not is one of the most pertinent questions to ask about them. This arises because such theories, being about the nature of political systems commonly called democracies, are assumed, fallaciously, to be necessarily democratic.

Now that some of the difficulties and confusions involved in defining democracy have been sorted out we can proceed to the definition itself. It was argued earlier that, despite the appearance of an intolerable vagueness, a wide acceptable general definition of democracy was possible. This is not meant to imply that there are no real disagreements about the meaning of 'democracy', or that a crystal-clear definition is possible. Rather, it is maintained that there is, in fact, some broad agreement about the general area of meaning covered by the term. But it is recognized that disputes exist about the precise position of the boundary. Moreover, there are differing interpretations of the nature of that which falls within the area of meaning—as was argued earlier.

The meaning of 'democracy' can be summed up in the phrase 'government by the people'.[14] We shall make this into a slightly more precise general definition, although it will involve the important additional idea that government implies decision-making. That is to say, it is asserted that a logically necessary condition of a person or group governing is that they decide what shall be done. The existence of a decision that X should be done is taken as the only satisfactory evidence of a will to have X done (aspects of this general point are discussed later).

Our general definition will now be suggested, and then various comments will be made upon it. A democracy is (or the term 'democracy' connotes) a political system of which it can be said that the whole people, positively or negatively, make, and are entitled to make, the basic determining decisions on important matters of public policy. This definition, it is maintained, encapsulates the meaning of 'democracy'— contains the more specific meanings that have been ascribed to the term[15] as well as adequately expressing the general meaning which usage usually gives it. If such is the case, then it can usefully be said that this is the meaning of 'democracy'.[16]

A number of amplifications and clarifications of this definition need to be made. The first concerns the phrase 'the whole people'. This means the whole of that group known as 'the people',[17] rather than a person, group or groups within—or outside the people (a king, for example, would usually be regarded as a person not 'within' the people, but 'above' them—and ruling over them). No particular conception concerning the extent to which the people form a corporate entity as distinct from a mere aggregate of individuals is directly referred to here. However, we shall see later that the notion of a decision by the people has important implications for such conceptions.

The second comment concerns the stipulation of entitlement—the inclusion in the definition of the phrase '. . . and are entitled to make . . .'. This refers to the presence of a constitution, or other system of basic norms,[18] which *authorizes* the making of determining decisions by the people. This distinguishes a democracy from systems in which the people, through civil disobedience, riot, general disorders, insurrection (or the threat of it), etc., influence political decision-making to such an extent that they are, in effect, making the basic determining decisions on important matters of public policy even though they have no authorization to do so. A weak and/or ailing dictatorship would be an example of such a system, as would an insecure military junta.

It is because this entitlement to (as well as the actuality of) decision-making by the people is a defining feature of democracy that in descriptions of democracy such great stress is often laid upon the constitutional-institutional mechanisms for bringing it about. That is to say, statements of the nature of democracy frequently include an itemization of the main official institutions which are involved in the effecting of a decision by the people : institutions which, at one and the same time, legitimize and bring about determining decisions by the people. Very often this itemization occurs as part of the very definition of democracy. The main types of institutions involved are responsible executives, representative legislatures and elections. Elections, particularly, are stressed —usually with the proviso that they be 'free' elections. *A Dictionary of Politics*, for example, refers to 'free choice at regular intervals between two or more parties; an election in which the electorate can only choose or reject a single list of candidates is not democratic in this sense of the word [the sense generally accepted in the West]'.[19] Further discussion of the relationship between the general concept of democracy and kinds of institutional arrangements and types of institutions which give effect to it will be found in Chapter 2 and in Chapter 7. All that needs to be done here is to reassert what was argued earlier : that there is often confusion between defining features and necessary—including logically necessary—conditions of democracy. The itemization of the institutional requirements of popular decision-making, then, should not be included in a *definition* since they are assertions of *necessary conditions* for such decision-making—and hence for democracy.

Although the entitlement of the people to basic decision-making enters into the definition of 'democracy', it should not, of course, be forgotten that the actuality of such decision-making is also a defining feature. A democracy is a political system in which not only are the people entitled to make the basic determining decisions, but in which they also actually do make such decisions because of this entitlement. It is by virtue of this that one distinguishes systems that are not in fact democracies despite the presence of the forms of democracy. Similarly, it can be, and frequently is, asked whether such political systems as the British and American really are democracies (we will be concerned with just such a question in Chapters 5 and 6). The point here is that the question can arise despite an acknowledgement of the entitlement of the people to make the basic decisions and of the presence of institutions embodying this entitlement.

The possession of the entitlement and the ability to make the basic determining decisions constitutes supreme power (see below). The term 'sovereignty' is often used to express this. The possession of supreme power by the people is frequently referred to as the 'sovereignty of the people' or 'popular sovereignty'. Definitions of 'democracy' often make use of such terms. However, the meaning of the term 'sovereignty' raises so many difficulties[20] that it is better to spell out the meaning a little more precisely—as we do in our definition by the use of the phrase 'basic determining decisions'. It is to an elucidation of the meaning of this phrase that we now turn as the third of the clarifications of the general definition of 'democracy'.

First of all the notion of a 'determining decision'. This is more or less self-explanatory : when something actually happens as a result of a decision to bring that event about, then such a decision is a determining decision. In the context of politics and political systems, one is usually concerned with decisions which bring about decisions and actions by other people. For example, suppose that Smith decides to do—and does—x, because Jones decides that x should be done by Smith. We would say, here, that Jones has made a determining decision of the type we are most interested in. The reasons why Smith should act in this way, and the relationship between him and Jones, raise complex and controversial issues concerning the concepts of power and authority. Suffice it to say that if Smith regularly acts in this way in relation to Jones, then we would usually say that Jones has, or is exercising, power over him. Of course, one of the reasons why Smith does what he is told to do might be that he recognizes an entitlement (perhaps, though not necessarily, a legal entitlement) by Jones to decide what Smith shall do. In this case we should say Jones had, and was exercising, authority over Smith. And this, as we saw just now, is the form of power we are often most concerned with in talking about democracy. It should be noted that it is not until Jones's entitlement to decide what should be done actually results in those things being done that we consider authority to be a form of power. As we saw it, it is supreme power of this kind that is most usually meant by the term sovereignty. Suppose Smith did not in fact carry out Jones's decisions, despite the latter's entitlement to have them carried out (perhaps because Smith did not recognize such an entitlement). In this case, we could say that Jones had authority without power. Now consider the converse : Smith does what Jones decides he should do even though the latter has no entitle-ment—perhaps because of fear of Jones. Here we would say that Jones had power without authority. This would often be called coercive power. In real life—and especially in political systems—different kinds of power and authority are usually mixed together (and often reinforce each other) in particular relationships. For example, a citizen commonly obeys his government in part because he recognizes that the government is entitled to require certain kinds of action of him, and in part because he is afraid of, or would dislike, the consequences of non-obedience. Moreover, part of the reason for the citizen's recognition of the govern-ment's entitlement is his appreciation of the fact that it can be backed up by coercive power. But the government only has coercive power because and in so far as the personnel of the instruments of coercion (army, police, etc.) will act in certain ways as a result of the govern-ment's entitlement to obedience. (In some cases, the government can directly order them to perform certain sorts of action, and in others there is simply a general duty to enforce the law.)

In talking of decisions on matters of public policy—decisions re-garding what the state shall do—we are, of course, no longer concerned simply with the relationship between two people. One of the great complications here is that a policy can be the outcome of a process rather than anything as specific and clear-cut as a decision. It is true that there are always decisions at crucial points by government per-sonnel, but such decisions themselves can result from, rather than significantly control, a flow of events. For example, many have argued that the United States never *decided* to engage in the Vietnam conflict, but was drawn into it. Again, the introduction of a prices and incomes freeze in Britain in 1972 constituted a reaction to events rather than an autonomous decision on policy.[21] Besides the fact that public policy can result from sometimes complex processes rather than 'decisions', there is the further point that a certain stage in the policy-formulating process is recognized as the crucial one at which it is said the state has acted—for example, a Bill is passed through Parliament, or a Minister or civil servant carries out some administrative act. As we have just seen, very often this cannot be properly referred to as the point of decision—as a governmental or state decision. We need, then, some term to signify the point at which the state is said to have acted but which does not imply that this was itself a decision—or the direct result of one—in the relevant significant sense. We shall use the term 'a determination' : the point at which the state is said to have acted is a determination of public policy.

A determination of public policy may not be, or may not be the result of, a decision. This has just been argued. However, it *may* be. Determinations are sometimes in a reasonably clear-cut way expressions of decisions. Take, for example, the acts of nationalization carried out by the 1945–51 Labour government, or the accession of Britain to the Common Market. In such cases it *is* a decision that results in public policy—in action by the state. And this is what is meant by a determining decision in the context of political systems : a determining decision occurs where it is one that results in a determination. A determining decision is thus an exercise of political power. A 'basic' determining decision is one that results in other, more specific determining decisions, but the nature of which is dependent on the basic decision. For example, a decision to set up a national health service could be described as a basic determining decision : further, significant decisions concerning the nature of the service, its financing, etc., how and when it is brought into being and so on—all these result from and are dependent on the basic determining decision. Thus, those who make (in so far as any are made) the important basic determining decisions in a political system have the supreme power. Or, to put the point another way, those who make these decisions are governing—in the wider sense of the term 'governing'. In the case of democracy it is, of course, the whole people who do this. Just how specific and how many, or what proportion of, basic determining decisions have to be made before it is said that supreme power is being exercised will depend upon what are considered the more important matters. In our definition of democracy, this is made explicit by actually incorporating the word 'important' into the definition (see also below).

One of the great difficulties involved in the concept of democracy is that of making sense of the notion of a decision by the whole people, given the great numbers of individuals and diversities and divergencies of views (and/or interests) involved. Aspects of the issues involved are discussed later, principally in Chapters 2, 4, 5 and 6, but one of the general points needs to be made here. This is that some would argue that the numbers and diversity of the people, together with the inherent complexity of all policy formulation in a modern state, make it impossible to say that the people make decisions (they would possibly argue that most determinations are not the results of decisions at all, let alone decisions by the people). In Chapter 5 we also meet the argument that it is because of their ignorance and apathy that the people cannot be said to be making decisions on matters of public policy. According to this argument, the activities of the electorate result in, or significantly influence, determinations of policy, but the electorate do not make determining decisions because no relevant *decisions* are made by them. In a sense they are being said (at least to some extent) to determine the determinations, but without there being determining decisions by the electorate.

We come now to the fourth of the comments upon our general definition—which is to point out that the definition achieves its generality by its 'escape clauses'. For instance, the phrase 'of which it can be said' is inserted to cover two views of the meaning of democracy. First, there is the now usual one according to which the people make determining decisions in a sense indirectly—by means of elections and representative institutions. Secondly, there is the conception of democracy in which the people directly make the determining decisions in some kind of face-to-face group, in some kind of general public assembly. Similarly, '. . . decisions on important matters of public policy' is an escape clause. Use of the word 'important' ensures that this phrase covers a gradation of views within the meaning of democracy. At one end there are those conceptions of democracy in which the people make the basic determining decisions on only a few salient matters, such as the appointment of the governors and the very broad lines of policy they pursue.[22] At the other end are those conceptions according to which the people make the determining decisions on all but the most routine of matters. Where indirect democracies are included, devices such as referenda—and perhaps the initiative and the recall—are seen as supplementing elections and representative institutions as a way of achieving this. Each case is covered by our definition, since the differing ideas regarding the scope of the popular decision-making would be included in differing criteria of 'importance'.

The phrase 'whether positively or negatively' is included so as to cover both the conception of the people initiating policy and of the people merely giving or withholding consent. In the first case, the people 'think up' and implement policies. In the second case, on the other hand, the policy proposals come from the government and/or those who are seeking to become the government. The people's role is to give or refuse consent to, or to choose among, the proposals (see the following two chapters). In many conceptions of democracy, both ideas play an important part.

There is one more clarification to be made concerning the meaning of an item in the proposed definition. This concerns the concept of 'the people'. This crucial concept is subject to differing interpretations. It has already been mentioned that the people can be seen simply as a collection of individuals or as some kind of organic unity or corporate entity. This will be discussed in Chapter 2. There is, however, another difference in interpretation or conception that cuts across this one. This concerns the proportion of the total society included in the meaning of 'the people'. That is to say, the concept of the people has varied in the parts and the extent of the society it has covered. 'The society' here is the one organized and delimited by the political system—called a democracy—in question.

The man in the street would usually assume that the concept of the people in definitions of democracy included the whole of society—all the members of the relevant society. If he were being precise he would say all the adult members. However, it is quite often pointed out that what has been meant by 'the people' has not always been as extensive.[23] The Athenian city-state of Ancient Greece—often seen as the original or the archetypal form of democracy—only included a minority of the society among the decision-makers. Aliens, slaves and women were excluded. Again, in the early meaning of 'democracy'—the sense in which the word is used by Aristotle—'the people' means the poor (more precisely, the poor who are not slaves).[24] This sense of the word was often adapted to equate 'the people' with 'the mob'. Aristotle's meaning stayed alive and was echoed centuries later in the Marxist–Leninist conception of democracy as the dictatorship of the proletariat.

Paradoxically, in the hands of some the concept of the people has at at times covered the middle classes[25] rather than the poor. One of the crucial factors here was the linking of property, or the ownership of property, with a full membership of society and the consequent right to participate in political decision-making. 'The poor' was not always equivalent to 'the working class(es)', since skilled artisans and so on were often included within this concept of the people. The relevant facts about the poor were usually seen as their alleged total ignorance and their lack of sufficient property. This latter, as just indicated, was held to mean that they had no 'stake in society', and were therefore in one sense not of that society.

Simple acceptance of this view of 'the people' as merely having different meanings implies that systems can properly be called democratic that are very different indeed.[26] Some of these systems would be such that power—the making of the basic determining decisions—was in the hands of a small minority of the adult population. For example, it would appear that, according to Schumpeter's argument, rule by a white minority, as in Rhodesia and South Africa, is to be counted as democracy : 'For fitness is a matter of opinion and of degree. . . . A race-conscious nation may associate fitness with racial considerations. And so on. The salient point . . . is not what *we* think about any or all of these possible disabilities.'[27] He argues that the salient point is what the society in question thinks. It is true that Schumpeter could respond here by saying that, in the cases of Rhodesia and South Africa, the majority—the excluded majority—of the society in question do *not* accept the criterion of exclusion from political power. However, this would be irrelevant to the basic argument : *if* the excluded majority accepted the criterion, then these countries would be deemed democracies despite the exclusion of a majority of the population from political power. In fact, however, it is not even clear that Schumpeter is implying that an excluded majority have to approve the criterion for their exclusion in order for the system to be a democracy. Rather, there seems to be an identification of 'what the society thinks' with 'what the people think'—i.e. the criterion of exclusion has only to be approved by the minority who are not excluded![28]

Can we accept this view that political systems with very different proportions of society sharing in political power are all democracies because of different meanings being given to 'the people'? The answer is surely no. And this is because the meaning of 'the people' is not an arbitrary matter. Even accepting that the meaning of 'the people' is not—or at least has not always been—'all the people in the society in question', it does not follow that its meaning contains no implication about the proportion of the society to be included. Perhaps the meaning of 'the people' could more accurately be rendered in the formula : 'as great a proportion of the society as are not unfit to partake in the making of the basic political decisions'. Schumpeter acknowledges this : as we have just seen, he justifies differing concepts of the people on the grounds that 'fitness is a matter of opinion and of degree'. But this is not all. The whole thrust of democratic theory, and of democratic thought generally, has, over the years, been towards enlarging the proportion of the society that engages in the basic decision-making. That is to say, the thrust has been towards urging that a larger proportion is not unfit to—and ought to—engage in the decision-making. In other words, a basic element in democratic thought has been to widen the concept of the people until it includes the whole society (or, at least, virtually the whole adult population—see below). The demand for universal suffrage has long been accepted as one of the most characteristic features of the democratic creed. There is in most democratic thought—and especially in radical democratic theory (see Chapter 3) —a moral presumption in favour of universal suffrage. And, indeed, the arguments used to justify universal franchise are often the same as typical arguments used to justify democracy itself.[29]

In short, there is a fundamental incongruity in asserting a meaning for 'the people' narrower than virtually the entire adult population. 'It really is an astonishing proof of confusion of thought that anyone who professes and calls himself a democrat should set to work to make arbitrary assumptions as to who the people are.'[30] It may be that this way of thinking is newer than the idea of democracy itself. It may be that this conflicts with the tradition of regarding Athens as the archetypal democracy. Nonetheless, this 'new' way of thought is now absolutely fundamental to democratic thought; and the Athenian 'democracy' is quite often viewed with some suspicion—as perhaps not really being a democracy—precisely because of the exclusions from political power mentioned earlier. Brown, for example, says of Athens : 'There was only government by a fragment of the whole people, and this was called democracy because a franchise so comparatively wide seemed remarkable in a world of oligarchies and tyrannies.'[31] There is sometimes hesitation about calling J. S. Mill a democrat—in part because he believed that some people should, initially at least, be excluded from the franchise (see Chapter 3).

It was noted just now that one of the most common of exclusions from the the concept of 'the people' has been a good half of the adult population, viz. women (J. S. Mill was, of course, a notable exception). But again, this exclusion is now generally regarded as undemocratic, and has been strongly opposed for this among other reasons. It may be that, for some, the concept of 'the people' is such that Switzerland could have been accepted as a democracy before its enfranchisement of women, while others would say it was definitely not a democracy precisely because women did not have the vote. And, indeed, many people did feel profoundly uneasy about calling Switzerland a democracy. The suffragette movement gained its strength not—or not just—from sympathy for women. Rather, the view became widespread that it was unjust and undemocratic to exclude women from the franchise. Unjust, because there was no relevant difference between men and women in this sphere; undemocratic, because the lack of relevant reasons for the exclusion of women meant that they ought to be included in the concept of 'the people'.

It can be seen, then, that the meaning of 'the people' (or, at least, the dominant meaning—see below) now includes virtually the whole adult population. There may once have been more restricted meanings, but these are best explained as superseded interpretations of an agreed formula (see page 15). But this is no arbitrary change. The reasons for the change are very much the same as those for believing in democracy in the first place. In this way the 'modern' meaning of 'the people' is more democratic—in a sense, it is the 'correct' meaning for the term in democratic thought. Moreover, it is not entirely true to say that this is the modern meaning of the term. The idea of supreme authority residing in the people is not restricted to democratic thought. What is specific to the democratic idea is that this supreme authority should actually be exercised by the people in the form of the making of basic decisions on policy. The non-democratic form of the idea of the supreme authority of the people has, then, involved no difficulties—about fitness or practicability—concerning everyone partaking in the policy decision-making. Here, then, 'the people' can without difficulty mean *all* the people. And this is what the term has usually meant. At the same time, it must be realized that concepts utilized are those such as the people as a corporate entity rather than as a collection of individuals; and 'virtual representation'.[32] This means that, in other ways, the ideas of the people and of the way in which they possess authority is very different from those found in democratic thought. Nonetheless, it remains true that, in *a* sense, which is significant, ideas of the supreme authority of the people have always involved a concept of the people that has covered all the people. Moreover, democrats have on occasion been chided for losing sight of this corporate idea of the people[33] (but see also Chapter 3 below).

The dominant meaning of 'the people' in the definition of democracy, then, covers all the people—or, more accurately, virtually the entire adult population. This qualification is necessary, for even the most ardent democrats do not include children, criminals or the insane among those entitled to vote.[34] It might be objected that this stopping point is as arbitrary as all the others, and that there is therefore no valid reason for not simply including the *whole* population within the meaning of 'the people'. However, it will be remembered that a more accurate formula for defining 'the people' was suggested above, according to which those not unfit to partake in political decision-making were those included in the concept. The point is, there are what would be accepted as compelling reasons for excluding children, criminals and the insane according to this criterion. They are, moreover, reasons which accord with the typical aspects of democratic thought that widened the concept of 'the people' in the first place. It may be believed that there might be some individuals in some categories—or, indeed, in all categories—about whom it might be generally agreed that they are unfitted to partake in political decision-making. But the only *categories* of individuals about which there is such agreement are children, criminals and the insane. The distinguishing features of these categories are the only characteristics that are very generally admitted to render an individual unfit to engage in basic political decision-making. Criminals, because they have excluded themselves from the community;[35] and children and the insane because they are simply not capable of the relevant thought processes. There may be dispute as to

where the lines are to be drawn : just how much 'irrationality' constitutes insanity, and just what age marks the beginning of adulthood (for
example, 18 or 21)? All are agreed, however, that a line comes somewhere. No one would give the vote to a person who, say, thought he
was Napoleon any more than they would to a three-year-old. These
categories of exclusion are therefore in accord with a central aspect of
democratic thought : a belief in the worth of all individuals and of the
consequent desirability of individuals sharing in political power,[36]
barring only those who *all* agree are completely unfit for such activity.
Statements of the dominant meaning of 'the people' refer, then, to the
adult population—and to virtually the whole adult population. The
exclusion of the insane, and possibly of criminals, normally constitutes
such a small contraction from the whole adult population that the
qualification 'virtually' will be dropped from any future references to
the meaning of 'the people'.

While it is true that the dominant meaning of 'the people' is 'the
whole adult population', a subsidiary meaning must also be recognized.
The Aristotelian meaning of the term has been so persistent that it
cannot be regarded as just another interpretation of the 'fitness criterion'. The notion of the people as 'the common people',[37] 'the poor'
or simply 'the non-wealthy' has been the most persistent and consistent
of the 'limited' interpretations of 'the people'. And still it has not died.
It must therefore be recognized as a separate—if subsidiary—meaning.
Sometimes, when a person says 'democracy', he means a system in
which basic political decision-making is in the hands of the poor.[38]
But the usual implication is that the poor are the most numerous—
indeed, this is the way in which Aristotle's conception arose. In
The Politics, III : 7, democracy is identified as (one kind of) the rule
of the Many; but in II : 8 it is argued that what makes a democracy
is the rule of the poor. It so happens that the poor are usually the most
numerous, even though it is not necessarily the case. Nonetheless, for
Aristotle, as for others, the assumption is that the poor are nearly always
the most numerous. In this way, then, there is a connection between
this and the dominant meaning of 'the people'. In this secondary sense,
the term may mean not all the people but that section of them—the
most numerous—that comes nearest to being all the people.

There is one more point to note before we leave the concept of the
people. This is that the conception of the people as the whole adult
population, plus the individualist view of collective entities inherent in
most democratic theories, has usually resulted in an equation of democracy with political equality. Indeed, equality has usually played a
central role in the democratic credo; that all men are created equal
was, for example, the first of the 'self-evident' truths of the American
Declaration of Independence. Thus power, being in the hands of the

people—all the adults—is commonly taken to imply an equal amount of power (voting power at least) in the hands of each individual person. 'Accepting democracy, i.e. people's power, as one's ideal, there is no reason for denying to any sane, law-abiding adult membership of the people and the possession of rights and duties. Thus, democracy, to be genuine, must be founded on the doctrine of equality.'[39] Some of the issues involved will be discussed at various points, but it is worth noting here the common association of democracy with political equality. Not only is democracy usually held to involve or to require it, but political equality is commonly held to be intrinsically good. There is, then, a 'double strength' to the belief in political equality among democrats. Indeed, so important is it often held to be, that democracy is sometimes *defined* in terms of political equality. It would, however, seem less confusing, and more accurate, to regard political equality as an associated desirable feature rather than as a defining feature of democracy. It is also sometimes seen as a logically necessary condition. Not least of the complications here is the uncertainty and controversy surrounding definitions of equality. There is not, however, the space to go into this question here.[40]

The concept of equality leads us on to the final point which needs to be made about the definition of democracy. This is that, as mentioned earlier, while it may be said that our definition is of the term in its usual, primary or dominant sense, there are also other senses. Very often what appear to be other senses of the word democracy turn out not to be different. However, this confusion does not always occur, and despite close connections with the dominant sense, it must be recognized that there are certain other usages persistent and consistent enough to yield different meanings. The meanings referred to here are those sometimes expressed by the terms 'economic democracy' and 'social democracy'.[41] There is a connection with the dominant meaning via the conception of equality. 'Economic' and 'social democracy'— although the meanings are sometimes a little hard to pin down—seem to be terms meaning systems or states of affairs in which there is economic and social equality (there is not always this distinction drawn between the two forms of equality, and these two additional senses of 'democracy' often tend to become merged). Now, democracy in the usual sense is often held to imply political equality. But it is also often held that political equality without economic and/or social equality is a façade. Either political equality by itself is 'not really' equality, or else economic and/or social equality are held to be necessary conditions for the existence of political equality.

Where 'social democracy' is given a meaning different from 'economic democracy' there is only the connection just noted with the predominant meaning of 'democracy'. Social democracy exists where there is social equality—roughly speaking, a classless society (or something approaching it) in which there are little or no differences in status or 'social advantages'. However, in the case of economic democracy there can be other connections with the predominant meaning. Economic equality is frequently taken to imply an equality of control over the economy or those aspects of the economy which particularly affect an individual, such as the conditions at, and the running of, his place of work. Such 'equality of control' implies, of course, increased participation or sharing in control by those at present excluded—the workers. Sometimes it means complete control by the workers. Indeed, 'economic democracy' can imply anything from increased consultation by employers with trade unions, through workers' control of factories, etc., within the framework of the state ('industrial democracy'), to anarcho-syndicalism, in which the state is superseded by autonomous units of production under the control of the workers. (For further discussion of workers' control, etc., see Chapter 9). Here we come back again to the idea of the determining decisions being in the hands of 'the people'—although 'the people' is usually meant in the subsidiary sense discussed above (p. 18). The difference between this 'economic sense' and the usual sense of 'democracy' is that, in the former, the control by 'the people' is in addition to, or instead of, control over the state's actions. The idea is that either there should be no state, or else that there are crucial dimensions of social economic life left unaffected by the state's actions. In either event, for 'the people' to have full power—power over the persons and/or circumstances that would otherwise govern their lives—they must control something other than, or in addition to, the state, viz. the factors determining economic conditions. Of course, both kinds of democracy can exist—and be recommended—simultaneously. And this is usually the case—except where the complete non-existence of the state is postulated. Nonetheless, they are two different kinds : one consisting in control by the people of the state, the other in control by the people of matters unaffected by the state.

It must be recognized, therefore, that there is also a social and an economic sense of 'democracy'—whether defined solely in terms of equality or whether alternative forms of popular control are also included. However, it does remain true that the sense expressed by our definition—the 'political sense'—is the primary one. Some would not, in fact, even accept the legitimacy of recognizing anything other than the political sense. Bryce, for example, spoke of democracy as being 'merely a form of government. . .'.[42] But, in any case, the political meaning is the primary and most important one in the sense that this is the meaning indicated by the great majority of uses of the term, both during modern times and in the past. 'It is clear that the traditional use of the term "democracy" from the time of the Greeks to the present day has been to describe a form of government. The evidence for this is overwhelming.'[43] Similarly, Plamenatz says that 'democracy, as the etymology of the word indicates, is above all a form of government'.[44] A detailed semantic analysis of 'democracy' concluded that 'one may consider "form of government" to be a conceptual characteristic of a relatively large group of democracy concepts. Every member of the group has at least that characteristic in common.'[45] The author of a development of this semantic research stated that 'the tendency to use "democracy" to signify a certain kind of rule, or a certain kind of government, may be generally regarded as a predominant trend'.[46]

This completes our discussion of the definition of 'democracy'. In Chapter 2, on the different sorts of democracy, we turn to an examination of some of the matters arising out of this discussion.

NOTES AND REFERENCES

1 This dispensing with definition may be part of the 'definitional fallacy' discussed below.
2 C. Perelman in *Democracy in a World of Tensions*, UNESCO symposium, edited by R. McKeon and S. Rokkan, Wesport, Conn., Greenwood Press, 1951, p. 296.
3 J. P. Plamenatz in *Democracy in a World of Tensions*, p 302.
3ª For a contrary view, see Q. Skinner, 'The Empirical Theorists of Democracy and Their Critics', in *Political Theory*, Vol. I, No. 3 (August 1973), pp. 287–306, esp. p. 298. (See also p. 178 below.)
4 The question of how the definition should be fomulated will be taken up shortly.
5 It might appear that a logically necessary condition is the same as a defining feature. But a defining feature is a component of the meaning of a term, whereas a logically necessary condition is a component of the object(s) to which the term is applied—it is a feature by virtue of which the term is correctly applied to the object(s). There can be agreement on the former while there is disagreement on the latter (such disagreement might, as indicated in the text, involve interpretation both of the meaning and of the object). For example, a disagreement about whether a plank of wood balanced on a log constituted a weighing machine would be a dispute about logically necessary conditions. All would agree on the *meaning* of 'weighing machine' (a machine for weighing objects); disagreement would be about whether such a contraption could be said to be 'for weighing objects' (one could in fact weigh objects on it in a crude manner).
   This distinction between meaning and logically necessary conditions is in some ways similar to that between meaning and criteria (see R. M. Hare, *The Language of Morals*, London, Oxford University Press, 1952 (paperback 1964), Chapter 6). However, there is a difference. Criteria are used in respect of adjectives rather than nouns and differing statements of criteria need not (although they may) involve dispute about what *are* the

criteria, whereas this is necessarily what happens in the case of differing statements of logically necessary conditions. For example, people can happily differ about the criteria for the application of the term 'exciting' without finding it necessary to determine which is the 'correct' view (and, of course, there need be no disagreement about the meaning of the word 'exciting').

6 Some combinations are not possible, and some are necessary. For example, a defining characteristic is specifically not an empirically necessary condition. An accompanying feature specifically is not a defining feature, but a defining characteristic could also be one that is deemed desirable (although there are complications here). If it is not a defining feature or a logically necessary condition, a desirable characteristic must, of course, also be an accompanying feature—although not all accompanying features are necessarily desirable.

7 But see the Preface to E. P. Douglass, *Rebels and Democrats*, Chicago, Quadrangle Books, 1965 (first published by the University of North Carolina Press in 1955).

8 A. Naess, *et al.*, *Democracy, Ideology and Objectivity*, Oslo, Universitets-forlaget, 1956, p. 101.

9 See, for example, P. Bachrach, *The Theory of Democratic Elitism*, Boston and Toronto, Little, Brown, 1967 (published later in London, University of London Press, 1969), p. 24; his reference to Dahl is perhaps a little unfair since Dahl at that point does not fully commit the definitional fallacy (although he verges on it): R. A. Dahl, *Modern Political Analysis*, Englewood Cliffs, New Jersey, Prentice-Hall, first edition, 1963, p. 73.

10 E. E. Schattschneider, *The Semisovereign People*, New York, Holt, Rinehart & Winston, 1960, p. 136. The question of the relationship between ideal models and political reality is discussed in Chapter 5.

11 It may be that the meaning (connotation) of a term can be learnt from, or established by, a consideration of its denotata, but this does not imply that meaning and denotata are equivalents—just as redness and pillar boxes, holly berries, etc., are not equivalents. On connotation and denotation, see J. S. Mill's *A System of Logic* (first published 1843, Book I, sections ii, v and vi.))

12 R. A. Dahl, *A Preface to Democratic Theory*, Chicago, Chicago University Press, 1956 (paperback 1963), p. 2. (Dahl adds that inquiry into the necessary conditions of democracy thus identified, is the other element in such theory.)

13 Bachrach, *The Theory of Democratic Elitism*, p. 24.

14 This is widely held to be the case. Selecting more or less at random, we find that Schnattsneider, for example, speaks of '. . . the most pervasive and widely accepted common definition of democracy as "government by the people" ' (*The Semisovereign People*, p. 142). *A Dictionary of Politics* begins the entry on 'democracy' thus: 'From the Greek *demos*, people, and *kratos*, power, meaning government by the people' (F. Elliott and M. Summer-skill, Harmondsworth, Penguin Books, first edition, 1957, p. 89). Lincoln's famous formulation was, of course, 'government of the people, by the people, for the people'. It should also be noted that the same idea is expressed by such formulations as 'control of the state—or control of the state's actions—by the people'.

15 There is, perhaps, a class of exceptions to this—see the discussion below (pp. 19–20). The more specific meanings that are referred to here are mainly those that ascribe differing roles to the people; e.g. a definite positive and initiating role—as in radical democratic theory (see Chapter 3). They are 'contained within' in the sense that qualifications—like the inclusion of the word 'important'—allow for different conceptions of the scope of the people's decision-making—see p. 13 below.

16 The argument is, then, that there is more than simply a 'family relationship' between different usages of the term democracy (with the qualification referred to in n. 15). The philosopher Wittgenstein suggested that there are family relationships between different usages of terms rather than 'essential meanings'. However, this does not rule out the possibility of a common element constituting *a* meaning, even if it is not an 'essential' meaning.

17 The question of the extent of this group is taken up later.

18 In Britain there are notorious difficulties in determining what is and is not specified by the constitution (if any), but it could well be argued that the constitution itself does not authorize decision-making by the people. However, such an authorization is, in an important sense, given by widely and strongly held beliefs about the proper functioning of the system. Moreover, such beliefs are effective—they actually play an important part in the way the system works, and this includes having an effect on the constitution (e.g. the convention that a government resigns if its party is beaten at a general election). These beliefs can be considered a variety of what A. D. Lindsay called 'operative ideals'. (A. D. Lindsay, *The Modern Democratic State*, Oxford, Oxford University Press, 1943, pp. 37–8.)

19 op. cit., p. 89.

20 On the concept of sovereignty, see W. J. Stankiewicz (ed.), *In Defense of Sovereignty*, New York, Oxford University Press, 1969. This includes both attacks on vagueness and ambiguity of the concept, and a reply to these attacks. The critical articles by S. I. Benn and W. J. Rees are reprinted from P. Laslett (ed.), *Philosophy, Politics and Society* (1st Series), op. cit. Rees argues that the term has become so vague that it should be dispensed with.

21 It is true that the introduction of a freeze involved considered decisions by the government (for example, the decision to prepare and introduce a Bill), but such decisions resulted from the flow of events, and were not those which the government would otherwise wished to have taken. The essential point is that 'decisions' of this kind are 'forced' by events, in contradistinction to decisions which are autonomously made and which initiate and control flows of events. (It is true that events are rarely completely controlled, or that there are no constraints upon decision-making—indeed, in a sense, there are always some constraints. However, there *are* significant differences of degree, and the distinctions just drawn can be viewed as involving useful analytical categories.)

22 There are some views of democracy according to which, apparently, a system is a democracy even if *no* sorts of determining decisions on policy are made by the people—the only requirement being that the governors are appointed (and removeable) by them. However, it is argued in Chapter 6 that either such views are not in fact what they purport to be (that, in fact,

popular decision-making on policy *is* included), or else that they are not after all views of democracy.

23 See, for example, J. A. Schumpeter, *Capitalism, Socialism and Democracy*, London, Allen & Unwin, 4th ed., 1954, pp. 243–5.

24 There are complications concerning the meaning of 'the people' in Aristotle's thought. The point here is that, according to Aristotle's classification (which departs in important respects from modern categories with similar labels), a democracy is a *polis* in which the poor rule (see *The Politics*, IV: viii). It is in this sense that the concept of the people as the poor is referred to as Aristotle's conception.

25 See, for example, D. Spearman, *Democracy in England*, London, Rockliff, 1957, p.87. Sometimes the meaning is not so much 'the middle classes' as something like 'responsible people'—see, for example, Voltaire's definition quoted by Schumpeter, *Capitalism, Socialism and Democracy*, p. 244n.

26 See, for example, ibid.

27 ibid.

28 See, for example, ibid., p. 245, where he writes: 'Must we not leave it to every *populus* to define himself?'—'*populus*' being the Roman word for 'people'.

29 See, for example, H. B. Mayo, *An Introduction to Democratic Theory*, New York, Oxford University Press, 1960, pp. 115–21; on p. 120, Mayo writes: 'In summary, I am inclined to think that today the universal adult suffrage is merely an inseparable part of the wider argument for democracy.'

30 I. Brown, *The Meaning of Democracy*, London, R. Cobden Sanderson, third edition, 1926, p. 44.

31 Brown, *The Meaning of Democracy*, p. 40.

32 See Chapter 2 for a discussion of these concepts.

33 For an influential assertion of this viewpoint, and for an analysis of the concepts just mentioned, see W. Lippmann, *The Public Philosophy*, Mentor Book edition, New York, The New American Library, 1956 (published in England by Hamish Hamilton), esp. pp. 32–8.

34 Paradoxically, 'the non-democratic concept' of the people is not even restricted in this way. In this concept the *whole* of the corporate entity is included. It is not just that fitness for decision-making is not at issue. It is also that the interests held to be 'virtually represented' are the real and long-term interests of society as a whole and of all the individuals, past, present and future. Apart from anything else, this implies that the adulthood as well as the childhood of any particular population of children is being considered. In short, the whole people is meant by 'the people' because no particular set of individuals is seen as constituting the whole people.

35 This category is not so self-evident as the other two. Many probably would not see too relevant a distinction between criminals and revolutionaries dedicated to the overthrow of the state, society or whatever. And they might well be reluctant to deny the vote to such revolutionaries. In any case, the deprivation of civic rights—albeit temporary—was not necessarily a part of the relevant penal policies. Perhaps, therefore, the concept of the people ought only to exclude children and the insane.

36 For a discussion of these and related ideas, see Chapter 8 on the justification of democracy.

37 It is this sense of the term that is being used when it is said of a politician that he is 'a man of the people'.

38 The conception of the people in class terms in Marxist–Leninist thought has already been mentioned. 'The people' tends to be equated with 'the proletariat'. See Chapter 2 for a discussion of 'Eastern European' conceptions of democracy.

39 Brown, *The Meaning of Democracy*, p. 45. See Sartori, *Democratic Theory*, New York, Praeger, 1965, Chapter 14, for a good discussion of the relationship between democracy and equality.

40 Besides Sartori, see, for example, B. Williams, 'The Idea of Equality', in Laslett and Runciman (eds.), *Philosophy, Politics and Society* (Second Series); R. H. Tawney, *Equality*, London, Allen & Unwin, 1964 (first published 1931): new edition with Introduction by R. M. Titmuss; J. R. Pennock and J. W. Chapman, *Equality*, New York, Atherton Press (Nomos IX), 1967; and J. Rees, *Equality*, London, Pall Mall, 1971.

41 See, for example, D. Pickles, *Democracy*, London, Methuen, 1970, Ch. 5.

42 Lord Bryce, *Modern Democracies*, London, Macmillan, 1921, Vol. I, p. 76.

43 G. C. Field in *Democracy in a World of Tensions*, p. 77.

44 J. P. Plamenatz in ibid., p. 305.

45 A. Naess, *et al.*, *Democracy, Ideology and Objectivity*, p. 58.

46 J. A. Christophersen, *The Meaning of 'Democracy'*, Oslo, Universitetsforlaget, 1966, p. 285.

CHAPTER 2

Different Sorts of Democracy

It was pointed out in Chapter 1 that a broad agreement on the meaning of 'democracy' is not incompatible with the existence of some important different conceptions of democracy (see p. 3). It is frequently believed that the term 'democracy' is used in significantly different senses. However, it seemed more accurate, and less confusing, to regard these apparently different meanings as indicating different interpretations of elements within a common meaning, and different interpretations of that to which the term was applied.[1] In this chapter, then, we shall look at some ways in which there can be such different interpretations, and how they nonetheless relate to the same general definition—the definition put forward in Chapter 1. In particular, we shall discuss two pairs of 'opposites'. These two pairs are usually labelled as 'direct' and 'indirect' or 'representative' democracy on the one hand, and as 'people's' and 'Western' or 'liberal' democracy on the other.[2]

The conceptions of direct and indirect democracy both fall within our general definition of democracy. That both can do so results from different interpretations of the notion of the people making decisions and of what constitute important matters of public policy. A direct democracy is a political system in which the people directly make the determining political decisions. 'Directly', in the sense that the decisions implemented are the ones actually made by—rather than being derived from the ones made by—all the people. This is usually taken to mean that all the people are present when the decisions are made and all partake—or have the chance to—in the making of them. As a result of this direct decision-making, the number of matters specifically decided by the people is high. Since the people *can* be assembled to make decisions, there is no reason[3] why all non-routine decisions should not be taken by them. An indirect democracy is a political system in which the people make the determining political decisions to an important extent directly. Some decisions are made directly at elections—ideas of the nature and scope of these varying with different sorts of democratic theory (see the following chapter). But many of the decisions are actually made by elected representatives of the people. Again, there are varying ideas concerning the relationship between such decisions and the opinions and interests of the people, but in all cases the representatives are deciding for (albeit in various senses) the people.

Direct democracy has always been, in a sense, the archetype of democracy. The first democracies—those of ancient Greece—were direct. They have also usually been highly esteemed. Because of the directness and extent of the people's decision-making, direct democracy is usually regarded as in some sense 'more democratic' than indirect democracy. For all these reasons, direct democracy has very often been held up as an ideal against which indirect democracy—and particular instances of it—has to be judged. And it should be remembered, as was pointed out in Chapter 1, that for a long time the term 'democracy' only meant what we now refer to as direct democracy. Despite the fact that it is commonly considered to be totally impracticable in modern conditions,[4] direct democracy therefore continues to exert an important influence upon thinking about democracy. For this reason it is worth saying something about it here.

We have seen that a direct democracy is one characterized by a high proportion of decisions being made by the people actually assembled together. It also follows from this that the people will be initiating decisions rather than simply accepting or rejecting proposals put to them by those who would govern them. The latter case would not accord with the notion of the people themselves directly constituting and exercising the political authority. It is true that, in the ancient Athenian democracy, the mass assembly 'decided only those issues framed by and put to it by the council'.[5] However, the composition and functions of this organizing council were such that it was an agent of the people rather than a separate body ruling over them (albeit with consent). The council 'represented a fair cross-section of the population, [and] it could be assumed that the views of the two bodies [council and assembly] would not be seriously in conflict'.[6] The council *was* the people—in microcosm. Even Sartori, who insists that the rulers and ruled were not identical, acknowledges that 'the difference between direct and indirect democracy is radical. . . . In direct democracy there is continuous participation of the people in the direct exercise of power, whereas indirect democracy amounts to a system of *limitation* and *control* of power.'[7]

Of course, the kind of political system indicated by the definition of direct democracy is not necessarily exemplified by only one political system that has existed, nor even just the democracies of a particular place and epoch. Rather, it is a model against which actual systems could be compared. Nonetheless, the model has a special relationship with the democracies of ancient Greece, and with that of Athens in the fifth and fourth centuries B.C. in particular—since it is about this that most is known. It was from a perception of these systems that the model was constructed.[8] But, as was indicated just now, the model has continued to exert a hold over democratic thought. Rousseau, writing in the eighteenth century, depicted a political system in which the people themselves directly made the laws (although he at times qualified this). Legislation—although not executive action—was to be directly enacted by the assembled people. 'Sovereignty, for the same reason as makes it inalienable, cannot be represented. . . . Every law the people has not ratified in person is null and void—is, in fact, not a law.'[9] There is a sense in which Marx and Lenin also regarded 'true democracy' as direct democracy. 'It was Marx's thesis (and also Lenin's) that true democracy could only be direct democracy.'[10] Although here, it should be noted, the directness of the democracy, in Marx's case at least, consisted not so much in the character of the decision-making in the state, as in the withering away of the state.[11] In this conception direct popular power consists in the ordinary people taking the exercise of power directly into their own hands. The people do what has to be done directly, individually and spontaneously. This is to be contrasted with the people exercising, not their direct unorganized power, but the power of the state—albeit by making direct decisions about what the state shall do.[12]

In more recent times there has been a resurgence of interest in direct democracy. The current vogue for 'participation' often involves a denunciation of representative institutions and a demand for direct involvement and decision-making by the masses—in the state and in other spheres (see Chapter 9). Students have been among the most vocal advocates of such views. 'The rebel students consider representative democracy a failure. Radical students in France and elsewhere argue for some kind of Utopia where everybody votes on everything that affects them.'[13]

As said before, it is commonly considered that direct democracy is impracticable in the modern state. And this must surely be the correct view. The arguments from size and complexity are unanswerable. It is true that a form of direct democracy could be obtained without attempting that which it would be absurd to attempt—assembling together all the citizens of a modern state. There could, for example, be a system in which television viewers, after watching some sort of debate or presentation of policy proposals, voted directly on the issues by means of buttons attached to their sets. This would not be beyond the wit of modern technology. However, such a system would omit a vital dimension of direct democracy as it is usually conceived : the positive initiation of proposals by the people. Even if technology could in some sense provide for this also, it is extremely doubtful whether it could ever be so effectively provided as in a face-to-face meeting of a manageable size. Moreover, this kind of system would still not survive the objection of complexity. It will be argued later that even one kind of indirect democracy—the sort postulated in radical democratic theory—is untenable because of the inability of the mass of the people to decide upon detailed complex issues (see Chapters 5 and 6). If this is so, direct democracy would be even more untenable. In fact, of course, direct democratic decision-making has actually existed only in the same situation where it can most meaningfully be demanded : in small units where face-to-face meetings are possible and where the complexity of issues is limited.

The Athenian *polis* contained under 50,000 citizens, of whom 3,000 to 6,000 actually attended the assembly; and the complex issues thrown up by modern society were absent. Similarly, the Swiss cantons idealized by Rousseau were simple communities small enough to enable all citizens to meet at intervals to legislate. The main modern examples of direct democracy in state institutions—the smaller Swiss cantons and municipalities and the New England town meeting[14]—are instances of regional or local government. Again, they are small enough for the citizens to assemble, and, not being concerned with central governmental functions, complexity of issues is limited.[15] Moreover, the 'directness' of the popular decision-making is diluted. Broad decisions are made by the mass meetings, but officials are elected to carry out and interpret these decisions in detail.

Direct democracy has, then, long been regarded by most—though not all—as utopian; and some would regard it as inherently undesirable anyway (see the discussion of 'participatory democracy' in Chapter 9). From the French Revolution onwards, indirect democracy came to be generally regarded as the only practicable form of democracy. We have already noted how this was reflected in a change in the meaning of 'democracy' (see Chapter 1). It is time, then, to look at the conception of indirect democracy.

As we saw on p. 27, indirect democracy means representative democracy : a political system in which the people elect representatives to act for them for certain purposes. Representation[16] was not, of course, a feature of ancient Greek democracy. This was not owing to its rejection, but to its non-existence. A system of representation could not exist since the concept did not exist. 'The concept of representation, particularly of human beings representing other human beings, is essentially a modern one. The ancient Greeks had no corresponding word, although they elected some officials and sometimes sent ambassadors—activities which *we* might say involve representation.'[17] As we saw just now, the great disadvantage of direct democracy on the ancient Greek pattern is that it is impracticable on a larger scale. And the idea of representation was later incorporated into democratic thought as a device for overcoming this disadvantage. The concept and practice of representation developed from their emergence during the Middle Ages. They were made use of in the flowering of democratic theory—beginning in the late eighteenth century—in incorporating representation into democratic theory. Indeed, in some instances representation was joyously seized upon as a miraculous solution to the problems of applying popular rule in large-scale societies. Tom Paine was of the view that, as the ancient 'democracies increased in population, and the territory extended, the simple democratical form became unwieldy and impracticable', though 'original simple democracy . . . affords the true data from which government on a large scale can begin. [But] it is incapable of extension, not from its principle, but from the inconvenience of its form.' However, the system of representation is the remedy for this defect of form, and 'by ingrafting representation upon democracy we arrive at a system of government capable of embracing and confederating all the various interests and every extent and territory of population'.[18] James Mill proclaimed that 'in the grand discovery of modern times, the system of representation, the solution of all the difficulties, both speculative and practical, will perhaps be found'.[19] As we shall see in the following chapter, not all theories of representative democracy view representation as simply overcoming the problems of size. Nonetheless, all theories would ascribe at least—if not only—this function to a system of representation.

An indirect democracy, then, is one in which the difficulties of direct democracy are overcome by having elected representatives—for certain purposes at least—acting in place of the people. To elucidate this, and to see how this accords with our definition of democracy, it is necessary to say something further about the concept of representation.

The first thing to be noticed is that there are concept*s*, rather than *a* concept, of representation—and this can cause much confusion. The terms 'representation' and 'representative' have varying meanings. Birch points out that a search for one underlying 'essential' meaning is misplaced,[20] although there are, of course, certain features common to more than one meaning (by virtue of which there is the one word 'representation' rather than different words that happen to have the same spelling). It is, however, possible to say that different conceptions of representation fall into three main categories. Birch talks of the three main usages of the term 'representation'. He specifies these as follows :
(1) to denote an agent or spokesman who acts on behalf of his principal;
(2) to indicate that a person shares some of the characteristics of a class

of persons; and (3) to indicate that a person symbolizes the identity or qualities of a class of persons.[21]

According to the first usage, a representative is one who is recognized as having a duty to promote certain interests or the wishes[22] of another (his 'principal'). A sales representative or a lawyer are examples given by Birch of this type of representative. There are, as Birch points out, a variety of relationships between 'agent' and 'principal' that are covered by this conception. In its second sense the term is used to denote that which has characteristics typical of some larger group or category within which it is included. This 'usage is well exemplified in the term "representative sample", which indicates a sample of the relevant population chosen by statistical methods so that the main characteristics of the population will be mirrored in the sample'.[23] The third usage is less central for our purposes. It indicates a person or object that 'stands for' something else in a way other than simply sharing the characteristics of that which it represents. This 'standing for' is well expressed by the term 'symbolize'. 'A symbolic representative calls to mind, or serves as a concrete embodiment of, a whole group or category of persons.'[24] Examples of representation in this sense would be provided by a piece of sculpture—representing, say, courage—and the British queen, representing the British nation. This also approximates to the original sense of 'representation',[25] and is to some extent reflected in the other usages. Even in the first two senses, a representative 'stands for'—in a very loose sense—that which is represented.

Not only does the term 'representation' have different meanings, but there are also, in the political sphere, different ideas regarding who or what is (or should be) represented. In other words, besides differing conceptions of the way in which persons or groups can be represented, there are differing notions of what persons or groups are to be represented. And this is to leave aside varying ideas about the use to which such representation is to be put in the political system as a whole. Although there are (sometimes close) connections between these different categories of ideas, there are a great number of possible combinations. Hence there are many different theories or doctrines of representation.

We are not, however, concerned here with all theories of representation. Because of the growth of democracy in the modern world, there is sometimes a tendency to assume that the idea and practice of representation is peculiar to democracy. This is not, however, the case. We have already seen that the idea and practice of representation have no especial connection with the notion of power being in the hands of the people. 'No doubt the contemporary popularity of the concept depends much upon its having become linked with the idea of democracy, as well as with ideas of liberty and justice. Yet through much of their history both the concept and the practice of representation have had little to do with democracy or liberty.'[26]

Our concern, then, is only with those notions of representation which occur in democratic theory.[27] This means that our interest here is restricted to conceptions according to which representation is a part of the way in which basic determining decisions are made by the people. Excluded, then, are conceptions in which less than the whole people are represented. So also are conceptions in which those represented— even though they be the whole people—make no decisions concerning how and by whom they are to be represented. Mere reflection or assertion (and even a consequent implementation) of the interests[28] or presumed opinions of those represented is not equivalent to the deciding by those being represented what it is that they want asserted and implemented. Even more is this true where the represented's interests are not promoted but merely taken account of. This was the case with the concept of 'virtual representation' influential in eighteenth-century Britain.[29] Admittedly this restriction to mere 'taking account' of interests was owing to the representatives' overriding duty to pursue the *national* interest. However, the determination and pursuit of the national interest was a task for the representatives alone. This was a feature of the Whig theory of representation—of which the concept of virtual representation was a part. Those virtually represent*ed* had no hand in the formulation of the general interest, and so this overriding of particular interests by the general interest was not a democratic feature in the manner of democratic theories inspired by Rousseau (see Chapter 5, p. 135).

Democratic conceptions of representation, then, are those in which the whole people are represented, and in which the people decide who are to be their representatives and, roughly, at least, what they are to do. Elections constitute the mechanism which, above all else, gives effect to this difference between democratic and non-democratic modes of representation. The people decide, by means of an election, how and by whom they are to be represented. That is to say, such decisions are made or expressed through the process of electing representatives.

Elected representatives can represent in any of the three senses of the term just outlined, although it is the first two which are the most usual. Birch is of the opinion that the fact of election is of such significance as to distinguish yet another sense of the term 'representative'. 'The description of elected members of a political assembly as representatives is best regarded as a specialized usage of the term. . . . The essential characteristic of such persons is the manner of their selection, not their behaviour or characteristics or symbolic value.'[30] It seems to the present writer, however, that while the fact of election is of crucial significance, it is an oversimplification to say simply that here is another sense of the term representation. Election is a vital part of the means whereby representation is actually achieved, rather than a part of the concept itself. To say of an elected member of a political assembly that he is a representative is to assert that he is an agent of his electors and/or that he shares some of their characteristics (symbolic representation is not usually meant). It is further implied that it is, to a large extent, because of, and by means of, his election that he stands in this relationship to those whom he represents. But this *is* to distinguish the relationship from the conditions for its achievement or maintenance.

Whether or not election is a means of achieving representation, or simply an aspect of it, as we shall see in the next chapter there are a number of ways in which election is conceived to help bring about representation. These fall within four main categories. First, there is the idea that election will ensure that only those persons will be chosen who say that they will advance the opinions or interests of the electors. Secondly, there is the idea that election will help to ensure that those chosen as representatives will have characteristics typical of their electors.[31] With each of these first two ideas the assumption is that the electors will only vote for such candidates as will be representative. The third conception is that of the electors ensuring that the representative will behave in the appropriate way after his election. The idea here is that a member of the assembly who does not in fact do what he was elected to do will not be re-elected by his constituents. This has the double effect of helping to ensure that most members will remain representative, and of removing any that do nonetheless become unrepresentative. These ideas concerning the continued representativeness[32] of the elected members rely on the notion that they will wish to be re-elected and that they will therefore see to it that they do nothing to prevent this. This conception is sometimes expressed in terms of the 'rule of anticipated reactions'.[33] A fourth idea concerns the insecurity of tenure implied by election. A representative will, it is argued, refrain from promoting legislation that will adversely affect him when he loses his special status and reverts to being an ordinary member of the public.

There are other ideas to be found concerning the relationship between election and representation, but most ideas fall within these four categories. Representation is provided not only by election,[33a] even where there are these relationships. Election powerfully reinforces rather than provides representation. It is basically the existence of the concept (and corresponding role) of the representative that governs the behaviour of he who is a representative. Nonetheless, performance of the role *is*, in the ways just indicated, very powerfully reinforced—and the role itself modified—by election. And it is through such conceptions of the place of election in representation that a system of representation becomes a part of democratic theory. It is because, and in so far as, election provides that the people decide the policy pursued by their representatives, that a system of representative government is democracy. It is true that our second category of ways in which election contributes to representation does not directly refer to electors' decisions on the representatives' policy. However, in democratic theory the point of a representative in Birch's second sense is that he will have the same opinions as (and therefore will pursue policies desired by) the group or groups that have the characteristics he typifies. Moreover, this conception of representation occurs in conjunction with the others. Representation secured by election means, then, that the basic decisions on policy are made by those who are represented : the people.

Four further important aspects of the relationship between representation and democracy will be taken up later. First, different notions concerning the degree of autonomy of the representative in relation to his electors are outlined in the next chapter. Secondly, these notions are often connected with differing views of the relationship between the national interest and the interest or interests of individual representatives' constituents. And these are reflected in differing conceptions of the duties of a representative towards each type of interest. These issues will also be touched upon in the next chapter. Thirdly, the questions of the extent to which there is a difference, and of the proper relationship between the representation of opinions and of interests, is referred to in the next chapter, while aspects of it are discussed in Chapters 5 and 6. Fourthly, the existence of political parties poses problems for an account of representation in terms of individuals representing constituencies. This will be looked at in Chapter 5.

It is now time to look at our other 'dichotomy'—that between 'Western' or 'liberal' democracy on the one hand, and 'Eastern European' or 'people's' democracy on the other. It was argued earlier that both these conceptions of democracy were within the meaning indicated by our general definition. The difference could not simply be dismissed as a case of different meanings being given to 'democracy'.[34] It is now necessary, therefore, to look at the nature of these two conceptions and to see how both relate to the general definition.

In broad outline, the difference between the two conceptions is as follows. In the concept of *liberal-democracy*, decisions by the people are seen as concrete choices by the people of alternative policies and/or governors.[35] An important corollary of the choice of governors is the ability also to remove them. The scope of government is also seen as limited in some way. As we shall see, there are some connections (as well as some tensions) between these two prongs of the conception.

According to the notion of *people's democracy*, the 'decisions' of the people are incorporated in a single popular will. This will of the people is expressed (and perhaps ascertained) by a single party and is executed by the government under the close guidance of the party. Limitation on the government is not necessary, and would indeed be regarded as undemocratic since it would constitute a limitation on the implementation of the will of the people. As we shall see, one of the ideas behind this theory is the Marxist–Leninist conception of democracy. However, this type of theory is not always linked only to communist countries and Marxism–Leninism. A similar theory is also to be found in the 'Third World'—what C. B. Macpherson calls 'non-liberal democracy : the underdeveloped variant'[36] (in contradistinction to 'non-liberal democracy : the communist variant').

We shall look first at the conception of liberal-democracy, but before doing this a clarification is necessary. In the next chapter we shall analyse what will be called liberal democratic theory, and distinguish it from what will be termed radical democratic theory. Both of these are theories that are applied to Western democracies (see Chapters 5 and 6). The point to be made here is that both theories' portrayals of democracy are contained within the concept with which we are at this moment concerned—the umbrella conception of liberal-democracy. (This will be qualified slightly, see p. 38 below.)

The liberal-democratic model rests on a view of society and the political system that is individualist or pluralist. The conception is not of the community as a corporate entity; rather, all that is seen to exist is a collection of autonomous individuals or groups.[37] This is the basis for the characteristic features of liberal-democracy already indicated. Autonomy of the individual or group implies protection from government interference—hence the idea of limited government. Where government does have to act, such action should accord with the wishes of the people. But the people simply consist of all the individuals or groups—and therefore it is the wishes of these units that have to be ascertained. This can only be done by allowing free expression of views and genuine choice at elections. It is a fundamental tenet of liberal individualism that an individual's views and decisions can only properly emerge if he himself can at some point make uninfluenced statements and choices (a similar assumption regarding group decisions and interests is involved in pluralism). Any divining by others of their 'best interests' or clarification of their 'real will' is ruled out unless it is subject to the check of actual choice on the part of those alleged to have the interest or will.

The making of free choices is seen, then, as a logically necessary condition of democracy. And it is this that leads to the emphasis laid by Western democrats on free elections.[38] Free elections are held to involve both unrestricted voting choice and unrestricted expression of opinion. As we saw previously, the notion of free elections and/or the institutional (and perhaps other) prerequisites for their existence is quite frequently built into the very definitions of democracy given by liberal-democrats.

Aspects of what is involved in the conception of free elections carry over into the other part of the notion of liberal democracy : the idea of limitation on the scope of government—the limited or liberal state. The liberal values limitation of the extent to which the state can control the individual or group—the preservation for them of areas of autonomy. This is the basic element in the liberal view of the state, although it can gain expression in different ways. The main examples are natural rights theory and Utilitarian theory. The former (exemplified by John Locke and Tom Paine) is in essence the view that every individual has a 'natural right' to do certain things, and not to be interfered with in doing them; and the latter (typified by Jeremy Bentham and James Mill) holds that each individual is the best judge of his own interest and that therefore each should be allowed to pursue his own interest in his own way. This latter view connects up with laissez-faire notions and the classical economists' conceptions of the desirability of the non-interventionist state. The idea here is that there will be harmony in the pursuit by all individuals of their interests : that the public as a whole will automatically benefit from every individual pursuing his interest. Because the public interest automatically results, the state need not, and should not, intervene.[39] But to return to the idea that the liberal notion of the limited state involves protection of the individual in many spheres from state interference. Many principles and devices have been brought into play to achieve such protection. Some of the most notable have been the separation of powers, the principles and practices of 'the rule of law', and written constitutions and bills of rights. The point here, however, is that, important among these ideas, has been the establishment of such civil rights as the right to free speech and assembly. These are also, as we saw just now, usually regarded as among the requirements for free elections. They thus have a double significance and value for liberal-democrats. This 'doubling-up' also means that some at least of the liberal and democratic aspects of the notion of liberal-democracy become tightly welded together.

So intermeshed have some of these aspects become that the other features of the liberal view of the state—such as the separation of powers and the rule of law—often come to be seen as part and parcel of the way in which a system is *democratic*. Yet, as has often been pointed out, the liberal state evolved before democracy was grafted on to it (mainly in the nineteenth and early twentieth centuries). 'In our Western societies the democratic franchise was not installed until after the liberal society and the liberal state were firmly established. Democracy came as a top dressing.'[40] The two types of aspect of liberal-democracy are, then, to an important extent separable. Indeed, it has fairly often been argued that there is tension between them and that democracy is a threat to individual liberty. Nonetheless, there *are* some logical interconnections. We have just seen an example of this, and there are others. A discussion of these important issues will be found in the appendix to the present chapter on pp. 51–4.

An important aspect of the idea of liberal-democracy is that of a dichotomy between the government and the governed. In contradistinction to the ideas of democracy based on Rousseau's thought, the government is often not really seen as an integral part of the community—as the agency through which the people act. Rather, the people are seen as *acted upon* by a body which is, in an important sense, separate from them, i.e. the government. For Rousseau, the governed and governors are the same. The people literally *govern themselves*—via and by means of the agency of the government. In the liberal-democratic model, on the other hand, the governed and governors are separate. The people are governed *by the government.* For Rousseau, a 'basic determining decision by the people' would consist in the people making a decision and then, in effect, *themselves* carrying it out through the agency of the government.[41] For a liberal-democrat, such a decision would consist in the government responding to a decision by the people regarding what they wanted *the government* to do. In the former conception, the people do what they wish to be done; in the latter, the people get the government to do what they wish to be done.

It should be understood that the liberal-democratic view of the polity in terms of a dichotomy between government and governed is a tendency only. The political system is not consistently viewed in this way—one of the reasons being the unsatisfactoriness of such a conception. It simply does not make sense to refuse to conceive of the government as, at least in some aspects, the instrument through which the community acts. And, because of this, the refusal is incomplete : there is a shifting back and forth between the 'dichotomous' and 'non-dichotomous' views. Nonetheless, the dichotomous view is on the whole predominant, and it can meaningfully be said to be typical of the idea of liberal-democracy. One of the reasons for this predominance is the individualist ontology typical of liberal-democracy, by virtue of which a collection of individuals rather than a community is discerned. It is hard to conceive of a large collection of individuals acting, except in the unlikely event of all doing the same thing at the same time. They would only normally be capable of asking (and there are problems enough with this idea) some small body (the government), capable of acting, to do things for them. The Rousseauist theory, on the other hand, involves the notion of the people as a corporate entity—a community (see below, p. 42). There is no difficulty connected with the conception of an entity acting.

This idea of the dichotomy and of the *government* acting—albeit doing what the people want it to do—can take a positive and a negative form. That is to say, it can take the form either of the people themselves initiating the proposals for government action, or of the government initiating the proposals for the people to accept or reject (or perhaps modify). The positive form can easily slide off into Rousseauist conceptions of democracy. It is but a short step from the idea of the government waiting to be told the wishes of the people—and then carrying them out—to the idea of the government as merely the agency of the people, the mechanism by which the people themselves govern. As we shall see, there are 'positive' liberal-democratic theories, and they do often have these affinities with, or merge into, democratic theories of the type based on Rousseau. However, the idea of liberal-democracy often takes the negative form.[42] And it is this form that most typically comes to mind when the idea of liberal-democracy is mentioned. Part of the reason is that it is in this type of conception that some of the clearest links exist between the liberal and democratic aspects of liberal-democracy. Thus, the idea of the people merely accepting or rejecting what the *governors* (actual or potential) propose to do overlaps very considerably with the idea of the government being firmly kept in its place. The people can be seen as the instrument—indeed, the best instrument—for limiting the scope of government activity. In this negative form of the idea of the dichotomy between people and government, the notion of the government responding to what the people want can be viewed in part as the government being prevented from doing things—the things the people do not wish it to do. Since the liberal-democrat typically presumes that the people do not want 'invasion of their liberties' by the government, the process of responding to the people's wants amounts to limitation of the scope of government activity and the protection of individual liberties. The government doing what the people want consists largely in its refraining from doing things. This sort of view is central to the political thought of John Locke (1632–1704)—the patron saint of liberal-democracy. For Locke the idea—or rather one of his ideas[43]—was that the governors should be removed by the people if their liberties were threatened.

There remains still in the people a Supreme Powere to remove or alter the Legislative, when they find the Legislative act contrary to the trust reposed in them. . . . And thus the Community perpetually retains a Supreme Power of saving themselves from the attempts and designs of any Body, even of their

Legislators, whenever they shall be so foolish, or so wicked, as to lay and carry on designs against the Liberties and Properties of the Subject.[44]

The negative form of the notion of a dichotomy between people and government is most usually expressed in the idea of 'government by consent' : the idea that the existence and activities of the government should be consented to by the people. And, indeed, liberal-democracy is very often defined or summed up as a system in which there is government by consent. Again, it is Locke who is the fountainhead of the idea for liberal-democrats. Locke linked the idea with a theory of society and government as being based upon a contract—a 'social contract'.[45] 'Of the leading contract theorists, Locke is usually taken to be especially the exponent of the theory that the authority of government is derived from and depends upon the consent of the governed.'[46] The theory is one of popular power : the government can be and do only what the people consent to. But, again, it is also a theory of limited government : the people will refuse to consent to improper invasion by the government of their rights and liberties. Locke is important in the 'history of the doctrine of consent' to a large extent because of his 'insistence on inalienable individual rights—life, liberty and property—and because, therefore, "consent of the governed" seemed to be associated with an impenetrable core of individual right and freedom, with "liberty against government", and with tight curbing of governmental power.'[47] In Locke democracy[48] and individual liberty become enshrined in the doctrine of government by consent.

The meaning of 'government by consent' is complex and vague. Here we will merely point out some aspects of the variation of meaning and indicate what portion of the area of meaning can be said to fall within the terms of our definition of democracy.[49] The meaning of 'government by consent' varies principally along two main dimensions. One dimension concerns that which the people consent to. At one end of the scale it is consent to the existence of government as such. This varies through consent to particular forms of government and particular governments to, at the other end of the scale, consent to the policies pursued by the government or even to particular legislative or administrative acts. The other dimension concerns that which constitutes consent. This varies from aquiescence under duress, through various kinds of manipulated, habitual and traditional aquiescence—and also the process of 'socialization'—to deliberate choice to submit, which may involve the giving of permission.[50] Partridge also includes within the notion of consent positive conceptions of the role of the people— where 'the government gives effect to the already declared will of the governed'.[51] He even suggests that Idealist doctrines of the 'real will'[52] are included.[53] However, this would seem to blur the significant distinction that is usually drawn between reacting to a proposal by someone else—which is usually implied by 'consent'—and seeking to have one's own proposal implemented. And Partridge himself admits that ideas of the 'real will' are not usually included within the general notion of consent.[54] At any rate, in this discussion the idea of government by consent will be applied only to such of these conceptions as give the people a negative role.

It remains only to indicate that portion of each dimension of 'government by consent' that falls within the meaning of 'democracy'. On the first dimension, only consent to the policies or particular actions of government can be said to accord with the notion of decisions on 'matters of public policy'. Consent to the existence of the form of government (and to government as such)—and/or to particular governments—may very well also occur in democracies. Such consent may even be a necessary condition for consent to policies or actions. But it does not itself constitute a democracy. Only consent by the people to the policies (and/or the particular enactments or actions) of the governing authorities brings a system of government by consent within the definition of democracy. On the second dimension, it is only conceptions involving deliberate choice that are 'decisions by the people'. Again, though, it may also be the case that the existence of consent of this kind is rendered more likely or more secure if other kinds of consent are also present. In summary, then, democratic conceptions of government by consent are those in which the government submits proposals to the people who give (or withhold) approval and permission for their implementation by governmental action. A necessary condition for this may well be that the government itself be consented to. It is, at least, part of the general idea of liberal-democracy that the people should have a choice of governors, and it would normally be conceived that such choice also implied consent. That is to say, choice of governors would also be seen as consent to the existence as governors of those chosen.

The conception—which we have just been discussing—of a negative role for the people is, as we said, the more clearly liberal form of the liberal-democratic idea of the dichotomy between government and governed. However, we also saw that it can take a positive form. We find this in radical democratic theory. Although, as we shall see in the next chapter, this owes much to Rousseau, it also has a liberal individualist form—even if there are inconsistencies and an incomplete separation from Rousseauist conceptions. In this form the individuals comprising the people still have a crucial sphere of independent autonomous action. This is characteristic of both main planks of individualist radical democratic theory : Utilitarianism and the kind of natural-rights doctrine typified by Tom Paine and Thomas Jefferson. The basic idea here is that of a government completely responsive to, and carrying out, the declared will of the people as being necessary for the promotion or protection of all the individual's interests or rights. The government is to be responsive so that it will not interfere unduly with individuals. The people initiate, but they initiate policies of (or which involve) non-interference with individuals—since, of course, non-interference is what all individuals desire.[55] The difficulty is that once government is postulated as the complete servant of the people, it is sometimes hard to retain the view of it as a hostile force that has to be kept within strict limits. There is, then, a fundamental ambiguity in radical democratic theory in conceptions of the relationship between the people and the government. This is largely due to an inability to perceive that the government can be the creature of the people as a whole while still being a body that orders the individual about. There is a failure to see that the relationship between *the people* and the government is not the same as the relationship between *the individual* and the government—and that, indeed, the relationship between the individual and the government is an important aspect of that between the individual and the people (see below for further discussion of this point). This is part of a fairly general failure of individualist liberal-democratic theory to come to grips with the conceptualization of what might appear to be the paradox that even where the people govern, they are still governed. Talk of majorities and minorities often obscures the fact that it is the same people who both govern (in a wide sense) and are governed. The paradox is more acute where the people are given a positive role, because there is then less obscuring of the fact that it is the people as well as the government who govern (albeit in a wide and in a narrow sense respectively). Again, it is in Rousseau rather than in liberal-democratic thought that these issues are properly focused upon.

Now that we have had a look at the conception of liberal-democracy, it is time to indicate the nature of 'people's democracy'. The primary concern of this book is with liberal-democracy. However, people's democracy is brought in here better to illustrate, by contrasts, aspects of liberal-democracy, and to show that there is an alternative conception of democracy. The validity of this alternative conception is also disputed.

As we have already seen, the basic idea involved in the notion of people's democracy is that of the people's will manifesting itself in the uninhibited activity of the government. Behind this lie the twin ideas of a single, unified will of the people and of a single unopposed party as the means of eliciting and securing the implementation of this will of the people. The basis of these ideas is to be found in Jacobinism and in Marxism–Leninism—with the notion of a single, unified will of the people being derived from Rousseau.

The idea of liberal-democracy rested, as we saw, on an individualist view of the polity. Inherent in this view is the possibility—indeed the near certainty—of the autonomous individuals having different views on public policy. The difficulties this raises for the notion of a decision by the people did not notably bother the earlier theorists. Where any difficulties were perceived, a rather simple notion of majority rule allegedly coped with them. Later thinking about liberal-democracy has been more troubled over the problem of disparate individual views and decisions (see Chapter 4). In the idea of people's democracy, however, there are no such difficulties. The individuals form a corporate entity[56] —the people. This entity has but a single will. This unified will is both a reflection and a component of the corporate character of the people : a single entity has a single will, but that which helps to make the people a corporate entity is the will of all individuals being the same. Apparent diversities of individual wills are, in a sense, less real. The *genuine* will of each individual is the same. This idea is expressed in Rousseau's famous conception of the general will. Here any diversity is seen as the result of individuals following their selfish interests; where they are united is in all willing the common good—this combined will being the general will. It is part of this conception that the will for the common good is the real and the moral will of the individual. Hence the will of the people is more real and more moral than any apparent individual wills that diverge from it. Submission by the individual to the will of the people is nothing but submission to his own real will. Also a part of this conception is the idea that there is a profoundly important distinction between two kinds of will of the people : the genuine will of the people (the general will) and—what might sometimes occur—the mere coincidence of selfish (particular) wills. 'There is often a great deal of difference between the will of all and the general will; the latter considers only the common interest, while the former takes private interest into account, and is no more than the sum of particular wills.'[57]

A later development of the idea was to conceive of some sections of society as having interests and a will different from (and hostile to) the major part. But it was part of such thinking to exclude these hostile elements from the conception of the people (compare the discussion above of the subsidiary concept of the people, pp. 14 and 18). The will of the people thus remained unified—and, indeed, part of its object was the elimination of the opposition of the hostile elements. In both the French and the Russian revolutions there was involved the idea of the masses—the people—rooting out any that remained of their erstwhile oppressors. In the case of the Russian revolution, this idea stems also from the Marxist notion of the dictatorship of the proletariat which follows the revolutionary overthrow of the bourgeoisie. This phase of the dictatorship of the proletariat is seen in

Marxist theory as transitional between the proletariat's revolutionary seizure of power and the final withering away of the state. In this phase the state apparatus, reconstructed, is used by the proletariat to destroy what remains of the bourgeois class. Only then—with the arrival of the classless society—can the state wither away. The proletariat are equated with the masses—the people. They either constitute the mass of the population or else are the revolutionary vanguard of the masses. 'On the continent of Europe, in 1871, the proletariat did not in a single country constitute the majority of the people. A "people's revolution" . . . could be such only if embracing both the proletariat and the peasantry. Both classes then constituted the "people".'[58]

In Marxist–Leninist hands, then, 'the people' become a class—or perhaps, initially, two united classes. They become an entity and have a will in the way that Marxism conceives of a class as an entity which develops a class-consciousness and a revolutionary purpose. For Marx, genuine democracy, as distinct from sham 'bourgeois democracy', comes into existence at this stage—after the proletarian revolution. It can be argued that Marx himself saw this as a kind of spontaneous stateless democracy that paves the way for the fully developed classless society : 'the dictatorship of the proletariat is in Marx the emergency self-government (for the period of the overt class war) of the proletariat itself and nothing more. And his democracy is a stateless democracy. . . .'[59] But there is no doubt that Lenin saw the dictatorship of the proletariat clearly *as* a dictatorship in which the proletariat used their reconstructed state to destroy the bourgeoisie at the same time as organizing themselves : 'The overthrow of the capitalist class is feasible only by the transformation of the proletariat into the ruling class, able to crush the inevitable and desperate resistance of the bourgeoisie, and to organize, for the new settlement of the economic order, all the toiling and exploited masses.'[60] Lenin's *State and Revolution* is devoted to exposing what he alleges is the fallacy of interpreting Marxism as meaning that the dictatorship of the proletariat is a stateless phase or one in which there is an interplay of divergent views; the will of the proletariat is unified, is triumphant and is implemented through the state. And, Lenin says, this is democracy—a system in which the people (the formerly exploited masses) rule, the form of rule being a dictatorial use of the state. 'The dictatorship of the proletariat, the period of transition to Communism, will, for the first time, produce a democracy for the people, for the majority', and 'democracy is a *State* which recognizes the subjection of the minority to the majority, that is, an organization for the systematic use of *violence* by one class against another, by one part of the population against another.'[61] There are also other concepts of democracy to be found in Lenin's thought,[62] but this one does seem to be dominant.

Marxist–Leninist thought also contains an analogue to the idea, embodied in Rousseau's conception of the general will, of the real will of the people not necessarily coinciding with their apparent will. In Marxism–Leninism, the real interest of the proletariat is their 'objective' class interest. But, in part because of the 'false consciousness' foisted upon the proletariat by the ideology of the bourgeois ruling class, they may very well not discern their objective class interest until a fairly late stage in the development of the proletariat as a class. For Marx, this comes with the development of class-consciousness. And once discerned, that which is in the interests of the class is overtly willed by the members of the class. For Lenin, however, the bulk of the proletariat will need firm guidance by the Communist party, at least until the last vestiges of the forces of capitalism have been destroyed.[63] The party—the revolutionary vanguard of the proletariat— is necessary to discern, proclaim and pursue the class interest. But it was Stalin who most explicitly developed the idea which amounts to the view that, whether or not the rest of the proletariat comprehend or accept them, it is the words and deeds of their vanguard that are in their objective ('real') class interests—and therefore what they really will.

But in order that it may really be the vanguard, the Party must be armed with revolutionary theory. . . . Without this it will be incapable of directing the struggle of the proletariat, of leading the proletariat. The Party cannot be a real party if it limits itself to registering what the masses of the working class feel and think . . . if it is unable to rise above the momentary interests of the proletariat, if it is unable to elevate the masses to the level of the class interests of the proletariat. The Party must stand at the head of the working class; it must see farther than the working class; it must lead the proletariat, and not follow in the tail of the spontaneous movement.[64]

In the notion of people's democracy, then, the will of the people consists of a single unified will—even if the contrary is indicated by social divisions or the apparent state of public opinion. It is also part of this idea that there should be no restrictions—such as constitutional limitations on legislation or government action—on the prosecution of the people's will.[65] Since the will of the people *is* the real will of every individual, there is no sense in the notion that individuals should in any way be protected from it.

As has already been indicated, it is also part of the idea of people's democracy that a party—but only a single party[66]—is necessary to elicit and to implement the people's will. The former process involves discerning the real interests of the people and, by means of organization and propaganda, bringing the people to a condition where the pursuit of these interests is fairly widely accepted and thereby made possible.

The latter activity involves the party in directing and supervising the governmental machinery of the state. The one-party state is thus a necessary part of the idea of people's democracy. A single party, with the functions just indicated, is a necessary condition for the expression and implementation of the unified will of the people.

As we have seen, this idea of the essential role of a single party is derived from the Leninist conception of the revolutionary vanguard. The party is the organizational instrument of the vanguard. But the idea of the enlightened vanguard had appeared earlier than this. It had arisen as a development of the Jacobin theory of democracy associated with the French revolution. Even the idea of the crucial role of a party was there in embryo.[67]

The idea of a vanguard party guiding the people is not incompatible with the idea of indirect democracy. Indeed, it is a necessary part of the theory that direct control should be in the hands of a body smaller than the people as a whole, viz. the party. However, there is the connection with Rousseau's thought, which, as we have seen, constituted a theory of direct democracy. And it is not at all clear that the party or its members are seen as representatives in the sense that there are representatives in the liberal conception of indirect democracy. The crucial idea is that of the unified will of the people. Because there are no differences of opinion or interest to be represented, there is no need for representation. The single will of the people simply has to manifest itself. If there is a need for a group to be in direct control, this is for the purpose of eliciting and implementing the popular will rather than for representing it. If such a group is to be conceived as representing, it would seem to be the third of the concepts of representation indicated by Birch (see p. 31 above) which is involved. The party acts as a symbolization, rather than as an agent or a 'sample', of the people. The will of the party is not directed by the will of the people; it *is* the will of the people.

In fact, in both the Jacobin and the Marxist–Leninist notions of democracy there has been some uncertainty about the place of representative institutions. There seems to have been an oscillation between two types of view. One involves liberal-democratic 'delegate theories' of representation (see next chapter). The other is an insistence on either straightforward direct democracy or the party-as-the-embodiment-of-the-people version of it just indicated.[68] Representative institutions were usually accepted as inevitably necessary, but the representatives were to be treated as potential enemies of the people and hedged about with restrictions embodying direct manifestations of popular power. 'Robespierre searched for safeguards against "representative despotism". They were two : constant popular control over the Legislative body, and direct democratic action by the people.'[69] We have already seen that it often looks as if Marx and Lenin are theorists of direct democracy (see p. 28 above). But, again, there is no complete rejection of representative institutions. Lenin, indeed, clearly accepted them, provided that they did in actuality secure unmitigated popular control of the processes of government. 'Representative institutions remain, but parliamentarianism as a special system, as a division of labour between the legislative and the executive functions, as creating a privileged position for its deputies, *no longer exists* [in the democracy Marx discerned in the Paris Commune]. Without representative institutions we cannot imagine a Democracy, even a proletarian Democracy; but we can and *must* think of democracy without parliamentarianism.'[70] The idea was that the representative assembly was to be the real power centre—a working body rather than a 'talking shop'—in direct control of administration as well as of legislation.

Both with and without an explicit consideration of the role of party, then, the idea of people's democracy has an ambiguous relationship with the idea of direct democracy. However, the guiding conception is clear. This is that there should be direct, unimpeded, expression and implementation of the single and all-powerful will of the people— whether or not this involves intermediate bodies of some kind or another. We can sum up the notion of people's democracy as one in which 'the basic determining decisions' of the people are unanimous and which directly determine state action. Such decisions may also be elicited, rather than overtly made by means of an institutional decision-making procedure. Elections in a people's democracy are for the purpose of ratifying rather than arriving at a decision. Hence a theory and justification of elections at which only one party puts up, or approves, candidates.

There is one aspect of the theory of people's democracy that has not so far been mentioned. This is not so much part of the conception of *democracy* (in the primary sense of the word, at least) as a theory to which the conception became attached. This is the Marxist theory of the determining role of the economic basis of society. This involves a view of political institutions and beliefs as being but part of the 'superstructure' (and consequently of economic power and the 'economic conditions' of the people as being more important that political arrangements) :

The sum total of . . . relations of production constitutes the economic structure of society, the real foundation, on which rises a legal and political superstructure and to which correspond definite forms of social consciousness. The mode of production of material life conditions the social, political and intellectual life process in general. It is not the consciousness of men that determines their being, but, on the contrary, their social being that determines their consciousness.[71]

This theory implies that liberal-democracy—'bourgeois democracy' —is a sham, because it leaves the economic power structure untouched.[72] Economic power remains in the hands of a minority—the bourgeoisie. Moreover, because of its economic power, the bourgeoisie also controls the political power: liberal-democracy is not even a political democracy. In a 'true' democracy—a people's democracy— economic as well as political power is therefore in the hands of the people. The former is a condition of the latter. But the direct economic power of the masses, which is conceived to result from the proletarian revolution, is also of great importance in its own right. This idea connects up with those of social and economic democracy generally (see previous chapter), and with the general socialist tradition's stress on economic and social equality. And, of course, from Rousseau onwards there have been interconnections between such ideas of equality and the conception of democracy that we have just been analysing.[73] In short, a theory of the desirability and crucial importance of equality of economic power is an essential part of the theory of people's democracy.

It was pointed out earlier that this book is primarily concerned with liberal-democracy rather than people's democracy.[74] This might be considered an arbitrary choice, or simply as reflecting the natural interests of Anglo-Saxons. (Continental democratic theory—i.e. non-Communist Continental democratic theory—is mainly liberal-democratic, but—being more influenced by Rousseau—it is so in a less clear-cut manner than Anglo-Saxon theory.[75]) It is, however, argued by liberal-democrats, of course, that liberal-democracy is better than people's democracy. If this is the case, it constitutes an additional reason for concentrating on liberal-democracy.

Very often the superiority of liberal-democracy is said to consist in the invalidity of the claims of people's 'democracy' to really be democracy. The present author broadly agrees with this argument, though some care is needed in stating it. One of the complications is that people's democracy is often attacked in the West for its illiberal rather than its undemocratic character—but often without such a distinction being explicitly made. It is true that, as we have seen, liberal-democracy merges to some extent the two conceptions after which it is named.[76] Nonetheless, it is a great aid to clarity if a distinction is (initially at least) made between two arguments. One is to the effect that, in people's 'democracy', the people cannot be said to govern, and the other is to the effect that, in such a 'democracy', individuals have no, or insufficient, liberty. This is not the place to go into all the complexities of the issues these arguments raise, but some salient points will be indicated.

First, the argument concerning individual liberty. As is shown in the appendix, conceptions of liberty and freedom can be developed in very different ways. But the important point would seem to be that, whether or not the idea of people's democracy incorporates an acceptable conception of liberty (and most Anglo-Saxons would say it did not), the nature of actual political systems based on this idea are in fact destructive of individual liberty in any sense. There is not the space to argue this in detail, but the central contention is that in practice, with the immense power derived from the unlimited authority of the 'general will', the party and government will in all probability rule in a tyrannical manner. Whether or not the pure ideas involved in people's democracy have some validity, the important point here is that they lend themselves to an interpretation that creates, or at least bolsters, a form of government that involves the arbitrary and cruel treatment of individuals by the powers that be.

This view is, in fact, an amalgam of two arguments which can be combined in ways that are not always entirely consistent. Nonetheless, both seem essentially correct—and if properly interpreted do reinforce one another. The first argument is to the effect that one should by-pass the question of the correct interpretation of the original, or most important, theorists or publicists. The essential point is that the body of thought that constitutes and underpins people's democracy has become a statement of, and a prescription for, totalitarian and arbitrary rule. It might well be that Rousseau—and even, perhaps, Lenin—is to be correctly interpreted in a very different way. However, the fact remains that an interpretation and tradition has arisen that gives total, virtually uncontrolled and arbitrary power to the government and the party.

The question of the 'responsibility' of Rousseau for the deeds or misdeeds of those who invoked his name is as relevant or irrelevant as say the question of the 'responsibility' of the Gospel for the expulsion of the Hugenots by Louis XIV. The continuity of a tradition matters more than the authenticity of the interpretation of the canon. And the totalitarian-democratic nature, or at least potentialities, of the Rousseauist–Jacobin canon stare into one's face.[77]

The second argument is to the effect that, whatever the guiding concepts,[78] a set of persons (the government and the party's leadership —which may be virtually identical) given power without effective practical restraints, will tend to abuse that power. One need not completely accept Lord Acton's dictum to the effect that all power tends to corrupt and absolute power corrupts absolutely. But one can still recognize that self-interest and/or individual ideas concerning the use to be made of power will tend to exert a dangerous influence upon those whose power is not effectively limited. One need not deny that there are other dimensions to government and to the state to accept at least this part of the classical liberal thesis. And even Rousseau insisted that, besides being an agent of the general will, the government (unfortunately) had its own particular will. Moreover, the two wills are in opposition : 'As the particular will acts in opposition to the general will, the government continually exerts itself against the Sovereignty.'[79]

The second form of argument against people's democracy is to the effect that political systems called such are not in fact democracies. Again the argument combines two prongs—the 'theoretical' and the 'practical'. The former rejects the notion that the idea of people's 'democracy' is democratic; the latter denies that the political systems alleged to be modelled on the idea are democracies.

The basis of the theoretical argument is the view that no sense can be made of the notion of a decision by the people unless the people are given the opportunity which contested elections provide to register different opinions and to make explicit 'empirical' choices between alternative policies and candidates for office. Such opportunities are not provided where elections are held merely to ratify the position of a single party. This, of course, is to restate a fundamental tenet of liberal-democracy. It is to reassert that a necessary condition for the manifesting of individuals' decisions[80] is that they should actually and explicitly be asked to make some. Admittedly, this is a necessary rather than a sufficient condition. Moreover this view need not, and should not, involve a denial of the Rousseauist distinction between selfish views (which may be transient) and a view of the common good. Nor should it involve a denial of the possible conflict between them, and of the superior relevance of the latter. Much of liberal-democratic theorizing is faulty in that it fails to come to grips with the crucial issues involved here (these issues are further discussed in Chapters 3, 5 and 6). However, even an 'enlightened' liberal-democratic view does involve two fundamental modifications of the Rousseauist conception (or conceptions often derived from Rousseau). First, that if, after asking for individuals' decisions regarding the common good, only particular or selfish[81] views are manifested, then these must be taken as the decision of the people regarding what the community should do. This involves considerable problems, but the salient point is that the people have *decided* that this is what they want (they want particular benefits promoted). Such a decision may be unwise—or even untenable—but it is the people's decision. Such a state of affairs is crucially different from one in which the people's decision is alleged to be embodied in the outcome of a struggle between pressure groups. Here, the people have not been asked to give their view of what the community should do, and so the combination of particular or selfish views does not amount to a decision by the people as to what it should do (see Chapters 5 and 6). The second modification consists quite simply in the contention that there can be genuine differences of view concerning what is for the common good. And, because of this, people actually have to be asked what their view is. Both these modifications, then, involve the idea that individuals have explicitly to say what their decisions are regarding state action. Such decisions cannot be deduced from an analysis (by theorist, party leader or whatever) of what is for the common good—whether or not the conception of the common good is modified by the idea of class interest.

The practical argument regarding the lack of democracy in people's 'democracies' is analogous to the one concerning individual liberty. Thus the argument is that whether or not the idea of people's democracy is valid, the political systems named after this idea are certainly not democracies. Even if the idea of the single, 'objectively determined', will of the people were valid, it would not follow that in the people's 'democracies' the party and government expressed and implemented this. As in the case of the argument concerning liberty, the contention is that governing personnel who have to submit to no practical regulation of their power, tend to develop a particular will of their own. In the people's 'democracies', then, it is not the will of the people but the will of the party leadership and/or the bureaucracy (or possibly the military leadership) which prevails.

It might be objected here that, even if people's 'democracies' are illiberal and undemocratic, they do at least secure economic power and equality for the people. Even if this were the case, however, it would not show these systems to be democratic—they might be better than democracies but they would not *be* democracies. But it is by no means clear that they would be better : would the lack of political liberty be counterbalanced by the economic freedom and equality? Even this, however, is not to penetrate to the nub of the issue. The fundamental point is that, if the arguments concerning the illiberal and the undemocratic character of the people's 'democracies' are correct, then economic power is not in the hands of the people. The kind of power which the governors of these political systems have involves a very considerable control by them of economic conditions as well as of the economy generally. If this is so, then it is not at all clear that it can be said that there is economic equality—not at least to the degree discerned by the supporters of people's 'democracy'. In liberal-democracies, on the other hand—when they really are democracies—the extent of economic inequality that can be perpetrated is limited by the political power of the masses. In a similar way, while there is undoubtedly a concentration of economic power into relatively few hands, the extent of this, and of the power it gives, is limited by the spread of political power (these and related issues will be touched on again in the last chapter). Thus, it can at the very least be argued that the economic inequalities of the liberal-democracies are not markedly greater than those of the people's 'democracies'. If this is so, then it can be confidently asserted that the virtues of liberal democracy—as compared to people's 'democracy'—clearly outweigh possible vices.

This statement of a belief in the superiority of liberal-democracy concludes the discussion of different sorts of democracy (further issues concerning the justification of democracy are discussed in Chapter 8). In the next chapter some of the different types of theory that lie behind the general idea of liberal-democracy will be outlined.

Appendix: Liberty and Democracy

There are many and complex issues involved in the question of the relationship between the concepts of 'democratic' and 'liberal', 'democracy' and 'liberty'. A proper discussion of them would itself take up a whole book. In this appendix an attempt will be made merely to indicate schematically some of the most salient considerations (including reference to the points already discussed in the text). The guiding theme is the question whether democracy and individual liberty are in conflict, or whether they interpenetrate one another.

'Democracy' has already been defined, but not 'liberty'. The question of the definition of 'liberty'—like that of 'democracy'—opens up great vistas of conceptualization and controversy.[82] Here there is space only for what will appear as somewhat dogmatic assertions. 'Individual liberty' will be taken to mean freedom of individuals in a social context.[83] 'Freedom' will be taken to mean self-determination: the free individual is the one who himself determines his actions. Different conceptions of freedom arise from differing accounts of the nature of self-determination and of the environment of the individual—and of the way in which the environment does or does not interfere with individual self-determination.

If one talks about the liberty of 'a people', as a collective entity, then democracy and liberty largely overlap. The self-determination of the people consists in its making its own determining decisions. In this way democracy and nationalism become associated: nationalism consists in the identification of a people as a nation and the demand that the nation become self-determining. However, as we have seen, liberal-democracy is individualist—individuals rather than nations or peoples are seen as the important (if not the only) entities. And the question at issue here is that of the relationship between *individual* liberty and democracy: the relationship between each individual determining his own activity and all the individuals determining what they all should do.

In some ways—or, at least, looked at in some ways—individual liberty and democracy intermesh. One of these ways we have already mentioned (pp. 38–40 above). This is an aspect of the negative form of the idea of a dichotomy between government and people. In this conception the people will decide that the government should be kept within limits, for this is what all the individuals will want. And this goes together with a conception of liberty according to which individual liberty consists in the absence of governmental restraints. Thus the people's power amounts to a guarantee of individual liberty. Such ideas as these lead to a fairly complete merging of liberalism and democracy. This is especially true of the theory of the American political system, stemming as it does so much from Locke. 'Americans *are* liberals, but they do not *call* their behaviour liberalism. The theory of their liberal practice is simply incorporated, in toto, in their theory of democracy.'[84]

There is another conception of the intermeshing of individual liberty and democracy which is associated more with the positive form of the government–people relationship. Here individual liberty is seen to consist not so much in the absence of governmental activity as in the individual participating in that activity. Individual self-determination incorporates determination (or rather a share in it) by the individual of the circumstances that mould his life—including the activities of the government. For example, Richard Price (an eighteenth-century radical democrat) said that 'in every free state every man is his own legislator', and he believed that 'no man is free unless he takes part in the procedures of government'.[85] Just as the radical form of liberal-democracy has affinities with Rousseauist democracy (see above, pp. 38, 40 and 41), so this conception of the relationship between democracy and individual liberty has affinities with the Rousseauist idea of freedom (see pp. 54–5 below). It is but a short step from asserting that individual freedom involves each individual in participating in the procedures of government to the idea that individual freedom *consists in* the submission of the individual to the outcome of those procedures: submission to a government which is implementing the general will.

Another way in which liberty and democracy become connected was demonstrated in the discussion of free elections. Here it was shown that what was seen as a logically necessary condition of decision-making by the people was also an important element in the limitation of government control of the individual (see pp. 35–6 above).

Despite these conceptions of close connections between democracy and individual liberty, important tensions or conflicts between the two have also been discerned.[86] The basis of this tension is to be found in the liberal conception of an opposition between state power and individual liberty: although a certain degree of state power is conceived as necessary to protect individuals from each other, individual liberty is said to exist where state power is absent. Democracy is a form of state, and as such does not do away with the conflict with individual liberty. The term 'democracy' refers to the location of the exercise of the state's power rather than to its limitation. 'Liberalism is above all the technique of limiting the State's power, whereas democracy is the insertion of popular power into the State.'[87] Now, as long as it is assumed that all the people wish to limit it, the insertion of popular power will limit the state's power—the first of the connections between democracy and individual liberty outlined above. But this assumption can be challenged. Moreover, the second of the connections outlined above rests on the assumption that all individuals will wish to act, or will wish the state to act, alike, and therefore that the people governing themselves is the same thing as each individual governing himself. This idea implies the *use* of state power, not its limitation. But this assumption is fallacious[88]—only a Rousseauist theory can consistently equate the will of each individual with the will of the people. In fact, failing a Rousseauist interpretation, it has to be accepted that it is usually the case that the wishes and therefore the wills of some individuals clash with those of others.

What is therefore counted as the will of the people cannot normally comprehend the wishes of all individuals (see Chapter 4 for a discussion of the issues raised by the notion of a collective decision generated from differing individual decisions). From an individualist viewpoint, then, the wills of some individuals must usually conflict with the will of the people. Hence, the use of state power that is determined by the will of the people must conflict with the wills of, and thereby limit the freedom of, some individuals.

This conception of an antithesis between democracy and liberty has typically been developed in three ways. One of these consists in focusing upon the threat to the freedom of minorities posed by the existence of majority rule. Given that unanimity rarely exists, the 'decisions of the people' are often seen as being constituted by the decisions of the majority. This has been a central feature of much democratic thought. But it would seem to follow from this that the minority are ruled despotically by the majority. Fear of the 'tyranny of the majority' has also been an important theme in thought about democracy—as evidenced by the writings of, for example, Madison, Tocqueville and J. S. Mill. Aspects of this question of majority rule and minority rights are discussed in Chapter 4.

The second way in which the conception of an antithesis between democracy and individual liberty is manifested consists in a development of the majority tyranny argument with respect to individuals rather than to minorities. The idea here is that, where the people rule, it means not that each individual rules himself but that he is ruled by all the rest.[89] 'The "self-government" spoken of is not the government of each by himself, but of each by all the rest.'[90] This idea is more accurately characterized as the individual *versus* the people (or the society or the community) than as some individuals *versus* the majority of individuals.

It has also been argued—by Tocqueville (1805–59), for example—that the atomizing of society into equal individuals characteristic of democracy reinforces this oppression of the individual by society. 'The same equality which renders [the individual] independent of each of his fellow-citizens taken severally exposes him alone and unprotected to the influence of the greater number.'[91] Both Mill and Tocqueville saw such oppression by society as occurring via the government and also by direct pressure on individuals. 'Like other tyrannies, the tyranny of the majority was at first, and is still vulgarly, held in dread chiefly as operating through the acts of the public authorities. But reflecting persons perceived that when society is itself the tyrant—society collectively, over the separate individuals who compose it—its means of tyrannizing are not restricted to the acts it may do by the hands of its political functionaries', since it acts also through the pressure of 'prevailing opinion and feeling'.[92] Moreover, this direct power is reinforced by the political power. 'The fact that the political laws of the Americans are such that the majority rules the community with sovereign sway, materially increases the power which that majority naturally exercises over the mind.'[93]

The third formulation of the antithesis between democracy and liberty arises from considering the great power of a government that is implementing the will of the people. In this formulation it is argued that to a considerable extent the government exercises its own power rather than that of the people. It acts in the name of the people, but in fact much of the time this merely enables it to exercise a great power of its own over individuals. According to this view, then, democracy—or, at least, the form of democracy—results in a straightforward oppression of individuals by the government. And this can happen because people are lulled into a false sense of security by the thought that government is in the hands of the people. 'Every man allows himself to be put in leading strings, because he sees that it is not a person or a class of persons, but the people at large, that holds the end of his chain. By this system the people shake off their state of dependence just long enough to select their master, and then relapse into it again.'[94]

In the face of these arguments many people feel that any inherent or 'natural' connections between democracy and liberty are insufficient, or else that such conceptions are mistaken. And it would, indeed, seem more satisfactory to maintain that for a democracy to be a liberal-democracy there should exist at least some of the traditional liberal limitations upon government.[95] If this is seen as a limitation of democracy—since it is a limitation of the instrument of the people's will—then so be it. This simply shows that liberal-democracy is an amalgam of different, to some extent conflicting, ideas. But as long as this is realized, the ideas can be allowed to modify each other and can be held in harmony rather than fundamental discord. Yet not all theorists or supporters of Western democracy would support this view. Some would discern sufficient 'inherent' connections between liberty and democracy, but others tend to stress the importance of what they see as the democratic aspects at the expense, if necessary, of the traditional liberal limitations on government.[96]

If liberal-democracy could be viewed as subject to illiberal tendencies, how much more might this be true of Rousseauist democracy—whether this be a tendency within non-Communist 'continental' theories of democracy or a part of the theory of 'people's democracy'. A government implementing the single all-powerful will of the people would seem to leave no room at all for a limitation on government control of minorities or individuals. And, indeed, a view of this kind of democracy as illiberal and totalitarian is common. This is exemplified by the title of J. L. Talmon's well-known book, *The Origins of Totalitarian Democracy*. It must, however, be realized that the Rousseauist notion of democracy is tied in with Rousseau's idea of freedom according to which individuals are perfectly free in a democracy of this kind. Those who see it as illiberal are viewing it in terms of the liberal's 'negative'—rather than Rousseau's 'positive'—concept of freedom.[97]

The difference between these two conceptions can be barely more than referred to here, but in very rough outline it is as follows. The negative concept of freedom sees individual self-determination as consisting in the individual doing what he wishes. But 'doing what he wishes' is conceived to include simply acting to fulfil his desires. The positive concept, on the other hand, sees individual self-determination as rational autonomy. The individual is self-determined when his actions are those that embody reasoned decisions rather than being reactions to the desire of the moment. The difference between the two conceptions is best illustrated by an example—albeit one that oversimplifies in order to bring out the contrasts. Consider the position of a person who has decided to give up smoking but who finds himself with a cigarette in front of him. The advocate of the positive concept of freedom would say that the self-determined individual is the one who would resist the desire for the cigarette and refrain from smoking it. But, such an advocate would argue, according to the negative concept, self-determination would consist in fulfilling the desire to smoke the cigarette—i.e., smoking the cigarette is, in an important sense, what he wishes to do. In terms of the positive concept, however, 'giving in' to desires in this way is not so much freedom as slavery—being a slave to one's desires.

The difference between positive and negative freedom translates itself into a political context. The negative concept implies—as we have seen—absence of governmental restraints: the absence of restraints upon individuals following out their various desires.[98] A liberal, it might be said, is one who values individual freedom in this sense. A crucial part of the positive concept, however, is the idea that the individuals' pursuit of their desires should give way to the rational guidance of the state. The state is the organization for the promotion of the common good. The promotion of the common good is the rational objective of all individuals, and therefore the state is seen as the manifestation of all individuals' 'rational will'. Hence the guidance of an individual by the state is not a limitation of his freedom but a vital part of it. Rousseau's conception of the general will incorporates these ideas and also contains the notion that the common good is actually (even if not apparently) willed by every individual: it is not merely that the common good is what would be the objective of those who thought about it—rather it is actually willed by everyone.

Seen in its own terms, then, the Rousseauist conception of democracy contains no negation of individual liberty. Indeed the opposite is the case— in such a democracy perfect freedom exists. Individuals are free because they are acting in accordance with their own rational wills. And there is a great deal in such a conception. This can be illustrated by a down-to-earth example. Although some British motorists carp about interference with the liberty of the individual, most would not regard the drinking and driving law in this light. Many a motorist in a pub will drink less than he would have done had the law not existed, but rather than seeing this as oppression, he will feel that he has acted in accordance with his true intentions. But as to whether or not the Rousseauist conception of freedom, and its relationship to democracy, is in some sense adequate—or even superior to the liberal-democratic view—the essential point is the one made earlier (see pp. 48–9 above). This is that a crucial failing in the use of the conception is its association in practice with tyrannical government. It would seem, therefore, that the traditional liberal-democratic view of Rousseauist democracy has in the end much to commend it—even if the issue is not nearly so simple as it is often made to appear, and even if in many ways Rousseau's thinking is far more profound than much of liberal-democratic thinking, and elements of it have to be accepted.

NOTES AND REFERENCES

1 It was, of course, acknowledged that there were *some* different meanings, and there was some discussion of this at the end of the chapter. But it should also be remembered that not all the apparently different meanings even indicate differing interpretations of the kind just mentioned. Some of these differences result from inabilities to define clearly, and some from confusions between questions of meaning and other questions—such as those regarding necessary conditions (see pp. 2 and 3–5).

2 There is some overlapping of these two distinctions, since people's democracy is to some extent identified as a kind of direct democracy (see below).

3 That is to say, no reason, given that it is already accepted that the people should make as many as possible of the determining decisions.

4 The modern conditions usually referred to are the size and complexity of modern states, and of the industrialized economies and societies with which they are associated. See Chapter 5 for further implications of such factors.

5 D. Pickles, *Democracy*, London, Methuen, 1970, p. 35.

6 ibid., p. 35. This is a prochronistic use of the concept of representation, and does not mean that the council consisted of elected representatives. Representation as we know it was an idea unknown to the ancient Greeks. See below for a discussion of the concept of representation. For a description of Greek democracy, see, for example, Pickles, *Democracy*, Chapter 2; Mayo, *An Introduction to Democratic Theory*, Chapter 3; A. H. M. Jones, *Athenian Democracy*, London, Blackwell, 1964; M. I. Finley, *Democracy Ancient and Modern*, New Brunswick, New Jersey, Rutgers University Press, 1973.

7 Sartori, *Democratic Theory*, p. 252.

8 A crucial difference—often overlooked—between ancient Greek and modern democracies should be noted. This is that the Greek *polis* was in important ways different from a state. Not only was it small—hence the term 'city-state'—but it was also an all-embracing community. There was not the separation of an important private sphere from the public political realm that is implied by the concept of—and existing within—a state. One result of this was that a high degree of 'participation' was likely in a democratic polis since the polis encapsulated very many aspects of a citizen's life. See Sartori, *Democratic Theory*, Chapter 12. But it is sometimes said that it was decreasing participation (and lack of military expertise) that were factors in the eventual downfall of Athens. See, for example, Pickles, *Democracy*, p. 39.

9 J. J. Rousseau, *The Social Contract*, Everyman edition, London, J. M. Dent, 1913, p. 78. The reader should beware of confusion. Rousseau in his own words rejects 'democracy' as undesirable and/or impossible of realization. See Book Three, Chapter 4 of *The Social Contract*. However, he is here using the term in a special sense (see Book Three, Chapters 2 and 3) to mean *administration*—direct executive action—by the people. This does nothing to detract from his conception of *legislation*, basic political decision-making, directly by the people—which would usually be called democracy. It should also be noted that, at times, Rousseau veers towards a conception of the people ratifying rather than initiating—as the cited quotation indicates. This is connected with his notion of the role of 'the Legislator' (see Book Two, Chapter 7). However, even when he is saying that the Legislator should propose laws to the people this is only for the purpose of better revealing to the people what it is that they really will—i.e. the purpose is to reveal the general will. The basic idea, then, is still the positive one of policy springing from the people.

10 Sartori, *Democratic Theory*, p. 426.

11 This would take place in the 'higher phase of communist society', when the

social conditions and productive forces would have evolved sufficiently to make this possible. At such time, the state—including its sham (bourgeois) democratic forms—could finally disappear. (See Marx and Engels, 'Critique of the Gotha Programme', *Karl Marx and Frederick Engels: Selected Works*, Moscow, Foreign Languages Publishing House, 1958, Vol. 2 (1951), esp. pp. 23 and 38–9.

12 Marx's conception did include some elected personnel, but these were to be very closely controlled by their electors. Bureaucracy, standing army and police were to be suppressed. See 'The Civil War in France', in *Selected Works*, Vol. 1, p. 519; and Sartori, *Democratic Theory*, p. 418. Lenin's idea of the meaning of the term 'democracy' is more confusing than Marx's. Lenin tends to shift between different uses of the term in rather a bewildering manner. On this, and generally on the concept of democracy in Marx and Lenin, see Sartori, op. cit., Chapter XVII, and Chrisophersen, *The Meaning of 'Democracy'*, Chapters IX and XVI. Also, see below, pp. 43–6.

13 J. Califano, *The Student Revolution: A Global Confrontation*, New York, Norton, 1970, p. 72, quoted in T. E. Cook and P. M. Morgan, *Participatory Democracy*, San Francisco, Canfield Press (Harper & Row), 1971, p. 1.

14 See, for example, C. J. Friedrich, *Constitutional Government and Democracy*, Waltham, Mass., Toronto and London, Blaisdell Publishing Co., fourth edition, 1968, pp. 240 and 243.

15 It is true that the Swiss cantons are regional, rather than purely local, governmental units (units, in fact, of a federation)—and as such more, and more complex, issues come within their purview. It is, indeed, often acknowledged that Swiss 'grass-roots' democracy is the most effective which exists. Even so, the cantons are not charged with the entire running of a modern state. Moreover, it is only in some smaller cantons—with the corresponding diminution in the complexity of issues—that direct democracy is practised. The qualification to the 'directness' of the democracy mentioned in the text should also be remembered. Lack of size and of complexity of issues to be dealt with also means that direct democracy can be practised in some non-state institutions. Students' unions are an example. Whether direct democracy is always desirable even where it is possible is, of course, another question (on this, and on the issues of size and complexity, see also the discussion of 'participatory democracy' in Chapter 9).

16 On the concept of representation, see A. H. Birch, *Representation*, London, Pall Mall, 1971, for a lucid and concise analysis. For more detailed discussions, see: H. F. Pitkin, *The Concept of Representation*, Berkeley and Los Angeles, and London, University of California Press and Cambridge University Press, 1967; and J. R. Pennock and J. W. Chapman (eds.), *Representation*, New York, Atherton Press (Nomos X), 1968.

17 Pitkin, *The Concept of Representation*, p. 3. Complex points are raised here about the relationship between concepts and political reality. The argument that concepts to an extent *constitute* political reality is mentioned in Chapter 5 (see n. 8, p. 147). But whether or not representation existed to some small extent in ancient Greek democracy, it certainly had no central role (hence, of course, its description as direct democracy).

18 T. Paine, *Rights of Man*, first published 1791/2; Pelican Books edition Harmondsworth, Penguin Books, 1969, pp. 199 and 202.

19 J. Mill, *Essay on Government* (written in 1820 as an article on 'Government' for the *Encyclopaedia Britannica*), Cambridge, Cambridge University Press, 1937, p. 34.

20 Birch, *Representation*, pp. 13–14.

21 ibid., p. 15.

22 Birch sticks to 'interests'. The relationship between interests and opinions in systems of representation is discussed in the next chapter.

23 Birch, *Representation*, p. 16.

24 ibid., p. 16.

25 See Pitkin, *The Concept of Representation*, pp. 3 and 241.

26 ibid., p. 2.

27 The object at this point is merely to outline the main concepts. Different theories of representation in democracy will be considered in the next chapter when different democratic theories are discussed. One of the main elements in these different theories is the degree of autonomy allowed to the representative in his relationship with those whom he represents.

28 The idea of the representation of group or sectional interests—which has a long history—has somewhat more complicated implications for this argument. However, it does not essentially alter the main point being made here. Aspects of the relevant considerations will be discussed in Chapter 6 where 'pressure group theories' of democracy will be discussed. On ideas of representation of interests, see, besides the works already cited, A. H. Birch, *Representative and Responsible Government*, London, Allen & Unwin, 1964; S. H. Beer, *Modern British Politics*, London, Faber & Faber, 1965; and 'The Representation of Interests in British Government: Historical Background', in *American Political Science Review*, Vol. 51 (September 1957), 613–50.

29 See Birch, *Representation*, pp. 51–2.

30 ibid., pp. 19–20.

31 Just which of the characteristics of the electors are considered relevant will vary with different democratic theories and circumstances.

32 Obviously this applies to the first rather than to the second of the previously outlined senses of representation. This, of course, was the sense that was utilized in the notion that election will ensure the choosing of those persons who will in fact advance the electors' opinions or interests.

33 C. J. Friedrich, *Constitutional Government and Democracy*, 2nd edition, Boston, 1941, pp. 589–91. See also Chapter 6 below.

33ª It is worth noting in passing that democratic selection of personnel need not be by election. Selection by lot was used in ancient Greece, although this method has grave disadvantages—in modern democracies, at least (for a recent discussion, see R. A. Dahl, *After the Revolution?*, New Haven and London, Yale University Press, 1970, pp. 149–53).

34 But this is—as we also saw—the account usually given. The fact that the quarrel over whether the Eastern or Western systems are to be called democracies is nonetheless seen as important, is often explained by the role of 'democracy' as a 'hurrah' word. Appropriation of the term is said to be

important because it expresses approval. The idea is said to be that if one can legitimize only the application of the term to one's own preferred type of political system, this will secure and/or increase the support for that type of system.

The argument above, that both conceptions are of democracy, does not imply that both are necessarily valid conceptions. Because a sympathetic statement of a conception falls within the definition of 'democracy', it does not follow that critical analysis will necessarily show the conception to be coherent and/or meaningful. Nor does it follow that the reality that is alleged to accord with the conception does in fact do so. This issue is taken up later.

35 As we shall see later (Chapter 6), certain modern theories of democracy which would describe themselves as liberal in a broad sense specify choice of governors *rather than* choice of policy. We shall discuss in Chapter 6 whether such theories can in fact properly be called democratic.

36 C. B. Macpherson, *The Real World of Democracy*, London, Oxford University Press, 1966 (first published by the Canadian Broadcasting Corporation, 1965), esp. Chapter 3.

37 Pluralist theories may be characterized here as those which view the basic elements of society as groups rather than individuals (but see Chapters 5 and 6, which also include analyses of the conflicts between individualism and pluralism). However, as in the individualist view, these elements are numerous and in an important sense autonomous. Pluralism shares some of the features of both individualism and collectivism. There is, broadly speaking, a division in political philosophy (and in political thought generally) between 'individualist' and 'collectivist' views of the structure of society. The former sees society as consituted by discrete and self-sufficient individuals and the nature of the society as derived from the characteristics of the individuals. The latter—which has affinities with ancient Greek political thought—points to the fact that individuals are born into an on-going society and that its customs, culture, etc. (indeed, the society itself), have a reality of their own. There is a corresponding emphasis on the extent to which the character of an individual is derived from the society—its customs, culture, etc. Examples of the individualist 'ontology' are provided by the political philosophies of Hobbes, Locke and J. S. Mill whereas the political philosophies of Rousseau (with some qualifications) and Hegel are examples of the 'collectivist' view. The individualist view often—as indicated in the text—leads to a liberal view of the state; but it does not necessarily do so, as the inclusion of Hobbes as an individualist indicates. Where a liberal view is derived, an individualist view of the structure of social reality is supplemented by a view of the moral worth of individuals and of autonomous individual activity.

38 For an excellent analysis of what is involved in giving an 'operational' account of the notion of a 'free election', see W. J. M. Mackenzie, *Free Elections*, London, Allen & Unwin, 1958.

39 Further discussion of such views of the relationship between individual and the public interests will be found in the next chapter, when reference is made to Utilitarian democratic theory. Similar issues are raised when we come to discuss group theories of democracy—see Chapters 5 and 6.

40 Macpherson, *The Real World of Democracy*, p. 5. But for a different view-point, see Sartori, *Democratic Theory*, Chapter XV, esp. pp. 358–60.

41 It is true that Rousseau says that the government is a body 'distinct from the people', but he also says that 'the public force needs an agent of its own' and that this is the government which is 'an intermediate body set up between the subjects and the Sovereign', i.e. between the people and themselves. The idea is clearly that the government is merely a mechanism by which the people *govern themselves*. This is also illustrated by the notion that the legislative power is the 'will which determines the act' and the executive power (that which the government exercises) is the 'physical power which executes it' (*The Social Contract*, Book III, Chapter 1).

42 It should, of course, be realized that actual perceptions of political systems frequently utilize both forms of the model—and often the Rousseauist one as well. What happens is that in talking or thinking about a Western political system, as within the idea of liberal democracy itself, people quite frequently slide back and forth between different sets of concepts.

43 There are a number of ideas to be found in Locke concerning the relation-ship of the government to the people. It is a matter for dispute how far they are consistent, but he does certainly at times even depart from the con-ception of the government as separate from the people, and views it as the agency through which they act (e.g. *Second Treatise*, para. 89, lines 9 and 10). This confusion, if it be such, is not so much the fault of Locke in particular as something that is inherent in the whole notion of a dichotomy between people and governors in a democracy. The question of whether Locke's theory *is* democratic will be discussed in the next chapter.

44 John Locke, *Two Treatises of Government*, a critical edition edited by Peter Laslett (Mentor Book edition, London, The New English Library, 1965), Second Treatise, Chapter XLLI, para. 149 (p. 413).

45 The idea of a social contract flourished in the seventeenth and eighteenth centuries. Basically, the idea involves the notion of man's original existence as that of a state of nature, without any regulation by the state. Even if not conceived as a historical fact, the state of nature was postulated as that which would exist if society broke down. Men exchanged, or would exchange, this for life in a state by means of contracting with one another to give up certain of their primordial freedoms in exchange for the benefit of the security and convenience thereby attained. Some social contract ideas involved the notion of individuals directly contracting to set up a government. Others involved two stages: first, a contract between indi-viduals to set up a society, and secondly, the setting up of a government with a contractual relationship between it and the society it then governs. Locke himself postulated a two-stage process, but the second stage involved the simile of a trust (the governors as trustees for the people) rather than of a contract (see the introduction by Peter Laslett to his critical edition of John Locke's *Two Treatises of Government*, pp. 127–8). (Locke also tended to use the term 'compact' rather than 'contract'—ibid., p. 126.) The idea of a social contract is connected with that of consent in that a contractual relationship implies consent to—and only to—that which is in the terms of the contract. For further discussion of the social contract idea, see J. W.

Gough, *The Social Contract*, Oxford, Oxford University Press, second edition, 1967.

46 P. H. Partridge, *Consent and Consensus*, London, Pall Mall Press (Key Concepts in Political Science series), 1971, p. 19. This book contains a lucid and concise discussion of the problematical concept of consent.

47 ibid.

48 As will be seen in the next chapter, it is a little uncertain how far it can be said that Locke's own theory is one of democracy. However, there are no doubts about its democratic implications or about the direct influence he had on later writers who propounded theories that were straightforwardly democratic.

49 See Partridge, *Consent and Consensus*, for further discussion of the concept of consent.

50 See ibid., esp. pp. 31–6.

51 ibid., p. 36.

52 See Chapter 3 for an indication of the nature of the mode of thought known as Idealism, and its relationship with democratic theory.

53 Partridge, *Consent and Consensus*, p. 36.

54 ibid.: 'But these idealist doctrines with their very special concept of will move far away from common-sense notions of consent and its possible meanings.'

55 This hostility to government is in part due to the fact that much of radical democratic theory originally arose as a reaction to what was seen as oppressive autocratic government. The notion of government as an alien and oppressive force upon the people remained. However, this conception excluded the notion of government as a mechanism to be actively used by the people—for example, to better their lot—an idea also attractive to radical democrats. This dilemma could be 'solved' by inconsistency, by moving from one notion of government to the other—often unconsciously. Compare, for example, Part One of Tom Paine's *Rights of Man* with Part Two, where such an interventionist idea as a state system of social security financed by progressive taxation makes its appearance. Because of the relative unawareness of these competing ideas, the difficulties they implied for the notion of individual liberty were not focused upon. It was not properly realized how governmental action for the benefit of the community involved interference with individuals. Only Rousseau's democratic theory could provide anything other than discomfort or inconsistency here (see below, p. 42). Any individualist theory of democracy tends to get into these kinds of difficulties: there is so often the tendency to subsume under the relationship between the people and the government relationships which are more accurately viewed as being between the individual and the people.

56 The Rousseauist conception is essentially collectivist, but it has profoundly important individualist aspects (in part because Rousseau himself moved to a collectivist conception of the community and its importance from within an individualist mode of thought). The society—the community—is a genuine corporate entity and not a mere collection of individuals: the individuals' nature is derived from their incorporation into the community. Nonetheless, within the community it is only individuals that do or should

exist. There are none of the ideas of the subtle balancing and blending of many intermediate groups (classes, estates, professions, etc.) characteristic of some other collectivist conceptions. Nor is there the focusing upon the web of custom, institutions and culture as components of the community that, for example, becomes so important in the Idealist successors of Rousseau. Indeed, these are ideas that are rejected by Rousseau. All that is left is the individual and the community or state. With a shift of vision the individualist view can easily re-emerge (although this can only happen if basic implications go out of focus). This is another reason for the affinities between individualist radical democratic theory and Rousseauist theory. Both were important in the French Revolution: Tom Paine and his thoughts were intimately involved and theories of natural rights were an important part of its inspiration—witness the Declaration of the Rights of Man prefixed to the Constitution of 1791. Indeed, it is possible to see liberal- and people's democracy as developing from a common set of ideas: 'the branching out of the two types of democracy from the common stem took place only after the common beliefs had been tested in the ordeal of the French Revolution' (J. L. Talmon, *The Origins of Totalitarian Democracy*, London, Heinemann (Mercury Books), 1961, p. 3).

57 Rousseau, *The Social Contract*, ed. cit., p. 23.

58 Lenin, 'The State and Revolution', in *The Essential Left*, London, Allen & Unwin, 1960, p. 182. In 1936 Stalin declared that since capitalist exploitation in the U.S.S.R. had ceased, the 'proletariat' had been transformed into 'an entirely new class'—'the working class of the U.S.S.R.' (J. Stalin, *Leninism*, London, Lawrence & Wishart, 1940, pp. 567–8). In Mao's China, where it was conceived that there had been a telescoping of the bourgeois and proletarian revolutions, 'the government set up by [the] revolution takes the form of a dictatorship of all "anti-imperialist and anti-feudal" forces, i.e. it is a multi-party government in which various parties represent different social classes'—F. J. Kase, *People's Democracy*, Leyden, A. W. Sijthoff, 1968, p. 138 (this book contains a discussion of the similarities and differences between the U.S.S.R. and people's democracies outside it).

59 Sartori, *Democratic Theory*, p. 419.

60 'The State and Revolution', p. 170.

61 ibid., pp. 227 and 220 (italics in the original).

62 See, for example, Sartori, *Democratic Theory*, pp. 420–5, and Christophersen, *The Meaning of Democracy*, pp. 252–60.

63 'The Communist Party alone . . . is capable of leading the proletariat in the most ruthless, decisive and final struggle against all the forces of capitalism'—'Theses on the Fundamental Tasks of the Second Congress of the Communist International' in *Selected Works*, London, Lawrence & Wishart, 1938, Vol. 10, p. 165.

64 *Leninism*, p. 73. It is true that Stalin also spoke of the will of the proletariat or working class as separate from the decisions of the party. However, this 'will' consists of deciding whether to carry out the 'guiding directions given by the Party' (ibid., p. 137). There can be little doubt that such 'decisions' are a foregone conclusion in Leninist–Stalinist theory and practice!

65 'The conception of constitutionalism is alien to the Soviet Union. Its ruling party is self-perpetuating, and it cannot be dislodged save by revolution.

Its powers are all-embracing and without limit. . . . Citizens have duties and obligations; such rights as they exercise depend on the precarious benificence of the ruling group'—M. Fainsod, *How Russia is Ruled*, London, Oxford University Press, 2nd edition, 1963, p. 349. (It is argued below that the theory of people's democracy must give rise to practice of this kind— which is, in some ways, alien to the theory.) See also F. J. Kase, *People's Democracy*, p. 82: 'Like the Soviet Constitution . . .[that of any other people's democracy] is not much more than a functional frame for the conduct of administration by the ruling oligarchy. The Western concept of the constitution as the essential instrumentality for the control of political power is entirely alien to the communists.'

66 The 1936 Soviet constitution in effect admits the exclusive domination of the Communist Party (Art. 126). Stalin himself said: 'A party is a part of a class, its most advanced part. Several parties, and, consequently, freedom for parties, can exist only in a society in which there are antagonistic classes. . . . But in the U.S.S.R. there are no longer such classes. . . . In the U.S.S.R. there are only two classes, workers and peasants, whose interests . . . are . . . friendly. Hence . . . in the U.S.S.R. there is ground only for one party, the Communist Party. In the U.S.S.R. only one party can exist, the Communist Party. . . .' (Report 'On the Draft Constitution of the U.S.S.R.' in *Leninism*, p. 579.) In other people's democracies, the existence of several parties is, in theory, recognized. These are united in a 'people's front'. However, only such parties as the communists find acceptable can exist (see Kase, *People's Democracy*, pp. 75–6).

67 Rousseau, of course, condemned parties as divisive and factious—and therefore as subverting the general will (see Chapter 5). And this view was reflected in the thought of Robespierre and Saint-Just. However, Rousseau's strictures applied most clearly to the conception of a party derived from a situation in which there is more than one party. The one-party idea clearly ties in with the conception of a single general will. The idea of a party of the vanguard is to be found in Robespierre's thinking, and more clearly in Babeuf's (see J. L. Talmon, *The Origins of Totalitarian Democracy*, esp. Part II, Chapter 3, and Part III, Chapter 4).

68 Part of the reason for the ambiguity in Jacobin theory is that its origins were intermeshed with those of aspects of liberal-democratic theory. See n. 56.

69 Talmon, op. cit., p. 98.

70 'The State and Revolution', pp. 189–90.

71 K. Marx, Preface to 'A Contribution to the Critique of Political Economy', in Marx and Engels, *Selected Works*, p. 363.

72 For a recent discussion of the Marxist conception of liberal-democracy, see W. R. Schonfield, 'The Classical Marxist Conception of Liberal Democracy', in *The Review of Politics*, Vol. 33, No. 3 (July 1971), pp. 360–76.

73 See, for example, Talmon, op. cit., esp. Part I, Chapter IV; Part II, Chapter V; and Part III, Chapters II and VI.

74 A variant—the 'underdeveloped variant'—of the idea of people's democracy will be referred to in the last chapter.

75 See Sartori, *Democratic Theory*, Chapter XI.

76 See appendix, for further discussion of the relationship between liberty and democracy.

77 J. L. Talmon, *Political Messianism, The Romantic Phase* (Vol. II of *The History of Totalitarian Democracy*), London, Secker & Warburg, 1960, p. viii.

78 This is not to deny that guiding concepts—in this case those concerning the party/government and their relationship to the people and their will—are important. Rather, it is to say that their effect is sometimes importantly modified by practice. Of course, the *overall* argument here is that the guiding concepts reinforce and are reinforced by the practice in question.

79 *The Social Contract*, ed. cit., p. 70.

80 It will be argued in the next chapter that a valid concept of democracy is necessarily individualist, at least to the extent that the specific decisions of particular individuals (those constituting the electorate at the time) are necessary components of 'a decision by the people'.

81 'Particular or selfish' here includes promotion of the interests of particular groups with which individuals may be associated.

82 Perhaps one of the best introductions to it all is M. Cranston, *Freedom: A New Analysis*, London, Longmans, Green, 3rd edition, 1967.

83 The terms 'liberty' and 'freedom' tend to be used interchangeably. However, the latter does have a wider, and more basic, meaning than the former. 'Liberty' implies freedom in relation to social and political institutions and/or the intentional activities of groups or individuals. Its meaning does not normally cover freedom of the self—or the individual will—in relation to other aspects of the psychological make-up of the individual, the general influence of social environment, or the physical environment.

84 Sartori, *Democratic Theory*, p. 358.

85 R. Price, *Observations on the Nature of Civil Liberty* (*Works*, London, R. Rees, 1816, Vol. VII), p. 6. D. O. Thomas, 'Richard Price and Edmund Burke', *Philosophy*, Vol. 30 (1959), p. 319.

86 The reference here is only to perceptions of (what their defenders see as) liberal democracies. The separate question of the relationship between democracy and liberty in Rousseauist democracy will be referred to below.

87 Sartori, *Democratic Theory*, p. 369.

88 See also n. 55 above.

89 This sort of idea of the domination of the individual by the people can take two rather different forms. In the first, each individual is seen as contributing to collective decisions. But, where the collective decision results from millions of votes, the contribution of each is so small that the decisions of the people can only appear as something other than his own decisions. In its second form, the idea is one of more explicit conflict. Here the focus is on those cases where the decision of the people actually conflicts with the wishes and decision of the individual.

90 J. S. Mill, 'On Liberty'; the publication here referred to is *On Liberty, Representative Government, The Subjection of Women*, London, Oxford University Press (The World's Classics series), 1912, p. 8.

91 A. de Tocqueville, *Democracy in America*, quotation taken from J. Plamenatz, *Readings from Liberal Writers*, London, Allen & Unwin, 1965, p. 217.

92 J. S. Mill, 'On Liberty', ed. cit., p. 9.

93 Tocqueville, *Democracy in America*, ed. cit., p. 217.

94 ibid., p. 234.

95 These do, of course, very explicitly exist in America—for example, the

separation of powers, the written constitution binding upon the governing authorities and the independent role of the supreme court. The position is not nearly so clear in the case of Britain. Indeed, it has quite often been argued that the sovereignty of Parliament implies the non-existence of any such limitations. However, the *de facto* special status of some laws, constitutional conventions and the norms of the political culture combine to provide analagous—if not so definite or effective—limitations.

96 See, for example, A. Ranney and Willmoore Kendall, *Democracy and the American Party System*, New York, Harcourt, Brace & World, 1956.Willmoore Kendall has even interpreted Locke in this light in his *John Locke and the Doctrine of Majority Rule*, Urbana, University of Illinois Press paperback, 1965. Continental views of democracy are more likely to be of this kind than are Anglo-Saxon views—see Sartori, *Democratic Theory*, Chapter XI: 'Empirical Democracies and Rational Democracies'; but see also the text in the paragraph which follows.

97 See I. Berlin's famous essay on 'The Two Concepts of Liberty', reprinted in *Four Essays on Liberty*, London, Oxford University Press, 1969.

98 As was pointed out before, liberals admit the necessity of some governmental restraints—in order that individuals do not interfere with each other's freedom. This is a case of some freedoms being invaded in order to preserve others: it is a matter of arriving at the optimum amount of—rather than complete—freedom.

CHAPTER 3

Traditional Theories of Democracy

In Chapter 2 we looked rather generally at the idea of liberal-democracy. In this chapter we shall look at some of the (not always compatible) elements and bases of the idea. In other words, we shall be concerned with some theories of democracy.[1] A theory of democracy —or democratic theory—is a body of thought that provides and analyses a conception of democracy together with an explanation and justification of the existence (or possible existence) of democracy so conceived. The analysed conception we may call a theory's model of democracy. There is also another use of the term 'democratic theory', as in the phrase 'empirical democratic theory'. In this sense it means a body of theory concerning the workings of actual political systems that are called democracies. We shall have occasion later to discuss some connections and contrasts between the two types of democratic theory.

There are, of course, different models of democracy which fit within the general idea of liberal-democracy; and there are the different democratic theories which contain them. These theories may very broadly be divided into traditional and modern, though these categories are not exhaustive. In this chapter we shall be concerned with what is usually called traditional democratic theory, together with a twentieth-century restatement and modification of it. Modern democratic theory will be considered in Chapter 6 in the context of an examination of responses to a critique of traditional radical democratic theory (although some types of theory—modern in the chronological sense—are to an important extent reassertions of this traditional radical democratic theory).

Traditional democratic theory proper—sometimes known as 'classical' democratic theory—consists of theories of democracy formulated in the late eighteenth and the nineteenth centuries. It is not usually taken to include—although it was often influenced by—the political theory pertaining to ancient Greek democracy. This is because it is usually felt that only theories of indirect democracy have been of any real relevance since the time of the ancient Greeks. Such theories did not really emerge until the late eighteenth century as part of the Enlightenment, although there had been an anticipation of them in the thought of the Levellers in the mid-seventeenth century.[2] The main lines of these theories were soon developed, and so the application of the label 'traditional democratic theory' is not usually extended beyond the nineteenth century. Some varieties of twentieth-century democratic thought have been in part a restatement of traditional theory (the 'citizenship theories' mentioned in n. 83, p. 96, and aspects of the radical critiques of modern systems that are discussed in Chapter 9). Other varieties are seen as constituting democratic theories of a different kind. Some of them are specifically reactions to traditional democratic theory, and these are the theories normally labelled 'modern'. These are discussed in Chapter 6.

Before looking at traditional democratic theory in a little more detail it is necessary to say something about John Locke. We have already seen (Chapter 2) that Locke's thought—particularly the *Second Treatise of Government* (first edition 1690[3])—is of great importance in the theory of liberal-democracy. The concepts involved, particularly those of consent and majority rule, have been at the heart of democratic theory. His theory as a whole has also been extremely influential in the Western democracies, particularly in the United States. 'The liberal theory of democracy . . . received its classical formulation with Locke. . . . The ordinary understanding of democracy in the United States today is basically Lockean, and his conception of democracy is still repeated in most civics textbooks.'[4] And yet it was stated above that traditional democratic theory was formulated in the late eighteenth and in the nineteenth centuries—thereby excluding Locke.

This somewhat paradoxical situation arises because it is not entirely clear whether Locke is to be classified as a democratic theorist. His political thought has both democratic and non-democratic aspects. Some of the democratic concepts have already been discussed, and others will be looked at later—notably the idea of majority rule (Chapter 4). The *non*-democratic aspect of Locke's thought consists in his failure to advocate universal suffrage. 'Locke made it clear that the masses were to have no share in the election of their representatives.'[5] The right to vote Locke held to be dependent upon the amount of taxes paid by a citizen. Non-enfranchised citizens were conceived to be virtually represented (see Chapter 2, p. 32, for a reference to the Whig theory of virtual representation). The whole people, including the unenfranchised masses, do have some direct power : they have an ultimate right to revolt should the governors abuse their trust; and it is the people who judge whether there has been such abuse.[6] This might be said to secure the sovereignty of the people.[7]

But whether or not this is so, it is doubtful whether the right to revolt brings the kind of system postulated by Locke within our definition of democracy (the difficulties of the concept of popular sovereignty were referred to when the definition of democracy was discussed in Chapter 1—see p. 10 above). There is room for different interpretations here, but it is certainly arguable that revolt—albeit 'by right'—does not constitute an *entitlement* to decision-making, not at least in the sense of an entitlement arising from the basic norms and institutions (see pp. 9–10 above). A revolt would usually be specifically viewed as a process that is unauthorized by the norms and institutions within—or in defiance of—which it occurs. Nonetheless it must also be pointed out that Locke did specifically recognize the possibility of democracy as a legitimate form of government.[8] Seliger characterizes this ambiguous relationship between Locke's thought and democracy by saying : 'Locke did not favour the permanent establishment of democracy. But its recognition as a legitimate and workable form of government enabled him to justify his advocacy of the right of revolt. . . .'[9]

It would seem, then, that it is quite possible to argue that Locke's political theory is not a theory of democracy.[10] The place of Locke in the theory of liberal-democracy is, rather, that his was a famous statement of liberal doctrine allied with which were ideas that were later easily developed into ones that were fully democratic. It is this that makes him a 'founding father' of traditional democratic theory (see below). Liberal democratic theory inherited the negative conception of the role of the people embodied in the notions of trust and consent. Radical democratic theory, on the other hand, emphasized some implications to be found in the right of revolt for the development of a more positive role for the people. Tom Paine's thought is, in many ways, a restatement of aspects of Locke in more radical terms.

To return to traditional democratic theory : as indicated, it divides into two main types—liberal democratic theory[11] and radical democratic theory. However, apart from those mentioned just now in the general characterization of traditional democratic theory, they have at least one feature in common : their individualism. This is in contrast to the pluralism of some modern theories. Both types of theory have a model of the political system in which the basic constituent elements are individuals only. Groups and institutions—as well as the society as a whole—are simply made up of, and take their characteristics entirely from, the set of individuals included within them at any particular time. Individuals are also given a great moral importance. That which is morally right is always that which is good for the individual rather than that which is good for the society, the state or some other alleged collective entity (the individualist view of the structure of society, while allowing that the two types of good may sometimes be mutually interdependent, usually has the effect of ruling out the notion that they are the same thing). This sort of view of the moral importance of individuals is often expressed in such terms as 'the individual ought to be treated as an end and not as a means'.

This characterization of the individualism—both 'descriptive' and 'moral'—of traditional democratic theory is something of an over-simplification. Not all of traditional theory consistently sticks within this framework, as is shown, for example, by J. S. Mill's perception of the general influence of society and the importance given to majorities in some conceptions of majority rule. Moreover, there are nineteenth-century theories—such as those of Madison and Calhoun—which specifically focus upon the role of groups, but which are obviously closely connected with the mainstream of traditional democratic theory. Nonetheless, this individualism is a predominant feature of both liberal and radical democratic theory. Other aspects of it will be touched upon at various points later.

What, then, is the difference between the two types of traditional democratic theory? It is basically one of a difference of role ascribed to the people in the respective models of democracy. In liberal democratic theory (hereinafter referred to as LDT) the people are given a negative role. As indicated in Chapter 2, this involves the people in little more than rather passively choosing between options presented to them. These choices concern both personnel and policies. However, the policy options are general and broad rather than detailed and specific. This is associated with the idea that the elected representatives have a greater knowledge—and more wisdom—than their constituents : they should accordingly have considerable autonomy in making political decisions while remaining within the overall control of the people. On the other hand, in radical democratic theory (hereinafter referred to as RDT) the people are given a positive role. Again, the meaning of this has already been indicated—the people actually initiate the policies. This involves the idea of representatives being closely controlled by their electors so that they are little more than messengers conveying the decisions of their constituents. In a word, they are delegates.[12] The electors, then, not only initiate, but make fairly detailed and specific decisions. Indeed, in RDT there is a sense in which the ideal remains a direct democracy. Representation is used merely as a device to deal with the problem of scale—as contrasted with LDT, where it is seen also as a means to 'refine and enlarge the public views, by passing them through the medium of a chosen body of citizens whose wisdom may best discern the true interest of their country'.[13]

An aspect of this positive role given to the people in RDT is the idea of popular participation. According to this, the people do not merely register their views on what is done or proposed by governments and/or representatives; they are also conceived to participate in the process of government themselves. Such participation is in some theories rather minimal, or not emphasized—in, for example, Tom Paine and the Utilitarians. Here it amounts to little more than voting[14] and discussion. The vote, it is true, is used 'actively' as a crucial part of the process whereby the people initiate policies. Indeed, it is by virtue of this 'active' use that voting is seen as participation rather than mere passive registration of views. However, in the case of other theories participation is specifically seen to consist of something more than simply casting a vote. It is these that can more properly be referred to as theories of participatory democracy (the present-day interest in participatory democracy is discussed in Chapter 9).

In participatory theories, then, the citizen does more than vote : he thinks about and discusses politics and he engages in activity that either forms or replaces part of the very process of government (for example, becoming a local councillor, helping to run community services). In such theories participation is seen as very important indeed—so important that a system of representation is only somewhat regretfully accepted as a necessary modification of (or supplement to) direct participation by the people. (Rousseau himself would not accept representation—see Chapter 2.) But in these theories participation is not just valued as the means, or an aspect of the means, by which the people make political decisions. Participation is also valued for its own sake—or, at least, for what are seen as its direct effects. The full development of the individual, the education of the individual and the creation or strengthening of bonds between the individual and the community—these are held to be some of the important results of participation.[15] The most important participatory theorist is Rousseau.[16] But, partly through his influence, individualist RDT also contains some theorists who ascribe an important role to participation : examples are Thomas Jefferson (1743–1826), the author of the American Declaration of Independence, and Richard Price (1723–91), well known in his own day as an English supporter of the American and French revolutions. (Price praised the French Revolution in a celebrated sermon, *The Love of Our Country*, which provoked Edmund Burke into replying with the *Reflections on the Revolution in France*.)[17] But within individualist traditional democratic theory it is John Stuart Mill who most specifically favours participation. Paradoxically, however, Mill is predominantly an exponent of LDT. This means that, in his case, conceptions regarding the function and value of participation are *not* combined with a theory concerning the positive role of the people.[18]

Despite J. S. Mill, however, the idea of popular participation in the process of government is primarily associated with RDT. As we shall see in Chapter 9, participation has recently come to the fore again as the key feature of what might be called new radical democratic theory. But to return to the differences between RDT and LDT. We can summarize these by saying that, in RDT, the people actively engage in the formulation of the policy the government is to pursue. In LDT, on the other hand, although there may be some participation in political activity—very important in the case of J. S. Mill—basically the people merely respond to proposed policies.[19] They also, of course, elect the governors, and some would characterize LDT primarily in these terms: the LDT model is one in which the people, rather than participating in government, elect persons to govern for them. This shows the folly of lumping RDT and LDT together as one theory, and calling it traditional or classical democratic theory, for the purpose of confronting it with modern analyses of the nature of political systems called democracies. LDT, of course, has one of the very features—the focusing upon election of personnel rather than detailed concern with policy—that 'modern' revisions of classical democratic theory have incorporated as a response to the modern analyses of political systems.[20] In fact it appears to be RDT that actually emerges as the theory that is challenged during the course of such confrontations. And later on it will initially be RDT that we shall very explicitly focus upon in this connection (see Chapter 5).

Before discussing RDT and LDT in a little more detail, it is necessary to say something about Rousseauist democratic theory. One often finds that Rousseauist theory is included under the label of RDT. However, as was pointed out in Chapter 2, we are concerned only with liberal-democracy—and we also saw that Rousseauist democracy is to be contrasted with this. Here, then, we shall be talking only about non-Rousseauist forms of RDT: forms of RDT that have an individualist basis. Nonetheless it should be remembered—as was also pointed out earlier—that the distinctions can become blurred. Statements of RDT can become very like Rousseauist theory at some points. Also, those who use RDT models very often slip backwards and forwards between individualist and Rousseauist forms. No statement of democratic theory, especially RDT, can really escape the influence of Rousseau.

The RDT and LDT models both consist of political systems in which the people make the decisions by electing individual representatives who then govern, or control those who do (the executive). In the RDT model, such election also constitutes a specific decision, or set of decisions, concerning what the representatives shall do. In the LDT model too the elections incorporate decisions by the people, but they are far looser and broader. To look in a little more detail at RDT and LDT, we shall look at some ways in which aspects of the electoral and governing process are treated. RDT and LDT are themselves both amalgams of the thought of particular theorists. There are differences between theorists in each category, apart from the similarities by virtue of which they are commonly grouped together.

We can conveniently illustrate the nature of, and some differences between, particular examples of LDT and RDT by indicating the ways in which three central questions are dealt with. The first concerns the nature of the individuals' decisions (which make up the collective political decisions of the people): are such decisions to be expressions of interests or opinions? The second question concerns the role of the representative: what is to be the relationship between a representative and his constituents? The third question also has to do with the role of representatives: what is to be the relationship between a role for a representative as promoter of his particular constituents' opinions and/ or interests and a role as promoter of the general interest of the state? These are questions which are intricately linked into a larger and even more central one concerning the nature of the relationship between the decisions of individuals and the 'decisions of the people'. This, however, is a question which is discussed later (particularly in Chapters 4, 5 and 6). However, the present discussion will serve as a useful preliminary for this later one.

First of all, then, the question of individuals' decisions and whether they express interests or opinions. We can say that an individual's interest(s)—or that which is in his interest(s)—is that which benefits him. One significant and complicating point is that an interest so conceived can exist independently of the recognition of it by the individual who has the interest. An opinion, on the other hand, is by definition what the individual who holds it conceives it to be (the question of its validity is, of course, another matter). This difference can have far-reaching implications. However, it is doubtful whether the interest–opinion dichotomy is an exhaustive categorization of the relevant areas of the individual's perception of, and relationship to, the world around him—although it frequently appears to be treated as such. Moreover, there are complicated relationships between interests and opinions, and in the thought of particular theorists the distinctions can become very blurred. Nonetheless, in a rough and ready way the drawing of this distinction indicates some important differences—at least of emphasis.

A decision which expresses an opinion is quite simply a decision to indicate that opinion and (in the case of the types of decisions we are interested in) that relevant action should be taken by the community.[21] A decision which expresses an interest is one that indicates a conception of what that interest is and advocates its promotion.

The notion of interests and their representation has been a part of widely varying political theories.[22] They have, for example, varied from those of Burke to those of Marx. But as was explained in Chapter 2, not all notions of representation fall within the general conception of democracy—let alone the more particular one of liberal-democracy. Many of the notions excluded are those of representation of interests. However, there remain many ideas of interest representation which do form part of an idea of democracy. We are concerned here, as part of a discussion of traditional democratic theory, with those primarily characterized by their individualism (but see the discussion of Madison and Calhoun below). We are here talking about ideas concerning the interests of individuals (and their expression and representation) rather than of sections or groups. The best-known and most influential source of such ideas in traditional democratic theory was Utilitarianism. Utilitarianism was a form of moral and political theory with a fairly long history. The conception of its length varies according to the particular definition of 'Utilitarianism' subscribed to, but it reached its best-known form, and was incorporated most clearly into traditional democratic theory, in the works of Jeremy Bentham (1748–1832) and James Mill (1773–1836).[23] Although somewhat shallow and often attacked, 'the utilitarian doctrine . . . is the greatest English contribution to moral and political philosophy' and 'the Utilitarians were once in England . . . the social and political thinkers whose ideas had the widest currency. . .'.[24] We may characterize Utilitarianism as asserting that pleasure is good and that the equal pleasures of any two or more men are equally good. From this was derived the famous criterion of moral action : that which is right is that which produces the greatest happiness of the greatest number.[25]

According to Utilitarianism, individuals usually or always seek pleasure, and they obtain it by fulfilling their desires (doing that which is pleasant). This is seen as the individual doing what benefits him— pursuing his interest. Such interests were sometimes seen in terms of wealth and power. 'The actions of men are governed by their wills, and their wills by their desires : . . . their desires are directed to pleasure and relief from pain as *ends*, and to wealth and power as the principal means. . . .'[26] Now, since only the individual concerned knows what desires he has, and he knows best how to fulfil them, it follows that each individual is the best judge of his own interest. And this is one of the axioms of Utilitarian theory (although it is arguable that, at certain points, Utilitarians have contradicted their own axiom—see below, p. 85). As Bentham puts it : 'There is no one who knows what is for your interest, so well as yourself.'[27]

In the democratic theory associated with Utilitarianism, then, the decisions of individuals express those individuals' conceptions of what is in their interests. We shall shortly take up the questions of the implications of this for the behaviour of representatives and of the relationship between individual interests and the general interest.

On the whole, Utilitarian democratic theory falls within the category of RDT : there may be some variations in Bentham, but James Mill's *Essay on Government* (apart from some odd notions about the extent of the franchise) is clearly an example of RDT.

In LDT the decisions of individuals are not usually seen as expressing interests. This is not so much because the concept of interest plays no part in LDT as because LDT tends to involve the view that ordinary men cannot fully know their own best interests. Wise representatives can know this better—but only if they are aware of the opinions and feelings of the people. It is thus opinions (or, at least, opinions and feelings) that are expressed by electors; and it is the representatives who, taking account of these expressions, decide what the interests of the electors are. The interests of individuals, according to this kind of view, do not consist simply in the fulfilling of their desires (and even Bentham at times adopts a similar view). Liberal democratic theory was in some ways associated with Burke's thinking. Edmund Burke (1729–97), a Whig, who has also often been hailed as one of the most profound of conservative thinkers, was not a democrat. LDT was in part, however, a descendant of Whig theories of representation. Moreover, much of Burke's thought forms part of a tradition of commentary upon the nature of the British constitution—including important aspects of the work of Montesquieu, Bagehot and Dicey—that is in important senses liberal. This tradition therefore overlaps with LDT, which is also a variety of liberal thought. Burke, indeed, propounded views on the duties of a representative that are still widely regarded as an authoritative statement of the proper role of a British M.P.[28] He made an important distinction between interest and opinion, and it is true that his conception of interest involved, and was connected with, non-individualist ideas alien to LDT. Nonetheless, Burkean and individualist conceptions of interest overlap (hence their coverage by the same term—'interest'), and Burkean ideas are often echoed in LDT. Burke held that a representative owed his constituents a 'devotion to their interests *rather than* to their opinions' and should if necessary maintain their 'interest even against [their] opinions'.[29]

For John Stuart Mill, the most influential British exponent of LDT, the concept of 'interest' did have some importance. He had quite a lot to say about class interest, and the representation of classes, for example. But even where it is opinions only that are involved, he still frequently talks of a relationship between constituents and representatives very much like that conceived by Burke. If electors have definite enough opinions, they should, ideally, vote for representatives 'who best [express] the voters' own opinions'; but otherwise they should vote for candidates 'whose abilities and character the voter most respects, and whom he most willingly trusts *to think for him*'.[30] Either way it is opinions—whether directly political, or indirectly political via a judgement of men—that the electors are expressing in these voting decisions.

In LDT, then, electors' decisions express opinions rather than interests. And this is so even where the concept of interest plays a part. There is, however, one important exception. Madison is an important figure in, or associated with, traditional democratic theory. Madison's political thought is clearly an example of what has been identified here as LDT, except that he ascribes such an important role to groups. It often looks as though his thinking has more in common with modern pluralist democratic theory than with individualist LDT. Nevertheless, unlike Burke, it is of groups of individuals that Madison mainly writes rather than corporate entities such as classes or estates of the realm. Moreover, although accepting the presence of groups as inevitable, unlike modern pluralists his aim is to tame them—to deal with 'the evils of faction'. At all events, Madison's thought, as expressed in his contribution to the *Federalist Papers* (first published in 1787–8), has a standing in the American tradition of thinking about democracy not unlike that of John Stuart Mill's *Representative Government* in British democratic thought.

Madison's thought, then, should be accepted as falling within the category of LDT. But, as indicated, in this case it is interests that are expressed by the people rather than opinions. Like the Utilitarians, he conceives of the individuals themselves knowing their interests, but unlike the Utilitarians he conceives of such interests in terms of groups ('factions'). It is the individual's conception of the interest of the group to which he belongs, rather than his particular individual interest, about which Madison is writing. Even so, due to the multiplicity of relevant groups to which individuals may belong, these are very much personal conceptions: 'For Madison, interests are multiple, shifting alignments, largely subjective. . . .'[31] It seems at times as if there is very little difference between Madison's 'interests' and the 'opinions' of other theorists of LDT. Indeed, the 'latent causes of faction' can exhibit themselves in 'a zeal for different *opinions* concerning religion, concerning government, and many other points . . .'.[32] There is, however, such a strong connection between opinion and that which benefits the holders of the opinions that the conception of interest(s) does seem to be the appropriate one.[33] But, in any case, the connecting of interests with opinions does not imply that there is no distinction between interests and important categories of opinions. It might be said that pursuing interests involves having opinions, but not all opinions are linked with interests: buying shares involves having an opinion on the state of the market, but, obviously, an opinion on, say, nuclear disarmament would not necessarily be linked with an interest.

Madison and the Utilitarians are the most important theorists in traditional democratic theory for whom the people express interests rather than opinions. We have seen that on the whole it is opinions which are expressed by the electors in LDT. But RDT is not constituted solely by Utilitarian democratic theory. It, too, contains theories in which the electors express opinions rather than interests—although this is usually implicit rather than explicit. Paine's political theory was at times essentially Utilitarian in character (e.g. in the second part of *Rights of Man*) : he 'was a sort of second cousin to the Utilitarians'.[34] However, he was not consistent in this line of thought and 'the most widely read part [Part One] of his most famous book, *Rights of Man*, is incompatible with Utilitarianism'.[35] Here he develops the argument that the purpose of government is the protection of the 'natural rights' of individuals. The only way to ensure that the government will do this, and *only* this, is to place it, via the representative system, in the hands of the people. The power of such government is delegated from the people—the nation. 'The right of a Parliament is only a right in trust, a right by delegation. . . . But the right of the Nation is an original right, as universal as taxation. The Nation is the paymaster of everything, and everything must conform to its general will.'[36] To retain and to exercise this right, the nation—'the people'—must have and express opinions regarding what the government shall, and shall not, do. And this means that the individuals who comprise the nation shall have and express such opinions, both directly and in the election of representatives. These will not have the particularity that characterizes interests, since Paine simply equates what is desired for the nation with the sum total of the desires of the particular individuals—and hence, by implication, the individuals' desires have a general (national) object. He fails to recognize the crucial problem of the relationship between the particular needs and views of particular individuals and the collective needs and views of the whole—the people, the community, the nation. Jefferson, although he occasionally talks in terms of interest,[37] thinks in much the same manner. Differences of view there may be, but these are to be dealt with by the operation of the majority principle, and the fundamental idea remains as the simple totting up of individual views to arrive at the view of the whole. 'Every man, and every body of men on earth, possess the right of self-government. . . . Individuals exercise it by their single will; collections of men by that of their majority; for the law of the majority is the natural law of every society of men.'[38]

Our second question concerned the role of the representative in relation to his constituents. Here the important line of division between different types of view marks the line between LDT and RDT. LDT is in part defined in terms of the representative's relative independence of his constituents in its model of democracy, as compared with the tight control exercised by constituents in the RDT model. In a word, as already indicated, the RDT model postulates delegates rather than representatives (in the non-generic sense). The generic sense of 'representation' primarily involved is the first of those indicated on p. 31 above, according to which a representative is an agent acting on behalf of a principal. However, the second sense (involving the sharing of characteristics) is also introduced.

As we have already seen (p. 69 above), LDT can be characterized as the form of traditional democratic theory in which the system of representation is seen as something more than a device to deal with the problem of scale. The system is also seen as valuable in that the representatives are deemed to have a greater wisdom and expertise than the man in the street. In LDT, representative institutions are seen as a way of combining the merits of democracy with the merits of rule by an educated and informed elite. J. S. Mill is in favour of 'Parliament . . . containing the very elite of the country'.[39] The view of the relationship between a representative and his constituents that this kind of theory involves is still usually summed up in Burke's famous words :

[His constituents'] wishes ought to have great weight with him [the representative]; their opinion, high respect; their business, unremitted attention. It is his duty . . . in all cases, to prefer their interest to his own. But his unbiased opinion, his mature judgement, his enlightened conscience, he ought not to sacrifice to you, to any man, or to any set of men living. . . . Your representative owes you, not his industry only, but his judgement; and he betrays, instead of serving you, if he sacrifices it to your opinion. . . .'[40]

In LDT, then, the public's views are not directly expressed and implemented. Rather they are refined and enlarged 'by passing them through the medium of a chosen body of citizens, whose wisdom may best discern the true interest of their country', and 'it may well happen that the public voice pronounced by the representatives of the people, will be more consonant to the public good than if pronounced by the people themselves . . .'.[41] In short, in LDT the people choose representatives to govern (or control the government) for them.

It might be wondered whether all this means that, after all, LDT is not properly speaking a *democratic* theory. However, despite the elitism and the independent and initiating role of the representatives, and despite the overlap with non-democratic theories, LDT's model of a political system does remain a democracy. It is true that 'Madison . . . goes about as far as it is possible to go while still remaining within the rubric of democracy'.[42] Nonetheless, he *does* remain within that rubric. Mankind, he says, has a 'capacity . . . for self-government'.[43] And even though the main mark of this 'self-government' is merely the appointment 'either directly or indirectly, by the people'[44] of those who govern, ideally 'all the adult citizens of a republic . . . determine the general direction of government policy'.[45] In other words, Madisonian theory depicts a political system in which the people make the basic determining decisions on important matters of public policy.

J. S. Mill had very real fears about the masses' lack of political wisdom, and he laid great emphasis on the need for high intelligence and skill in government. Consequently, he stressed the need for initiative and freedom of action on the part of the governors (the government, and those to whom it is directly responsible—the representatives). Indeed, he goes so far as to say that it is not that 'the people themselves govern, but that they have security for good government'.[46] But despite this—and despite his belief in more votes for the more educated electors[47]—the type of political system favoured by Mill seems on the whole to be a democracy. Certainly, his thinking has since been utilized as democratic theory. Mill 'grasped fully and firmly' the democratic idea 'despite many saving clauses'.[48] The security for good government consists in the ultimate control—the ultimate decisions on policy—being in the hands of the people. The people dismiss their rulers not out of whim but when they judge the 'devotion of those rulers to the interests of the people [to have] become questionable'.[49] 'The meaning of representative government is that . . . the people . . . exercise through deputies periodically elected by themselves, the ultimate controlling power. . . . This ultimate power they must possess in all its completeness.'[50] For Mill 'the people ought to be *masters*, but they are masters who must employ servants more skilful than themselves'.[51]

The LDT view of representation is best summed up by Hanna Pitkin :

The wonderful theoretical advantage of representation as Liberalism sees it, then, is this: representation makes it possible for each to participate in government as the final judge of whether his particular shoe pinches; yet it allows the rulers to use their wisdom and information to further people's true interests, where direct action would be misguided by short-range, hasty decisions. And, at the same time, representation makes it to the interest of the ruler to act in the interest of the subjects—not to give in to their passing whims, but to act in their true interest. For if he gives in to their passing whims, they will not really be pleased; the shoe that looked so attractive in the store will turn out to pinch. Only if he uses his wisdom to promote their true, long-range interests will they be truly pleased, and support him at the polls.[52]

In contrast to LDT, the representatives in RDT are but delegates. 'It is clear that [Paine] thought of elected representatives as delegates of the people.'[53] That is to say, the representatives do not exist to exercise their own judgement and initiative, but to overcome the inconvenience in the modern state of all the people meeting 'on every occasion as at first, when their number was small, their habitations near, and the public concerns few and trifling'.[54] In short those elected to the representative assembly are there simply to convey the wishes of their constituents, and to act as the latter would have acted. The members of the assembly are to 'act in the same manner as the whole body would act were they present'.[55] Jefferson's view was slightly different. While he often appeared to be in favour of as close an approximation to direct democracy as was possible, he also recognized that men of an intelligence greater than that of the ordinary man were needed for many of the affairs of government.[56] His answer was to recommend direct participation wherever possible, and governed by representatives where not : such representatives to be appropriately competent and frequently elected. '. . . Action by the citizens, in affairs within their reach and competence, and in all others by representatives, chosen immediately, and removable by themselves constitutes the essence of a republic [i.e. a democracy].'[57]

The logic of Utilitarianism—or at least, important aspects of it—also leads to a delegate view of representation.

In much of Utilitarian thought, each person is the only reliable measure of his own interest; no one else can know what it is as well as he does. Hence no representative can ever act in your interest contrary to your wishes. In any event, he probably would not, because he himself is motivated by his own interest [i.e. he wishes to retain office]. But even if he were acting altruistically, he could never know your interest as well as you know it, so he could only act in it by following your express directions.[58]

Although at times Bentham himself retained a role for the independent judgement of the representative, James Mill argues unequivocally for the subordination of the representative to his constituents.[59] Although it is part of Mill's theory that the electors will 'make choice of such persons as will act according to their wishes',[60] the key idea concerns the reinforcement of the efficacy of such choice. This is the conception, central to Utilitarian theory, of the identification of the interests of the governors and the governed : the idea that it must be ensured that the representatives have the same interests as their constituents. *have (utilitarian) their interests*

There can be no doubt, that if power is granted to a body of men, called Representatives, they, like any other men, will use their power, not for the advantage of the community, but for their own advantage, if they can. The only question is, therefore, how can they be prevented; in other words, how are the interests of the Representatives to be identified with those of the community?

Each Representative may be considered in two capacities; in his capacity of Representative, in which he has the exercise of power over others, and in his capacity of Member of the Community, in which others have the exercise of power over him.

If things were so arranged, that, in his capacity of Representative, it would be impossible for him to do himself so much good by misgovernment, as he would do himself harm in his capacity of member of the community, the object would be accomplished.[61]

The way to achieve this is to have frequent elections. Only those representatives who, in the judgement of the electors, properly pursued their constituents' interests would be re-elected. Thus it would be apparent that any representative promoting his own interest would remain a representative for a short time only. And 'the smaller the period of time during which any man retains his capacity of Representative, as compared with the time in which he is simply a member of the community, the more difficult it will be to compensate the sacrifice of the interests of the longer period, by the profits of misgovernment during the shorter'.[62]

In Utilitarian democratic theory, then, the representative pursues only the interests of his constituents; the constituents themselves are the judges of what these are; therefore the representative does only what his constituents wish him to do. The Utilitarians conceived interests as possessed by individuals, but it is worth noting a theory similar to Utilitarianism in its treatment of the role of representatives, but which deals with group or sectional interests. This is the theory, important at least in America, put forward by John C. Calhoun in his *Disquisition on Government* (1853). Like Madison, Calhoun accepted the idea of the representation of sectional interests. But, unlike Madison, he thought that representatives should *merely* reflect these interests and act *primarily* as spokesmen for their constituents. Control by elections would make 'those elected the true and faithful representatives of those who elected them instead of irresponsible rulers as they would be without it; and thus by converting it into an agency and the rulers into agents, to divest government of all claims to sovereignty and to retain it unimpaired to the community'.[63]

The third of our central questions dealt with in traditional democratic theory concerned the relationship between the representative's role with respect to his constituents and that with respect to the national interest. Is the representative merely to promote the opinions and/or interests of his particular constituents, or is his primary function that of identifying and promoting the *national* interest? Is there, indeed, a conflict here at all?

The answers to these questions are closely connected with the answers to the previous question concerning the relationship between a representative and his constituents. Thus, in LDT the representative, while bound to listen carefully to his constituents, has an overriding duty to pursue the national interest. This ties in with the notion that the representative knows better than the electors. Where opinions only are involved this is simply a matter of the representative's opinion regarding the national interest being wiser than that of his constituents. Where interests are involved it is slightly more complicated. The representative has a duty to promote the particular interests of his constituents,[64] but—where there is apparently a clash—this is overridden by his duty to the national interest. However, this would not really be a clash of interests. At least in the long term the national interest is in *everyone's* interest. The idea is that such clashes of interest are apparent only : the particular interests are in fact (where there is a conflict) not the genuine long-term interests of those involved. It is an important aspect of the representative's superior wisdom that he can see this even when his constituents cannot. The system remains democratic since in the last resort the electors can still get their way, whether or not their view is mistaken. It is always possible for the electors to refuse to re-elect those representatives whose conduct they do not like. However, since that which is discerned by the representatives' superior wisdom is more likely to actually be in everyone's interest, and since this will in time be made clear to the electors by the representatives, it is unlikely that any disagreement between constituents and representatives will persist. Where it does persist, it could well be that the representatives are not acting as they should be, and that they deserve to be removed. (It will be remembered that a significant idea to be found in LDT held that the point of representative government was that it allowed security against misgovernment.)

Again, it is the Whig theory of representation that LDT has adapted. 'The essence of [the Whig view of the role of representatives] was that, if Parliament were to be the centre of political power rather than merely a check on the king's power, the member of Parliament would have to be free to do what he thought best in the national interest rather than act merely as an agent for his constituents.'[65] Again, it is Burke's speech to the electors of Bristol that is most often quoted in this context :

Parliament is' not a congress of ambassadors from different and hostile interests, which interests each must maintain, as an agent and advocate, against other agents and advocates; but Parliament is a deliberative assembly of one nation, with one interest, that of the whole—where not local prejudices ought to guide, but the general good, resulting from the general reason of the whole. You choose a member, indeed; but when you have chosen him he is not a member of Bristol, but he is a member of Parliament.[66]

Despite this view of the difference between pursuit of the national and of particular constituencies' interests, there is for Burke no real conflict here. This is because when properly discerned and adjusted, the particular interests combine to form the national interest. ('The interests of the realm, added together, compose the interest of the realm.'[67] Madison, however, viewed matters rather differently. We have seen that he, too, conceived of representation in terms of interest. But, unlike Burke, he did see the national interest as something over and above the particular interests. Somewhat paradoxically, though, he also thought it an important part of the representatives' duty to simply reflect and promote the interests of their constituents. Nonetheless, the superior wisdom of the representatives consisted mainly in their ability to see also the national interest. The representative, therefore, had two rather incompatible roles—to reflect particular interests and to rise above these and pursue the general interest. However, this rather uncertain idea of the general interest and its realization was buttressed by another. Madison set greater store by this; indeed, he had little faith in the ability of enlightened representatives to promote the general interest successfully. 'It is in vain to say that enlightened statesmen will be able to adjust these clashing interests, and render them all subservient to the public good.'[68] This other idea was that of balancing different interests against one another so as to neutralize them. Reason, and the general interest, might then have a chance of prevailing. 'Burke considers representation as a device for arriving at the right solution in Parliament and enacting it, with hopes that the people will eventually accept the action. Madison, by contrast sees representation as a way of stalemating action in the legislature, and thus in society, until wisdom prevails among the people.' Representation, then, 'was a way of bringing dangerous social conflict into a single central forum, where it can be controlled by balancing and stalemating'.[69]

John Stuart Mill also thought at times in terms of securing the correct balance of interests in the representative assembly so that no one interest should prevail.[70] However, his main concern was to secure the election as representatives of persons with 'instructed minds'. Such persons would be the representatives of those likewise with instructed minds (a minority within the community at large), but because of their wisdom, they would also have a general role. This would be to discern the general interest and to induce the other representatives to promote it. These representatives with instructed minds would be in a minority. Nonetheless they might hold the balance between representatives of sectors of the population with particular interests (mainly classes); or else—more likely—they would form the necessary point of opposition to the otherwise dominant majority. Either way, what they lacked in numbers would, in part at least, be compensated by their superior qualities of intellect and knowledge. 'The instructed minority [of representatives] would, in the actual voting, count only for their numbers, but as a moral power they would count for much more, in virtue of their knowledge, and of the influence it would give them over the rest.'[71]

In so far as J. S. Mill was concerned with the representation of opinions rather than interests, there was really no problem regarding the particular *versus* the general. To talk of the interest of something other than the whole *is* to distinguish that interest—and therefore its representation—from the interest of the whole. On the other hand, there is no necessity for the *opinion* of a part of the whole (individual or section of individuals)—or of its representation—to conflict with the interest of the whole. Indeed, the opinion (or opinions) in question may very well embody a view of the interest of the whole and the desirability of its promotion. This was just what Mill hoped for from 'the instructed minds' and their representatives.

It was not, however, simply that Mill hoped that instructed minds would disregard the local interests of geographical constituencies (sectional interests are disregarded almost by definition—it is part of his idea of instructed minds that they are those who see beyond sectional interests). Rather, he favoured the institutional recognition and re-inforcement of the reduced relevance of geographical constituencies and the reduced importance of the representation of their interests.[72] Thus Mill strongly commended a system of proportional representation pro-posed by Thomas Hare.[73] The effect of this system is to allow electors to choose for whom to vote from candidates throughout the country. The opinions and qualities of the candidates would be voted for; hence it would be these that as representatives they would be promoting and utilizing. Where this happened, geographical constituencies would in effect cease to exist and the representation of their interests would thus cease to be part of the function of representatives (although some would continue to have the function of looking after the interests of important localities).[74]

In RDT there is, typically, no particular issue concerning the duties of a representative regarding his constituents and the national interest. This is because, as we have already seen, the *sole* duty of a representative (delegate) is to convey his electors' opinions and/or their own con-ception of their interests. Now, this meant that the problem of the particular *versus* the general did not get discussed at this point, and remained as a general issue unrelated to the particular question of the role of representatives. In the case of those radical democrats who thought in terms mainly of opinions and their representation, the problem tended simply to be ignored (see also p. 76). It was assumed that what individuals decided in favour of would constitute the national interest. (This is part of a general failure to perceive that the whole people are not the same as a single individual 'writ large', and that there are fundamental problems regarding the relationship between particular individuals and the sum total of individuals.) (As has been pointed out before, there is a tendency in these theories to assume that all important issues regarding impingement upon the individual's pursuit of his inclinations, concern his relationship with the government rather than with the people as a whole.)

In Utilitarian democratic theory the problem is again obscured. Again it is typically not a matter of the relationship between a representative and his constituents as contrasted with his relationship with the pursuit of the national interest. It is true that there is an issue—an important one—concerning the connection between particular interests and the general interest. However, this is seen in terms of the general interest and its relationship to the particular interests of the governors and of individuals as such rather than to those of groups of electors (geographical or otherwise).

According to Utilitarian theory, each individual has—and knows and pursues—his own particular interest. Also a part of Utilitarian theory at times is the view that the general interest is simply the particular interest of every individual : the particular interests are simply 'added together'. The idea that individual interests are harmonious in this way, and are best realized by leaving each individual unfettered in the pursuit of his interest, has already been mentioned (p. 36 above). It reached its most famous expression in the classical economists' notion of laissez-faire—and in particular in Adam Smith's conception of the 'invisible hand' that ensured that the pursuit of private gain resulted in the promotion of the interests of society as a whole. According to such views as these, there seemed little need for government of any kind—even democratic government. However, other aspects of Utilitarianism did, somewhat inconsistently, recognize that government was necessary. As Hobbes had earlier postulated, it was conceived that life without government would be insecure. Individuals would be in mutually destructive competition for limited resources. In other words, individual interests are not naturally harmonious and need to be 'artificially' made so.[75] This is the task of government. 'Government . . . is to make that distribution of the scanty materials of happiness, which would insure the greatest sum of it in the members of the community, taken altogether, preventing every individual or combination of individuals, from interfering with that distribution, or making any man to have less than his share.'[76] But now there is a problem : the government will be composed of persons who, like all individuals, will have and pursue their own private interests. We saw earlier (pp. 79–80 above) how this problem is solved : the representative system was conceived to get over this difficulty and ensure that the interests of the representatives are made to coincide with those of the community as a whole. The idea was that if the people control their rulers, then the interests of the people rather than of the rulers will be promoted. (not so !)

There is, of course, a crucial difficulty in this argument. Government is necessary to control the clash of particular interests amongst the people at large. How then can the people at large have *an* interest, and have control of the rulers to ensure its promotion? James Mill seemed unaware of this difficulty. 'Sometimes the Utilitarians simply ignore this difficulty, speaking of the people only as a unified whole with one interest [thereby contravening the individualist basis of Utilitarianism]. That is James Mill's solution, and one sometimes used by Bentham.'[77] Bentham also had a more sophisticated side to his theory. This involved a recognition of individuals having shared public interests as well as ethically inferior selfish private ones. It also involved a contradiction of the original axiom that each man is the best judge of his own interest, and a departure from the delegate view of representation.[78] It is, however, the simple—and inconsistent—theory exemplified by James Mill that has been regarded as the typical Utilitarian legacy.

We noticed earlier that Calhoun's theory of representation was like that of Utilitarianism, but based on groups rather than individuals. And we shall conclude this look at traditional democratic theory by noting that, like Utilitarianism, Calhoun's theory has shortcomings in its treatment of the relationship between the general and particular interests. Like Utilitarian theory, he tended to assume, erroneously, that the general interest consisted simply in the promotion—or rather, in his case, the protection—of all particular interests. Indeed, the very point of his theory was to emphasize the necessity of giving adequate weight to all particular interests. The danger was not so much that the pursuit of particular interests might block out the general interest, as that some particular interest or interests might block out other particular interests. However, a somewhat diluted and conservative theory of the general interest could be said to be involved in this idea of a process of mutual checking. According to Calhoun, the political institutions should be such that it is 'impossible for any one interest or combination of interests or class, or order, or portion of the community, to obtain exclusive control', thus preventing 'any one of them from oppressing the other'. This forces the different interests 'to unite in such measures only as would promote the prosperity of all, [since this is] the only means to prevent the suspension [by mutual veto] of the action of the government;—and, thereby, to avoid anarchy, the greatest of all evils'.[79]

Before leaving traditional democratic theory we must say something —very briefly—about the assumption of rationality. It has often been said that traditional (or 'orthodox') democratic theory suffers from an unrealistic assumption about the rationality of ordinary men. Cobban, for example, refers to what he sees as

... certain defects in orthodox [traditional] democratic theory. These lie, above all, in the psychological assumptions on which it is founded. Growing up under the influence of the intellectualist psychology of the eighteenth century, it naturally saw the individual as an intelligent, self-determining being, who uses his intellect to analyse his needs, and on the basis of this analysis decides on the appropriate mode of action and puts it into effect by a deliberate act of the will.[80]

Is there such an assumption of rationality in traditional democratic theory; and if there is, is it a defect? The second of these questions is taken up in Chapters 5 and 6. Indeed, one of the issues central to the discussion of the adequacy of traditional democratic theory in the light of modern political science is the idea of a lack of correspondence between the assumption of rationality and the portrayal of actual behaviour as given by political science. The answer to the first question will be briefly suggested here.

'Rationality' is a vague and complex concept. Many apparently different definitions of it can be found. Nonetheless, common to many of them (or, at least, to the meanings given by the actual usages of the term) is the idea of the obtaining of objectives by the use of reasoning based upon adequate relevant knowledge. An irrational man would be one who had no particular objectives, or who did not think logically or use relevant information in attempting to achieve such objectives as he did have.

Now, it seems that traditional democratic theory assumed, or stated, that men should and could make extensive use of reason in ordering their conduct. Even those who, like Sheldon Wolin, point to liberalism's rejection of reason in the positing of the *ends* of conduct, acknowledge the classical liberal's belief in reason's 'role of determining the most efficient means to achieving the ends proposed by feeling'.[81] LDT, then, as an aspect of liberalism, at least assumed this much about the role of reason. And even if it could not be enlarged by education, it was assumed that, by education, this role for reason could be realized in all men. However, the extent of this posited use of reason in LDT is not always as great as is sometimes supposed.[82] Moreover, the possession and use of adequate relevant knowledge is often explicitly denied— indeed, this is part of the very point of LDT's limitation of the control of representatives by their electors. It is by no means clear, then, that LDT assumes the rationality of the ordinary man. If it does so, then it is often a very diluted kind of rationality. (Although, whether or not consistently, it can on occasion become 'undiluted': Mill's espousal of Hare's form of proportional representation assumes great knowledge and use of reason in deciding who to vote for from a bewildering variety of choices. True, the primary purpose of this system of election was to give proper representation for the instructed minority, but it was not thought that they would be the only ones to make proper use of the system.)

In RDT, on the other hand, there is an unequivocal assumption of rationality. Inspired by the Enlightenment and its faith in human reason, RDT contains political theories that assume that the ordering as well as the understanding of the polity is to be achieved by the use of reason. This is largely shared by LDT; but RDT also supposes that all (or the great majority) of individuals engage in, or are capable of, rational activity—including political activity. This is both explicitly stated,[83] and anyway assumed by the content of the theories. RDT's model of democracy is such that the presence of rational citizens is logically required for its existence. As is pointed out in Chapter 5, it cannot be said that the people—all the individuals—are making the kind of specific policy choices postulated as part of the RDT model unless they actually know and think about what they are choosing. In other words, it is a logically necessary condition for the existence of the kind of democracy portrayed by RDT that the electors be rational —that they make reasoned choices based upon adequate relevant knowledge.

There is, however, one important qualification to this assertion of the requirement of rationality in RDT. In the form it was stated just now, it presumes that the concept of *elector* can be used interchangeably with that of *citizen*. This is reasonable, given the crucial place of elections in the RDT model (the place of elections in theories of democracy will be discussed in Chapter 6). However, it could be questioned whether such interchangeability could be pressed any further in the direction of generality. An elector is not the same as an individual : the concept of elector contains but an aspect (albeit an important one) of an individual's total existence. And the point here is that rational *voting* behaviour is not necessarily the same as rational behaviour. What constitutes rational voting behaviour is more or less implied by the concept of voting and the particular kinds of democratic theory in which it is utilized : between them, they specify fairly clearly what sort and level of knowledge is 'relevant' and 'adequate'. In the case of RDT, this is a knowledge of the issues and policies before the voters at an election (see Chapter 5). What constitutes rational behaviour as such is not similarly given by a model of democracy itself (although a conception of this is built up in a political philosophy as a whole). And it is possible to question whether it is rational to engage in the activity described at rational voting behaviour (in effect, some modern theories of democracy contain this argument). An analogy would be the deck-chair addict who questioned the rationality of engaging in 'rational gardening' or the well-off but busy and unmechanically minded house-wife who would consider it irrational to set about, or make an attempt at, rationally repairing and overhauling household gadgets herself. Aspects of this point of view will be discussed in Chapter 6. RDT does not, of course, contain this distinction between categories of rational behaviour, for, as was just indicated, it assumes or asserts man to be rational in all spheres of conduct. Moreover, RDT implies the importance of all engaging in political activity—particularly voting. Rational behaviour would therefore include rational voting behaviour.[84]

To the extent that traditional democratic theory assumes or asserts man to be rational, the question of whether he *is* rational becomes important. But this question, and the implications of the answers to it, are considerably complicated by the existence of the distinction just indicated : the distinction between a general view of man as rational and the concept of instrumentally rational political participation that is a logically necessary condition for the existence of the kind of democracy portrayed by RDT. These issues are taken up in Chapters 5 and 6.

This concludes our discussion of what is commonly known as traditional (or classical) democratic theory. However, one other stream of thought within traditional political theory must be mentioned. This is philosophical Idealism ('Idealism' with a capital 'I' refers not to an optimistic belief in the role of ideals in ordering life, but to the philosophical view that ideas rather than matter constitute the ultimate reality). Plato and the German philosopher Hegel (1770–1831) are perhaps the most important of those who, in different ways, developed Idealism as a political philosophy. But it was the English philosophical Idealists, most notably F. H. Bradley (1846–1924), T. H. Green (1836–82) and B. Bosanquet (1848–1923), who brought Idealism into English political theory (it never really took root in America). The main relevant characteristic of this mode of thought[85] is the connection with Rousseau and the general will, although the general will becomes something often referred to as 'the common will' or 'common interest'. However, despite this connection, it cannot be said that Idealist political theory is democratic even in the sense that Rousseau's political theory is. This is because the concept of decisions by the people is not a part of the theory. The 'common will' is embodied in the institutions, traditions and political culture of the society rather than in decisions by individuals : it comes not from the political decisions, but is constituted by the thought involved in those decisions.[86] Such thought—ideas and concepts concerning the community and what it should do—is present in, and derived from, society. As such it is common to all members of the society. It becomes 'will' by being 'internalized' and willed by individuals.

Such a type of political theory is not anti-democratic. Rather it is too general to be either democratic or anti-democratic. It amounts to a theory of the state as such, rather than of a particular kind of state. It is quite compatible with—and some theorists, such as Green, would use it in conjunction with—a democratic theory. It is just that such Idealist theory does not itself constitute a theory of democracy. The specific element missing is the notion of decision—decisions concerning what the state shall do. To the Idealist, it matters little how and by whom actual decisions are taken : it is the nature of the entity within which the decisions are taken that is important. But a theory of democracy is a theory about who makes the decisions : a democracy is a political system in which the basic determining decisions are made by the people as a whole.

This idea of decision has individualist implications. Part of the very concept of ' a decision' is the notion of an *act* of the human mind. Such an act can only take place 'within' an individual : only an individual (or an individual's) mind can act. Indeed, only an individual has a mind. A 'determination' (see pp. 11–13 above) of group action might be loosely spoken of as a decision by that group. But such a determination—if it in fact results from a corresponding decision at all—might be the outcome of decisions by but a few members or only one member of the group. For it to be said that the group as a whole had decided, it would be necessary for all the members[87] to have, in some sense, made the decision. It may be very significant for a determination to result from certain processes that integrate the activities and thoughts of all the members. Such integration may even be a necessary condition for the making of decisions by all. But it does not itself constitute the making of such decisions.

A decision by the people, then, implies decisions by all the individuals who are included in 'the people'. A corporate conception of the people is compatible with this conception. But only by dint of accepting an individualist view as far as *decisions* by the people are concerned. It may be that the corporate entity of the community is more significant than the particular collection of individuals it manifests itself in at any one time. But, in that case, if there is to be a democracy the presently existing people have to make decisions on *behalf* of this corporate entity. Lippman is right to remind us that the electorate—or even the whole population—that exists at any one time is not the same as the corporate entity, existing over time, which constitutes the community and is sometimes called the people[88] But in denying that the former have the right to make decisions, he is denying that democracy ought to exist. 'Democracy' does not merely imply a political system in which authority is vested in the people or in which the policies pursued are in the interest of the people (the public interest). It implies that the authority is actually exercised by the people in the form of the people making decisions on policy. Such decisions can only be made by individuals. To this extent, democratic theory is necessarily individualist. (As we have seen, much of traditional democratic theory was characterized by a more fundamental individualism in that the *only* operative conception was of the people as a collection of individuals.)

Idealist political theory is, then, not merely too general to be democratic theory; it is also true that it is 'too collectivist' (see n. 37 on p. 59
for meaning of 'collectivist'). It does not incorporate the notion of all
the individuals making 'decisions by the people' on public policy.
Rousseau was a collectivist, but his collectivism was modified (albeit at
times obscurely) by the idea of all the individuals actually taking part
in the decision-making.[89] As we saw just now, Idealist political theory
transforms the general will from something that emerges from the
people deliberating into that which is embodied in the political institutions and culture within which decision-making takes place.

There is, however, a twentieth-century tradition of thought which
has been much influenced by the English Idealists and which *is* specifically democratic. We might call this neo-Idealist democratic theory. It
is exemplified in the work of A. D. Lindsay and Ernest Barker.[90] The
Idealist influence is apparent in the notion of a 'spirit of the common
life'. This is something other than the particular interest of any group
or person, and is not to be found by merely adding together separate
individual opinions or interests. 'What matters is not primarily what
any one wills, but the discovery of the spirit of the common life and
what it demands, and then the willing in accordance with it.'[91] Such
discovery is made by a process of discussion. Indeed, discussion is what
makes a system a democracy. Decisions by the people—as expressed in
elections—can only occur as a result of (and as part of) a process of
discussion. 'Men can agree on common action which yet leaves each
to live his own life. . . . How that can best be obtained can be discovered
by discussion, in which the one-sidedness of particular views can be
eliminated and a principle of common action discovered which each
can feel does justice to what was vital to his own contention.'[92] Barker
argues that 'we may say that the process of political discussion begins
originally with the action of political parties, which debate and formulate their programmes as the issues for electoral discussion, and then
proceed to select and propose their candidates as the exponents of those
programmes. Discussion is then carried forward to the electorate, which
chooses between the programmes, after the grand debate of the general
election, by the simple act of choosing between the candidates and thus
constituting a majority in favour of one of the programmes.'[93]

Despite the Idealist influence, such theories have sufficient individualism to be democratic. Obviously, the thoroughgoing individualism
of much traditional democratic theory has been significantly modified,
but an important aspect also remains.[94] As Thompson points out,
'individuals are the units from which opinions must be solicited'.[95] The
process of discussion is one which involves individuals. But the crucial
point here is that there comes a point where a decision is made by the
people—albeit one that is embedded in the discussion process. And

such a decision is—as by definition it must be (see above, pp. 89–90)—constituted by the decisions of individuals. (See Chapter 4 for further analysis of the relationship between the discussion process and the notion of a decision by the people.)

It may also be noted here that such decisions by the people are of the broad general kind found in LDT rather than the specific ones of RDT.[96] Lindsay also emphasizes the 'shoe-pinching' argument (see Chapters 6 and 8 below) in his conception of the role of the people. Furthermore, he says that, primarily, the people pass judgement on what the government has been doing, rather than directly choosing what a future government shall do : 'The vote at a general election is primarily a judgement on results. . . .'[97] Both of these will be seen to be important ideas in the discussion of the 'factual validity' of democratic theories in Chapter 6. As was indicated earlier, Chapter 6 will also contain an outline of what might be termed modern theories of democracy. But, for the moment, we shall turn away from outlining the general nature of democratic theories, and take up some problems connected with them. This will form the subject of the next two chapters. The problems are raised by traditional democratic theories, but possible answers to them are also, of course, to be found in modern democratic theories. Indeed, the modern theories were to some extent provoked by the problems discussed in Chapter 5. Chapter 6, then, will also be concerned in part with further analysis of the difficulties connected with democratic theory.

NOTES AND REFERENCES

1 Henceforth, unless otherwise indicated, when the terms 'democracy', 'theory of democracy', etc., are used it will be 'liberal-democracy', 'theory of liberal-democracy', etc., that will be meant.

2 See, for example, G. P. Gooch, *English Democratic Ideas in the Seventeenth Century*, Cambridge, Cambridge University Press, 1954.

3 Although, as Laslett has shown, actually written some ten years earlier: see the Introduction to his edition of Locke's *Two Treatises of Government*, ed. cit.

4 K. A. Megill, *The New Democratic Theory*, New York, The Free Press, 1970, p. 25.

5 M. Seliger, *The Liberal Politics of John Locke*, London, Allen & Unwin, 1968, p. 285.

6 See, for example, *Second Treatise*, Section 240 (p. 476 in Laslett edition).

7 See, for example, ibid., Laslett's Introduction, p. 128, and W. Kendall, *John Locke and the Doctrine of Majority Rule*.

8 *Second Treatise*, para. 132 (p. 399). There is a complication in that the concept used is the original one of—what would now be called—direct democracy (see p. 5 above.)

9 M. Seliger, *The Liberal Politics of John Locke*, p. 218.

10 For a powerful expression of the contrary view, see W. Kendall, *John Locke and the Doctrine of Majority Rule*.

11 A point made earlier should be remembered. This was that the general idea of liberal-democracy is more general than that contained in what is usually referred to as liberal democratic theory. Thus it is not only liberal democratic theory that contains a model which falls within the general idea of liberal-democracy. This terminology carries obvious risks of confusion, but it is adopted here because it is the one that is very widely used and the attempt to avoid it would probably breed greater confusion.

12 Somewhat confusingly this point is often put by saying that they are delegates *rather than* representatives. It would seem that there is a meaning of 'representative' here which is generic, according to which a delegate is a type of representative, and another which is specific, according to which a delegate is contrasted with a representative (in this sense a representative would be but one kind of representative in the generic sense).

13 James Madison, in *The Federalist* (No. 10), London, J. M. Dent (Everyman edition), 1911, p. 45.

14 The role—a very central role—of elections in democracy will be discussed in Chapter 6.

15 See, for example, Carole Pateman, *Participation and Democratic Theory*, Cambridge, Cambridge University Press, 1970, esp. Chapters 1 and 2.

16 For a succinct account, see ibid.

17 On the thought of Jefferson and Price, see, for example, S. K. Padover (ed.), *Thomas Jefferson on Democracy* (Mentor Book edition), New York, The New American Library, 1946; and D. O. Thomas, 'Richard Price and Edmund Burke: The Duty to Participate in Government', *Philosophy*, Vol. 30 (1959), pp. 308–22.

18 It might be argued that there is an inconsistency in Mill's thought here: see, for example, Pateman, *Participation and Democratic Theory*, pp. 31–3.

19 The responses of the people will also be anticipated in advance so that the people will have *some* 'positive' influence. This point—which has already been mentioned (p. 33 above)—will be discussed in Chapter 6.

20 See, for example, F. Marini, 'John Locke and the Revision of Classical Democratic Theory', *The Western Political Quarterly*, Vol. 22, No. 1 (March 1969), pp. 5–19.

21 For the sake of completeness one should add that it might be non-action, or resistance to action, which is desired.

22 See, for example, Pitkin, *The Concept of Representation*; S. H. Beer, 'The Representation of Interests', *American Political Science Review* (1957), op. cit., and *Modern British Politics*; and Birch, *Representation*, Chapter 5.

23 For a lucid and not overlong account of the nature and history of Utilitarianism, see J. Plamenatz, *The English Utilitarians*, Oxford, Blackwell, 1949. James Mill's son, John Stuart Mill, is generally acknowledged to be a more important thinker than his father or Bentham. He is also often regarded—and regarded himself—as being a Utilitarian. However, he modified the theory to such an extent that it is doubtful whether it is meaningful to classify him as a Utilitarian. 'There is not much left of Benthamite Utilitarianism when John Stuart Mill has completed his

defence of it. What is left is, strictly speaking, not Utilitarianism at all . . .'—
ibid., p. 144. Certainly, as far as his explicit writing on democracy is
concerned, he falls into a different category from Utilitarianism for the
purposes of the present discussion.

24 Plamenatz, *The English Utilitarians*, p. 145.

25 See ibid., p. 2, for a more rigorous and extended definition.

26 James Mill, *An Essay on Government*, ed. cit., p. 27.

27 J. Bentham, 'A Plan for Parliamentary Reform', *Works*, ed. J. Bowring,
Edinburgh, 1843, III, p. 33; quoted in Pitkin, *The Concept of Representation*,
p. 198.

28 When they are so regarded they are abstracted from the non-democratic
aspects of Burke's thought—in particular the conceptions of 'virtual'
representation, acceptance of a limited franchise and his view of the
political incapability of the great bulk of the people.

29 Quoted in Pitkin, *The Concept of Representation*, p. 176.

30 J. S. Mill, *Considerations on Representative Government*, World's Classics edition,
op. cit., p. 257 (italics added).

31. Pitkin, *The Concept of Representation*, p. 192.

32 *The Federalist*, ed. cit., No. 10, pp. 42 and 43 (italics added).

33 'As long as the connection subsists between [man's] reason and his self-love,
his opinions and his passions will have a reciprocal influence on each other;
and the former will be objects to which the latter will attach themselves.'
Moreover, the divergencies of interest arise from property. 'From the
protection [which is the first object of government] of different and unequal
faculties of acquiring property, the possession of different degrees and kinds
of property immediately results; and from the influence of these on the
sentiments and views of the respective proprietors, ensues a division of the
society into different interests and parties'—*The Federalist*, ed. cit., No. 10,
p. 42.

34 Plamenatz, *The English Utilitarians*, p. 86.

35 ibid., p. 88.

36 T. Paine, *Rights of Man*, ed. cit., p. 142. Paine did not mean by 'general
will' what Rousseau meant. Paine merely uses it as a synonym for 'will of
the people'.

37 e.g. 'Enable [the whole mass of the people] to see that it is their interest to
preserve peace and order, and they will preserve them'—Padover (ed.),
Thomas Jefferson on Democracy, 1946, p. 23. But even here it is the interest
of the whole people, rather than particular individual or group interests
that is being referred to.

38 Padover (ed.), *Thomas Jefferson on Democracy*, p. 15. See following chapter
for a discussion of the majority principle.

39 J. S. Mill, *Considerations on Representative Government*, ed. cit., p. 258.

40 E. Burke, *Speech to the Electors of Bristol, November 3, 1774*, quoted in S. I.
Benn and R. S. Peters, *Social Principles and the Democratic State*, London,
Allen & Unwin, 1959, p. 341.

41 Madison writing in *The Federalist*, ed. cit., No. 10, pp. 45–6. It is true that
Madison goes on to say that 'on the other hand the effect may be inverted'
and that the representatives may be such as to betray the interests of the
people (p. 46). However, this is a matter of ensuring—or rendering prob-

able—the election of representatives of the right kind, rather than of casting doubt on the principle that the people ought not to govern themselves directly.

42 R. A. Dahl, *A Preface to Democratic Theory*, p. 32.

43 *The Federalist*, ed. cit., No. 39, p. 190.

44 ibid., p. 191.

45 Dahl, *Preface to Democratic Theory*, p. 31. At that time the meaning of the word 'democracy' was usually restricted to what would now be called direct democracy (see also above, p. 5). The term 'republic' was often used to mean what we would now call indirect or representative democracy.

46 J. S. Mill, *Dissertations and Discussions*, London, Longmans, 1859, Vol. I, Appendix, p. 470.

47 In *Representative Government* Mill also favoured certain exclusions (the illiterate and those who paid no direct taxes) from the suffrage. However, these were only seen as temporary measures (to be gradually rendered unnecessary by the extension of education and changes in the system of taxation) and not as detracting from Mill's belief in the principle of universal suffrage.

48 J. S. Schapiro, 'John Stuart Mill, Pioneer of Democratic Liberalism in England', in *Journal of the History of Ideas*, Vol. 4 (1943), pp. 141–2.

49 *Dissertations and Discussions*, p. 471.

50 *Considerations on Representative Government*, ed. cit., p. 211.

51 *Dissertations and Discussions*, p. 471 (italics added).

52 Pitkin, *The Concept of Representation*, p. 205. See Chapter 8 for a reference to the 'shoe-pinching' argument. The basic idea is that only the wearers (the people) know where the shoes pinch (the effects of state action).

53 Birch, *Representation*, p. 53.

54 Paine, *Common Sense* (1776), quoted in W. Harrison, *Sources of British Political Thought*, New York, Macmillan, 1965, p. 125.

55 ibid.

56 See E. P. Douglass, *Rebels and Democrats*, Chapter 15, for the view that Jefferson, although ambiguous in his thought, was not a radical democrat. Douglass is concerned in this book with the difference between revolutionary democrats (who subscribed to the views of Paine) and the Whig leaders of the American revolution (who were more concerned with the limitation of power and the protection of the social order than with political equality and majority rule). He concludes that from a survey of Jefferson's activities during the Revolutionary period 'it would appear that on the whole [Jefferson] leaned more toward eighteenth-century Whiggism than toward eighteenth-century democracy' (p. 311).

57 Padover (ed.), *Thomas Jefferson on Democracy*, p. 18.

58 Pitkin, *The Concept of Representation*, p. 159.

59 ibid., p. 148., and p. 277n.

60 James Mill, *An Essay on Government*, ed. cit., p. 43.

61 ibid., pp. 37–8.

62 ibid., p. 38.

63 John C. Calhoun, *Disquisition on Government*, quoted in Birch, *Representation*, pp. 84–5.

64 The 'particular interests' may be particular to a geographical area (one, or

a group of constituencies), or to a section of society. There may be considerable overlap between the two categories—as when particular economic interests are located predominantly in particular geographical areas (e.g. 'mining constituencies').

65 Birch, *Representation*, p. 37.
66 Quoted in Pitkin, *The Concept of Representation*, p. 171.
67 ibid., p. 186.
68 *The Federalist*, ed. cit., No. 10, p. 44.
69 Pitkin, *The Concept of Representation*, pp. 195 and 196.
70 See, for example, *Considerations on Representative Government*, pp. 245–6.
71 ibid., p. 263.
72 He did not totally exclude geographical representation, but gave it a secondary importance. 'Though the Parliament of the nation ought to have as little as possible to do with purely local affairs, yet, while it has to do with them there ought to be members specially commissioned to look after the interests of every important locality . . .'—ibid., p. 257.
73 ibid., pp. 254–71.
74 Hare's electoral system did not totally abolish geographical constituencies. It allowed electors to continue to vote in, and have representatives for, geographical areas if they so wished (the minority in each area, however, could still vote for a candidate more to their liking somewhere else in the country. It was by this sort of provision for minorities that Mill sought to secure the representation of those with instructed minds.) (ibid., pp. 257–60.)
75 For an extended discussion of Utilitarianism in general, and of the relationship between the natural and the artificial identification of interests in particular, see E. Halévy, *The Growth of Philosophical Radicalism*, London, Faber & Faber, 1954.
76 James Mill, *An Essay on Government*, p. 4.
77 Pitkin, *The Concept of Representation*, p. 202.
78 See ibid., esp. pp. 203–5. Pitkin concludes that Bentham ends up with a view of representation like that of J. S. Mill and Burke (p. 205).
79 John C. Calhoun, *A Disquisition on Government*, *The Works of John C. Calhoun* (ed. R. K. Cralle), published under the direction of the General Assembly of the State of South Carolina, 1851, Vol. I, pp. 25–6 and 38.
80 A. Cobban, *The Crisis of Civilisation*, London, Jonathan Cape, 1941, p. 151.
81 Sheldon S. Wolin, *Politics and Vision*, Boston, Little, Brown, 1960, p. 332.
82 See, for example, F. Marini's discussion of Locke: 'John Locke and the Revision of Classical Democratic Theory', art. cit.
83 Godwin (an extreme radical democrat whose theory bordered on anarchism) perhaps stated this most explicitly: man 'is a reasonable creature, capable of perceiving what is . . . right', and 'a person arrived at maturity, takes an extensive survey of the consequences of his actions, therefore he is eminently a voluntary and rational being . . .' (W. Godwin, *An Enquiry Concerning Political Juctice*, quoted in D. Fleisher, *William Godwin, a Study in Liberalism*, London, Allen & Unwin, 1951, p. 74, and in A. E. Rodway (ed.), *Godwin and the Age of Transition*, London, Harrap, 1952, p. 129). Godwin believed that the abolition of outmoded forms of government would reveal and give proper expression to man's inherent rationality.

Paine also believed this: 'There is existing in man, a mass of sense lying in a dormant state. . . .' Democracy would end this dormancy: 'the representative system diffuses such a body of knowledge throughout a nation, on the subject of government, as to explode ignorance and preclude imposition'— (Paine, *Rights of Man*, ed. cit., pp. 198 and 206.) Utilitarianism involves an idea of men as rational as part of the very concept of individuals knowing what their interests are and deciding how best to pursue them. An assumption of rationality was expressed by James Mill in the following words: 'every man, possessed of reason, is accustomed to weigh evidence, and to be guided and determined by its preponderance. When various conclusions are, with their evidence, presented with equal care and with equal skill, there is a moral certainty, though some few may be misguided, that the greater number will judge right, and that the greatest force of evidence, wherever it is, will produce the greatest impression'—*Liberty of the Press*, quoted in Halévy, *The Growth of Philosophical Radicalism*, p. 410.

84 Another point to note here is that RDT typically does not focus upon actual electoral systems. It therefore tends to ignore the limitation of choice implied by electoral systems' structuring of voting options (contrast Hare's system, and its espousal by J. S. Mill). Typically, then, RDT implies full freedom of electoral choice of political ends and means—i.e. fully rational choice. (I am indebted to Professor P. W. Campbell for drawing my attention to this point.)

85 On English Idealism, see M. Richter, *The Politics of Conscience: T. H. Green and His Age*, London, Weidenfeld and Nicolson, 1964. The main relevant works of the thinkers mentioned are: F. H. Bradley, *Ethical Studies*, 2nd edition, London, Oxford University Press, 1927 (paperback, 1962); T. H. Green, *Lectures on the Principles of Political Obligation*, London, Longmans, 1917; and B. Bosanquet, *Philosophical Theory of the State*, 4th edition, London, Macmillan, 1923.

86 See, for example, the quotation from Bosanquet in A. D. Lindsay, *The Modern Democratic State*, London, Oxford University Press, 1943, pp. 243–4. In particular: 'The general will cannot be identified with the decision of a community by vote upon any simple issue. Every such decision is an expression or consequence of the general will. . . .'

87 As we shall see in Chapter 4 there are numerous difficulties connected with the fact that it is rare for identical decisions to be made by all.

88 See W. Lippmann, *The Public Philosophy*, esp. pp. 32–8. See also Chapter 1 above, pp. 16–17.

89 It was argued in Chapter 2 that the theory of 'people's democracy' was invalid in part because it had moved away from the idea of the people actually making decisions.

90 See esp. A. D. Lindsay, *The Essentials of Democracy*, London, Oxford University Press (2nd edition), 1935, and *The Modern Democratic State*; Ernest Barker, *Reflections on Government*, London, Oxford University Press, 1942. There are also numerous twentieth-century democratic theorists who do not fall within the categories of what is termed modern democratic theory in Chapter 6. Some have affinities with Lindsay and Barker. To an extent, all are reasserting and restating aspects of traditional democratic theory. D. F. Thompson in his *The Democratic Citizen* (Cambridge, Cam-

bridge University Press, 1970) categorizes them as citizenship theorists and contrasts citizenship theory with elitist democratic theory. The latter accepts and/or prescribes a very limited role for the mass of the people (see Chapter 6). Citizenship theory is characterized by a belief in a fairly active political role for the people (see Thompson, op. cit., Introduction and Chapter 1). Some of the most important of these 'citizenship theorists' discussed by Thompson are L. T. Hobhouse, G. D. H. Cole, Harold Laski (some of his work), John Dewey, T. V. Smith, Yves Simon, R. M. MacIver and C. J. Friedrich (see Thompson's notes in op. cit., pp. 190–2, for a list of the relevant publications).

91 A. D. Lindsay, *The Modern Democratic State*, p. 241.
92 Lindsay, *The Essentials of Democracy*, pp. 35 and 36.
93 Ernest Barker, *Reflections on Government*, pp. 37–8. Barker then traces further stages of the discussion process in parliament and cabinet.
94 See ibid., pp. 153–4.
95 Thompson, *The Democratic Citizen*, p. 91.
96 See, for example, Barker, pp. 43–4 (although he admits the possibility of occasional specific decisions on major matters); and Lindsay, *The Modern Democratic State*, pp. 267–86.
97 *The Modern Democratic State*, p. 272.

CHAPTER 4

Problems Within Democratic Theory

In this and the following chapter we shall be concerned with some problems posed by democratic theory. In Chapter 5 we will begin a look at the difficulties which arise from the application of theory to reality, while in the present chapter the subject is certain problems that arise within democratic theory itself.

These problems all stem from one central difficulty : how can many and different individual decisions be combined in such a way that it may be said that all the individuals have made a single decision (or set of decisions)? In a democracy, the political decisions—the basic ones, at least—are made by the whole people. As we saw in Chapter 3, a decision by the whole people (sometimes referred to as a 'collective' or 'social decision') can only mean a decision made up of the decisions of all the individuals comprising the presently existing people. But such decisions usually differ. This is a problem raised by traditional democratic theory, but, as can be seen, it is one common to all democratic theory. Moreover, traditional theory sometimes ignores it and there are aspects of it that have only really been taken up in modern times.

It is, however, with the problem as it arises from traditional democratic theory proper that we start. This means that, to begin with, two important assumptions are made : the one concerning the individualist structure and functioning of the political system, and the other concerning the incorporation of virtually the entire democratic process into the electoral process and its direct effects. Both of these assumptions are characteristic of traditional democratic theory : in Chapter 3 we saw that the individualism of most non-Rousseauist traditional theory was more basic than the minimum implied simply by the notion of a decision by the people,[1] and the electoral assumption will be referred to later (suffice it to say that central to individualist traditional theory is the idea that decisions by the people are made by their voting at general elections). However, these assumptions are not by any means confined to traditional democratic theory : they have retained an extremely important place in much twentieth-century thought about democracy. Indeed, as we shall see, a significant form of contemporary theory is concerned with the quasi-mathematical problems of combining votes—the assumption being that this is an important matter since the democratic process is encapsulated in elections. Nonetheless, we shall see later that one way of responding to the problems concerning the notion of a collective decision is to modify, challenge or abandon these assumptions. This is done to some extent by both neo-Idealist and some modern democratic theory (the former response will be discussed in this chapter; the latter will be taken up in Chapter 6).

The problems we are here concerned with, then, arise from the combining of individual votes into a 'decision by the electorate'.[2] The individualist assumption implies that each person's vote is the expression of a distinct individual decision : two or more individuals might well vote the same way, but this would be the result of entirely separate decisions to do the same thing rather than to those decisions reflecting a previous merging of ideas.[3] Here it is the distinctness and diversity of individual decisions that is being focused upon, rather than the problem of the relationship between the individual and the common good. In the end—as Rousseau saw—the two categories of problem cannot be separated. However, the individualist assumption can imply such a separation (or else the denial of the existence of a problem about the common good) : a denial, in effect, of the existence of a general interest. (See pp. 84–5 above for the Utilitarian notion of the 'general interest' as consisting merely in some sort of addition of individual interests.) For the time being we shall not question this individualist assumption; hence we shall, for the moment, ignore the concept of the general interest. At this point it can be assumed either that the general interest is the concern of the representatives rather than the electors (so that the issue translates itself into that of the relationship between a representative and his electors),[4] or else that there is no separate problem. The latter could be the case because either it is conceived that there is no 'general interest' apart from the addition of individual interests, or else that votes already embody a conception of the general interest (they may express opinions rather than interests—see Chapter 3). In the following discussion we shall initially use the terminology of many modern analyses and side-step the question of whether it is opinions or interests that are involved by saying that votes express preferences. However, as we shall see later, such conceptualization is oversimple and begs important questions.

The problem of the idea of a collective decision can now be stated (or, at least, the problem as it arises when the conceptualization is simply in terms of individuals having preferences). If all individuals' preferences were the same, there would be no problem : the decision of all (the collective decision) would quite simply be the same as ('the sum total of') all individual decisions. The difficulties arise because such unanimity is a very rare occurrence—so rare that any viable theory would have to assume its non-existence. Given the non-existence of unanimity then, how can it be said there is *a* decision (or set of decisions) by all?[5]

Although this problem was, of course, implicit in traditional democratic theory, it was not always explicitly taken up. RDT was often more interested in demonstrating *that* the people should rule than with ticklish questions of *how* they could be said to rule : the contrasts with monarchical and oligarchical rule tended to be given more importance than the 'internal' problems of democratic rule (other than those of asserting popular control over representatives). When the problem was focused upon, it was usually only the majority–minority issues that were discussed. In LDT the power—or potential power—of the majority became a major worry (see p. 53 above). Other aspects of the problem were not really taken up in traditional theory. Thus it is only comparatively recently that there has been much discussion of such issues as those raised by considering individuals' rankings of preferences, and by taking note not just of votes but also of the intensity of preferences that lie behind them.

The idea of power in the hands of a majority is one that can raise some general issues. These arise primarily from the question of whether, and if so why, the majority ought to rule. But before these are looked at, one 'solution' to the majority-rule problem has to be disposed of. This is the argument that, in fact, owing to such factors as apathy, ignorance and the relative autonomy of politicians once elected, a majority does not rule. This is, for example, put forward by Dahl,[6] who then comes to the conclusion that democracy is characterized not by majority, nor by minority, rule, but by minori*ties* rule.[7] However, such ideas as these will be considered in the next two chapters rather than here. They arise from the confrontation of theory with reality rather than from within theory (traditional democratic theory, at least). The meaning and theoretical significance (not to mention the logical possibility) of majority decision-making have to be known before it makes sense to consider the significance of its possible non-existence in the empirical world.

To return, then, to the questions raised by the idea of majority rule. The first point to notice is that the assertion that state decisions ought to be made by a majority of the people does not follow from the proposition that decision-making groups ought to use majority voting. A further premise is needed for this conclusion : one to the effect that the people ought to constitute the decision-making group within the state.[8] Clearly, though, our purpose here is to consider majority decision-making by the people. But this leads into another point.

Justifications of majority decision-making by the people are intimately tied up with justifications of democracy itself. If it is held—as it frequently is—that the rationale of the method of majority decision-making is that a decision by a majority is the nearest approach to a decision by the whole, then it follows that what justifies decision-making by a majority of the people is that which justifies decision-making by the whole people. The latter types of justification are discussed in Chapter 8; and it is the 'majority-approximates-to-the-whole' rationale that is discussed here.

Although justifications of majority rule are frequently incorporated into justifications of democracy in the way just indicated,[9] it appears that this need not always be so. It need not be accepted that the decision of a majority of the people should be regarded as a decision of the people.) In such cases the question of whether—and if so, why—majority rule is justified would become, initially, at least, separated from the justification of democracy. Arguments used here include those to the effect that majority rule preserves social peace (since, without it, a majority would in any case be strong enough to get its way—by disrupting the system[10]), and those maintaining that majority rule is not 'unfair' since the minority have a chance to convert people to their point of view and thus become the majority.[11] This latter argument is not so much an independent, or 'positive', justification as one that buttresses others. Indeed, it is difficult to prise away any arguments from connections with justifications of democracy or the 'majority-approximates-to-the-whole' argument. (There is a logical category of arguments to the effect that majority rule is neither equated with, nor a condition of, democracy, and that it is desirable. But few have been moved to supply members of this category.) Even what is perhaps the most widely raised moral question about majority rule—the question of the extent to which minority rights ought to be preserved from infringement by a majority—becomes inextricably interconnected with general questions about the nature and justification of democracy. And, in fact, this question about minority rights shades off into two others: (a) the relationship between individual rights and governmental power in a democracy; and (b) the extent to which the views of *all*—not just of a majority—have to be accommodated before it can be said that there has been a decision by all. The first of these questions was covered in Chapter 2; the second is taken up here. Discussion of the justification of majority rule thus becomes absorbed into the analysis of related topics.

In this chapter, then, we are concerned with the concept of majority decision simply as regards the part it has been seen as playing in solving the 'non-unanimity problem'. The question to be answered is whether, and in what sense, the decision of the majority can be regarded as the decision of all.

The majority decision principle is based primarily on a simple line of reasoning : where unanimity is lacking, i.e. where preferences are divided, it is the greater rather than the lesser number of preferences that should prevail since the greater number is nearer to being the whole number. In other words, if there is no unanimous decision, it is the decision of either the majority or the minority that has to be accepted. The majority decision is accepted because it *can be counted as* the decision of all,[12] for the majority decision is nearer to being this than is the decision of the minority. This argument is frequently buttressed by another which in some ways looks similar. This is to the effect that since the majority is the greater number, they constitute the greater force and will, in any case, eventually get their way—i.e. if it came to a fight the majority would win ('we count heads in order to avoid breaking them'). Locke makes use of this as the basic argument in his statement of the majority principle, although he supplements it with others. For Locke a community is created by unanimous consent, but thereafter it should act by majority decision-making :

For when any number of men have, by the consent of every individual, made a Community, they have thereby made that community one Body, with a power to Act as one body, which is only by the will and determination of the majority. For that which acts any Community, being only the consent of the individuals of it, and it being necessary to that which is one body to move one way; it is necessary the Body should move that way whither greater force carries it, which is the consent of the majority: or else it is impossible it should act or continue one Body. . . . And therefore we see that in Assemblies . . . the act of the Majority passes for the act of the whole, and of course determines, as having by the Law of Nature and Reason, the power of the whole.[13]

Here the 'greater force' idea is reinforced by, or based on, an argument from natural law[14]—a type of argument used later by, for example, Jefferson : 'Individuals exercise [self-government] by their single will; collections of men by that of their majority; for the law of the majority is the natural law of every society of men.'[15]

The 'majority-is-nearer-to-being-all' argument was also used, for example, by Bentham[16]—and this and the 'majority-is-stronger' argument have continued to predominate in democratic theory. Strictly speaking another, complementary, argument has often come in as well. This is simply to the effect that for the democrat there is no alternative to majority decision-making. It is well expressed in Abraham Lincoln's words : 'Unanimity is impossible; the rule of a minority, as a permanent arrangement, is wholly inadmissible; so that, rejecting the majority principle, anarchy or despotism in some form is all that is left.'[17]

These, then, are the arguments that form the basis in democratic

theory for the 'majoritarian' answer to the question we are here concerned with : how, in the absence of unanimity, can it be said that
decisions are made by *all* the people?

How convincing are these arguments? Do they provide valid answers
to this question posed by the lack of unanimity? Let us look at
the 'Lincoln argument' first. This may be an argument for majority
decision-making, but it is not one for counting the decision of the
majority as the decision of all. It is, in fact, of the form : all the
available alternatives are ruled out, therefore it must be majority
decision-making that is compatible with democracy. But such reasoning
is invalid. The fact that only the majority method of decision-making is
left implies no more than that *if* it is compatible with democracy, then
it is the only method which is. It could just as well be that *no* method
is compatible with democracy. The 'Lincoln argument' could, indeed,
be seen as a demonstration of the impossibility of the existence of
democracy.

The 'majority-is-stronger argument' is similarly invalid. Again, it
may be an argument for majority decision-making,[18] but this does not
in itself mean that such decision-making is compatible with democracy.
It does not follow from the assertion that, in the end, the majority's
decision will prevail, that this decision can be counted as the decision
of all. All that seems to follow is that in such cases there are no decisions
by all, only decisions by a majority. Similarly, the idea that trials of
strength should be short-circuited by counting votes does not itself
show that the decision expressed by the majority's votes can be taken
as the decision of all. It might be objected that this is to ignore the
idea of a body naturally moving 'that way whither the greater force
[within itself] carries it'. But this is to presume a corporate conception
of the people : only thus can the greater force (the majority of individuals) be seen as *within* the whole rather than in contradistinction
to it (i.e. on an individualist account the whole is simply '*all* the
individuals'). An ambiguity, or rather a confusion arising from slipping
between different conceptions of the people (see n. 12, p. 120), is
'exploited' here. With the corporate conception, the whole people (an
entity) can be said to have acted even if only a minority (or just one
person—as in a medieval kingdom) had *decided* what that action should
be. But a collection of individuals as such (the individualist conception
of the people) can only be said to have acted if all have decided and
acted in the same way.[19] The following, invalid, argument seems
implicit in the 'whither-the-greater-force-carries-it' idea. The people
act, in the corporate sense, on the decision of a majority. But, using
the individualist conception, if the people act it must follow that all
the individuals decided so to act; therefore the decision of the majority
'must', in some way, be the decision of all. The 'natural movement'

argument is thus based on confusion and does not save the 'majority-is-stronger' idea.

We are left, then, with the primary argument: the decision of the majority is to be accepted because it comes nearest to being the decision of all. But this argument really will not do either. It looks plausible at first sight only because, or in so far as, it is an *overwhelming* majority that is thought of. It seems perfectly acceptable to treat a decision by 999 people out of a group of 1,000 as if it were a decision by the whole group. Or a decision by 990; or 950; or, perhaps, 900. But what about 850, or 700, or . . .? Certainly, by the time you come to 501 (the smallest possible majority, but a majority nonetheless) the idea becomes ridiculous. It seems purely arbitrary to select the decision of the 501 rather than that of the 499.[20] There is no reason why a decision by anything less than an overwhelming majority should be counted as the decision of the whole. It is at this point that the 'Lincoln argument' is usually brought in. But to no avail—this argument is also deficient.

It would seem, then, that it cannot be maintained that the decision of a majority can be counted as the decision of all. It is necessary, therefore, to consider possible responses to the apparent failure of majority decision-making to provide an answer to the non-unanimity problem.

One response consists essentially in a closer look at the concept of majority decision-making and what it implies. In the statements so far of the majority principle, an important distinction has been obscured. This is the distinction between stating a *rule* or *method* for making decisions, and stating that decisions are made by a certain group of people. Stated as a rule, the majority decision-making principle asserts only that when a decision on policy alternatives is to be taken, that alternative which secures the greatest number of votes should be chosen.[21] It does not follow from the use of this rule that there is any one group which constitutes 'the majority' and which is on the winning side in every vote. 'The majority' can be a purely mathematical term without implying anything about those who make up the relevant number as each issue is decided: taking decisions by majority vote does not imply that all decisions are taken by *a* majority. In short, use of the majority decision-making rule does not necessarily mean majority rule.[22]

It could well be that the mathematical majority is in each case made up of a different aggregate of individuals (although there would, of course, have to be some overlapping of the membership of the different aggregates). In the 'ideal' case—which would, in a sense, be the extreme case—every individual would have 'a turn' in the majority. And over the stream of decisions as a whole all individuals would have equal turns. Moreover, because of the continual 'shifting in and out' of the majority, no grouping of individuals could be said to be 'ruling over' others—even in the relatively short run. It would only be *all* the individuals that could be said to be 'the decision-making group'. To make a slightly different point, all individuals would have the same say in the stream of decisions as a whole, and thus the content of the stream would presumably reflect (and equally reflect) the preferences of all individuals.[23] Even if it is arbitrary to assume such a state of affairs in the short run, it could be argued that it is the median towards which there will be a tendency in the long run.

There is a good deal to be said for this argument. It is difficult to maintain, however, that it is an argument for majority decision-making as such. It is only necessary that there be a decision-making rule such that all individuals have equal turns at having their preferences adopted as particular issues come up for decision. Such a rule could be one of random selection of decision-makers, or some formula carefully worked out to give each individual an equal number of turns in the winning preference grouping. Moreover, such rules as these would, by definition, more precisely specify the 'ideal' case (towards which there is, at best, only a tendency with the majority decision rule).

It must, however, be recognized that such rules as those just indicated would probably lead to an entirely unacceptable lack of integration in policy outcomes—in fact, complete incoherence in state activity would be likely. And it is arguable that such incoherence is incompatible with the idea of *decision*-making by anybody. Moreover, in a group the size of a modern electorate it would hardly be practicable to operate rules of this kind. Thus after all it does seem that, failing unanimity, the majority decision-making rule is the one that must be used to achieve the 'equal say' state of affairs (or an approximation to it). This is, however, to ignore one further difficulty: the notion of 'a stream of decisions' would apply to a direct democratic process rather than to one of elections at relatively long intervals. Between elections it could be said that the particular combination of individuals who made up the majority at the previous election was ruling—that it had made the decisions for the inter-election period. But even if we ignore this for the moment, the 'equal say' argument rests on a further questionable assumption: that there are no majority groupings of individuals who have similar preferences on a number of issues. In the extreme case there could be a majority grouping in which the individuals had the same preferences on every issue up for decision. It would then always be the decisions of these same individuals which determined state policy. In other words, majority decision-making here *would* imply decision-making by *a* majority. Moreover, in real life such sharing of preferences usually arises where the relevant individuals form a definite group (rather than just a category or grouping) with a common outlook or interest on political issues. In such situations it is quite apparent that, far from the people as a whole making the decisions, there is domination by one group. Group domination of this kind is most likely to arise (or, at least, become most apparent) where there are two obviously defined and opposing groups—for example, the Protestant majority and the Catholic minority in Northern Ireland, or—to an extent—the white majority and the black minority in the United States. It is true that such clear-cut divisions are the exception rather than the rule, but the existence of fairly stable groupings of individuals with similar expressed preferences *is* usual in Western democracies. This can be seen in the general stability of electoral support for political parties (see Chapter 5). Parties both reflect and generate such groupings. Typically, they reflect, with varying degrees of 'accuracy', definite groups or coalitions. Where there is basically a two-party system, as in Britain and America, this means that the electorate is usually divided between *a* majority and *a* minority[24]—and even this assumes that which is not always the case : that the 'winning' party will have received a majority of votes (see p. 126 below). Admittedly there is sufficient variation (not, normally, entirely explicable by demographic factors) in electoral support for control to change hands : for the minority to 'become the majority', and vice versa. This point of crucial significance will be commented upon later. It does not, however, get round the fact that until and unless such a change takes place, decision-making is in the hands of a group smaller than the whole people.[25] Decision-making by alternating majority groups, whatever its benefits, is not the same as decision-making by the whole people. We should also remember here the difficulty just now put on one side : the difficulty of applying analyses of this kind to decision-making by means of relatively infrequent elections. At least from one election to the next it would have to be said that there was rule by a fairly definite group.[25]

It seems, then, that this attempt to 'rescue' the majority decision-making principle fails. Another type of rescue attempt takes the form of distinguishing different kinds, or 'degrees', of majority. If the majority principle fails primarily because it loses its plausibility when the majority ceases to be overwhelming (see above), would not a rule that stipulated an overwhelming, rather than a simple, majority be the answer? More specifically, it could be required that a determination would only be made when a proposal received two thirds—or, better, three quarters—of the votes.

There are two sorts of (or two aspects of essentially the same) difficulty with this idea. The first is that, precisely as the majority becomes more plausible in one sense, it becomes less so in another. The larger the required majority becomes, and therefore the more nearly it is the same as all the people, the more difficult it becomes to obtain it. It can be immediately appreciated that, for example, a 99 per cent majority rule would be utterly impracticable. To put the point another way, the more nearly the rules specify the ideal goal of unanimity, the more nearly do those rules become as unrealistic as this ideal goal.

Another aspect of this objection to the rule that proposals should secure a qualified (i.e. more than a bare) majority, is that it does not even ensure that decisions are always made by a majority. A failure to obtain the required qualified majority could mean that the minority had imposed a veto on the action favoured by a majority (e.g. if a 55 per cent majority were needed, then a minority of 46 per cent could block action). Dahl develops essentially the same point in his analysis of Madison's discussion of the dangers of 'tyranny' by factions :

For if more than a bare majority is required to enact policy, then a minority of the appropriate size can veto any policy it dislikes. If the freedom of some majority is already curtailed in such a way that only positive governmental action will eliminate that deprivation [e.g. the clearance of slums and the provision of social security], and if a minority with a veto dislikes the measures proposed to increase majority freedom, then by exercising its veto a minority can maintain deprivations of the freedom of a majority and hence can tyrannize over it.[26]

Calhoun explicitly developed and recommended this idea of minority veto with his principle of the 'concurrent majority'. This principle would require that the different groups (interests) within the community would each have to approve a measure by a majority of their own members before its adoption. Contrasting it with what he called the numerical majority principle, Calhoun said that 'on the contrary [the concurrent majority principle], regards interests as well as numbers, considering the community as made up of different and conflicting interests . . . and takes the sense of each, through its majority or appropriate organ, and the united sense of all, as the sense of the entire community'.[27] Calhoun's idea was that, to avoid the complete stalemating of government action which such mutual vetoing would seem to imply, the various 'interests' would be forced into agreeing on *something* (see p. 85 above). Thus it would seem to be virtually unanimous decision-making that Calhoun is after—despite its impracticability. (This way of putting it involves an oversimplification; nonetheless the charge of impracticability still stands. 'Forced' general agreement is not the same as—and its occurrence is more likely than—a general coincidence of 'original' preferences, but it can nonetheless be very difficult to obtain. See pp. 117–18 below, however, for a discussion of points that are of great importance and which are very closely connected to some which arise here.)

The failure of these rescue attempts would seem to imply that the majority principle must be abandoned—at least as a means of providing *by itself* a plausible account of how the many individual decisions can be combined into a collective decision, a decision by all the people. However, an important question poses itself here : why should it be assumed that the problem of non-unanimity must be seen entirely in terms of the majority principle? Why should lack of unanimity be taken to imply that there is a simple split between a majority and a minority? Is it not possible—and, indeed, far more likely—that there will be numerous sets of preferences instead of a simple division into two? Supposing a decision is to be made on what resources to devote to, say, defence. Individuals with preferences on this might well be 'strung out' along a scale varying from those who wanted no provision for defence to those who wanted, say, half the national income to be spent on it. Here there are divisions of preferences, but it does not make sense to say there is a majority and a minority. This is an exceedingly important point, and aspects of some of the issues it raises will be taken up later. But, for the moment, we shall stick with the terms in which the majority principle—and its failure—pose the problem. After all, even accepting that one cannot always talk of majorities and minorities, there almost invariably comes *a point* where a straightforward count of those 'for' and 'against' has to be taken. This is especially true of large groups—such as 'the people'. At some point, if there is to be a *decision*, a particular proposal has to be put and all the various preferences will have to be adapted into preferences for and against the proposal submitted. Thus there will be a majority and a minority (or else an exactly equal division between those for and against).[28] The majority problem thus remains.

We are now in a position to see that the majority principle (at least as a sufficient condition for collective decision-making) cannot be rescued. But the difficulties involved in the attempt to show that there can be collective decisions despite the existence of differing individual preferences apparently go even deeper. Even if the majority principle were acceptable, these further difficulties would still arise. In fact, statements of them will often assume the validity of the majority principle as such : the difficulties are those that arise in attempting to show that even *majority* decisions can take place.

These difficulties—quite often ignored in discussions of democracy— will only appear when an important restrictive assumption, implicit in the discussion so far, is relinquished. This assumption is that the voters each have only one preference (or one preference regarding each issue up for decision)—or, at least, that account need only be taken of the first choice of each voter. But, of course, it is by no means clear that voters will have only one preference regarding possible outcomes of the process of decision. Nor is it clear whether, if voters have more than one preference, account should be taken only of the first of these. Suppose that the question of the penalties for murder became an election issue.[29] And suppose that preferences were split into three groups : (a) those for no capital punishment; (b) those for capital punishment for certain cases of murder only (e.g. the murder of policemen and prison warders); and (c) those for capital punishment for all murders. Now, individuals having these preferences will not only have first preferences. A voter who would most prefer capital punishment for all murders might well prefer restricted capital punishment to none at all if what he most preferred was not to be brought about. Other combinations will also exist (and some of those whose first preference was for 'unrestricted' capital punishment might have (a) as second preference on the grounds that, for example, distinguishing between murders for the purposes of punishment was illogical and/or unjust). It seems entirely reasonable, if not essential, to say that the 'decision of all' (the 'social preference') should be a combination of all voters' *preference rankings*, rather than just of their first preferences.[30]

It seems necessary, then, that summations of preferences should take into account preference rankings. There are, however, notorious logical difficulties involved in the attempt to achieve this. Knowledge of these difficulties goes back to Condorcet in the eighteenth century. But they have not been widely recognized and analysed until quite recently. The starting-points for most analyses have been Duncan Black's *The Theory of Committees and Elections*[31] (once described as 'one of the most important books on political theory to be published this century')[32] and Kenneth J. Arrow's *Social Choice and Individual Values*.[33]

The difficulties centre on the transitivity of preferences. Preferences can be said to be transitive where a preference ranking of three or more objects of preference can be deduced from a direct knowledge of preference relations between pairs only. Using the notation 'aPb', etc., to mean 'a is preferred to b', etc., then preferences for a, b, and c are transitive where we can validly write : if aPb and bPc, then aPc. The whole idea of preference rankings implies the transitivity of preferences. And, as Riker says, 'we often define rationality as the ability to order preferences transitively. Certainly we think a man terribly confused if he says he likes Socialists better than Democrats, Democrats better than Republicans and Republicans better than Socialists.'[34] The assumption of the transitivity of all preferences has been challenged,[35] but it does seem that it would, in many cases, be difficult to deny their transitivity.

The difficulties—or the problems of the summation of preferences—are analysed in what has become known as the theory of social choice, and are crystallized in the 'paradox of voting'. 'The problem arises in its simplest form in the so-called paradox of voting which occurs when voting on pairs of alternatives does not result in a transitive social preference even if all the individual preferences are transitively ordered.'[36] Suppose three individuals (or groups of individuals) have the preference rankings : (1) aPb, bPc and aPc; (2) bPc, cPa and bPa; and, (3) cPa, aPb and cPb. Now, 'adding by pairs according to the rule of simple majority voting, it is apparent that two voters (1 and 3) prefer a to b and that two (1 and 2) prefer b to c. One might therefore expect that the majority preference would be aPc. But in fact two voters (2 and 3) prefer c to a. This is the paradox : that the summation of transitive preferences sometimes produces a circular result.'[37] This type of outcome renders a 'majority decision' impossible to obtain. But it is worth noticing that it is not just majority decision-making which is 'invalidated'. 'One might be tempted to suppose that the paradox of voting is an imperfection in the particular system of majority voting and more ingenious methods could avoid it. But unfortunately this is not so.'[38] Arrow, in fact, goes on to state a general impossibility theorem. The details of this need not detain us here,[39] but in essence the theorem amounts to a demonstration of the impossibility of arriving at a valid social preference, given certain conditions.

These conditions have been taken as constituting logically necessary conditions for the existence of democracy. Therefore it would seem that the theorem proves the impossibility of democracy. 'Put crudely, what Arrow has done is to show that strict democracy is impossible.'[40]

Is it to be accepted, then, that majority decision-making (let alone democracy) is impossible? One possible response is to deny that it matters if majority decisions *are* intransitive. It has been argued that 'intransitivity of majority decisions may prove to be a positive virtue in a democracy since the occasional inconsistency of majority decisions makes democratic rule more palatable to the minority'.[41] However, apart from any doubts about the effectiveness of this as a protection for minorities, it does not solve our problem : there would remain a clear sense in which any 'majority decision' could be spurious (i.e. would not have a special claim to reflect the preference of the majority).[42] Given that transitivity remains a problem, and given the conditions of the type specified by Arrow, there does not seem to be any way of avoiding the paradox. After a detailed and thorough review of the subject and the post-Arrow work in the field, Pattanaik comes to the conclusion that 'a general review of the different aspects of the problem leads one to the conclusion that no clear-cut solution has been found for Arrow's paradox'.[43]

This voting problem may not, however, constitute an insoluble problem for democracy. It remains possible to challenge the validity of Arrow's conditions—or, at least, the notion that they constitute logically necessary conditions for the existence of democracy. And, indeed, it has been asserted that 'the logical possibility of many kinds of democracy is left unscathed by the theory of social choice'.[44] And it does seem that it is too rigid a conception of the nature of democracy (even on strictly individualist assumptions) that requires all of Arrow's conditions to be rigorously fulfilled.

One method of voting which does not satisfy all the Arrow conditions, but which nonetheless may reasonably be accepted as a democratic decision procedure, is the rank-order method.[45] With this method voters numerically weight their preferences so that their first choice is given the highest number and their least preferred alternative the lowest, with the other preferences appropriately ranked and numbered between the two. The figures submitted by all voters are added together and the alternative with the highest score 'wins' and is deemed the alternative chosen, or decided upon, by the voters. This was the method Borda proposed in 1781.[46] It has its drawbacks,[47] but nonetheless seems reasonably satisfactory.

Another approach is to relax the Arrow condition which implies that a decision procedure is valid only if it can cope with all possible orderings of preference by individuals. It can be argued that, in practice, people's preference scales tend to be restricted to those that exhibit a certain harmony. Such preference scales have been described by Black as 'single-peaked' (because of the manner of their representation on a graph).[48] 'Black . . . proved that simple or special majority voting produces a unique transitive ordering if the whole set of individual orderings are single-peaked.'[49] Moreover, it is arguable that political viewpoints are very likely to be single-peaked clusters of preferences,[50] and that therefore elections in states are very likely to be 'saved' from the Arrow theorem. It should be noted that the existence of political parties helps to order preferences in this sort of way. It could further be argued that a virtue of the two-party system is that it simplifies this whole problem of the rationale of collective choice. By presenting just two comprehensive alternatives, such a system makes social choice more coherent and comprehensible.[51]

Another approach is to abandon the assumption that there is to be only a single ballot and that voters are stuck with simply and straightforwardly expressing their preferences. Black, Arrow and their successors have, of course, discussed procedures involving more than one ballot, but they have not paid much attention to the use of strategy and skill by voters. Instead of just registering their preferences, voters could adapt their votes to influence the changing situation as the balloting proceeds. This might require voting against one's preference at some stages so as to influence the *final* result in the right direction. In this way the social preference could be obtained while avoiding some of the problems involved in simply 'reading off' (or, rather, working out) the implications of individuals' preferences. All this would involve great sophistication on the part of the voters, who would be presumed to use information and logical reasoning to devise sometimes highly complex voting strategies. This approach is set out in what has been described as 'an exquisite little book' : *Theory of Voting*, by Robin Farquharson.[52] It is an important line of analysis. However, in view of the sophistication of voters it assumes, it is more applicable to committees (and perhaps to legislatures) than to the electorates of modern states. The nature of actual voting behaviour will be discussed in Chapters 5 and 6, but it should be pointed out here that a general election in a modern state is on too large a scale, and incorporates too complex an amalgam of matters needing decision, for voting to be subtle and finely judged.[53] Voting in such elections cannot consist of more than blanket responses to the whole complex of questions posed.

Another way of challenging Arrow's theorem is to question the validity of his third condition. This is known as the 'independence of irrelevant alternatives', but what interests us here is that the question of its acceptability 'boils down to . . . questions [concerning] . . . intensities of individual preferences',[54] and whether intensities should be reflected in social decisions. It seems reasonable, if not imperative, to argue that if a set of individuals prefers alternative x, and another set of the same size prefers y, but the preferences for x are more intense than those for y, then x is more preferred than y. And this argument could even hold if the set preferring x was smaller than that preferring y. However, this is often overlooked in democratic theory.[55] And Arrow's theorem—as the third condition implies—also assumes the irrelevance of preference intensities. But this means that if preference intensities *are* taken into account, then the impossibility theorem no longer holds.[56] 'Quantities' of preference can in principle be added together in a way that orderings of preferences cannot.

It would appear, then, that not only should preference intensity be taken into account, but that, when it is, majority decision-making is seen to be possible—the Black and Arrow difficulties are overcome. Yet the introduction of preference intensity raises difficulties of its own. First of all, it must be decided whether an alternative which is 'most preferred', even if only a minority prefer it, is to be the social choice. (Despite its denial of the majority principle in one sense, this would be analogous to it in another : in both cases the idea is that the greater quantity prevails—but see the following paragraph.) But it is here that the real difficulties begin. Although there is a sense in which quantities of preference can, in principle, be added together, in practice such problems arise as to suggest that such addition is impossible.[57] The basic difficulty is one of measurement. How can a measurement of preference be devised to give the appropriate weight to intensity as well as to quantity (the number of persons holding the preference(s) in question)? How can a meaning be attached to a 'unit of preference intensity' anyway? Which is the 'winning preference' where, say, sixty people have a slight preference for alternative x and forty intensely prefer y? Difficulties of this sort are exemplified in the question posed by Dahl : is it 'possible to construct rules so that an apathetic majority only slightly preferring its alternative could not override a minority strongly preferring its alternative'?[58] Dahl concludes that his 'analysis strongly suggests, although it does not prove, that no solution to the intensity problem through constitutional or procedural rules is attainable'.[59] The question now arises of whether it is sensible to try to deal with intensity in this quasi-mathematical way. But this becomes part of the general question of the adequacy of the strictly individualist assumptions of the whole analysis in this chapter so far. This question is taken up shortly.[60]

It was said just now (before the difficulties were indicated) that the recognition of preference intensity—because it disposed of the Arrow theorem—might appear to reinstate the majority principle (in its own right, that is : we have still not solved the non-unanimity problem). However, many would argue that taking account of preference intensity is to be *contrasted with* the majority principle,[61] or else that it disposes of the special character of the majority decision-making rule. This latter argument is used by James Buchanan and Gordon Tullock in their book *The Calculus of Consent*.[62] This book is of especial interest here as it brings us back to the previous question of the 'democratic validity' of the majority principle itself. There is little point in trying to reinstate the majority principle if it is itself defective as an instrument of democracy as our previous argument apparently showed it to be. Buchanan and Tullock, however, purport to show us a way of resolving this problem. Their argument (or an important aspect of it) is, in effect, that majority decision-making can be avoided since unanimity, or an approximation to it, is after all feasible.

According to Buchanan and Tullock, then, it is only if differences in preference intensities are ignored that the majority principle has any claim to a special status. 'When all individual preferences are of assumed equal intensity, simple majority rule will insure that the summed "benefits" from action will exceed the summed "losses".'[63] But if intensities are not equal, then this 'equation' will no longer hold. And it is unanimity (or an approach to it) that Buchanan and Tullock seek to establish in the place of majority decision-making.

In essence their argument is based on a challenge to an assumption lying behind the whole discussion so far in this chapter. This is that the preferences of individuals are fixed data : that the decisions of individuals indicating what they prefer can only reflect simple, static and purely individual preferences. Buchanan and Tullock, on the other hand, bring in the simple but important idea that individuals, recognizing they have divergent and often incompatible preferences, will seek to reconcile these by a process of bargaining. They replace the conception of some preferences (or sets of preferences) triumphing over others by the notion of preferences being modified by interaction with one another. In this way unanimous decision-making is possible, and not only possible, but best (since it best furthers everyone's interest), for the bargaining process can end up with all agreeing on a course of action ('all preferences being the same').[64] It is an essential part of this idea that attention should be paid not to 'single issues, taken one at a time and separately', but to 'a series of issues'.[65] This enables bargaining —or, more specifically, 'logrolling'[66]—to take place. A series of issues, and the different initial preferences with regard to them, provide the 'raw material' out of which bargains can be constructed. Differential intensity comes in again here. Unless intensities are unequal, no vote-trading can take place.[67] But, given intensity variation, then a voter can accept 'a decision contrary to his desire in an area where his preferences are weak in exchange for a decision in his favour where his feelings are stronger'.[68] The authors recognize that this type of process is fully possible in only relatively small groups—such as representative assemblies. Nonetheless, they contend that 'implicit logrolling' can be said to take place at general elections, via the agency of parties. Parties 'make up a complex mixture of policies designed to attract support. In so doing they keep firmly in mind the fact that the single voter may be so interested in the outcome of a particular issue that he will vote for the one party that supports this issue, although he may be opposed to the party on all other issues.'[69]

Buchanan and Tullock's book is valuable in so far as it focuses upon bargaining. This is in part because it is a process that can be important, but also because it is a reminder of the crucially important general point that it is artificially narrow and misleading to be restricted to the static and purely individual idea of preferences. However, the general argument of the book cannot be accepted. One of the basic reasons for this is that it is, itself, blinkered by an unmodified and excessively individualist idea of the polity.[70] (This tends to be a characteristic of all attempts to apply an 'economic analysis' to politics—although in welfare economics itself many of the same fundamental difficulties occur. The general point here is that it is a fallacy to maintain that social reality can be quantified, except at a relatively superficial level.) It can never get to grips with the real nature of interaction between individuals, and the extent to which this is shaped by the nature and requirements of the political structures in which they find themselves.

It is not only criticisms of this very general kind which are applicable to *The Calculus of Consent*. In his book *Political Argument*[71] Brian

Barry subjects Buchanan and Tullock's work to a close and damaging scrutiny. Barry develops a number of arguments, some of which do not even challenge Buchanan and Tullock's terms of reference—that is, arguments which are designed to hold even if the extreme individualist assumptions are accepted. There will be no attempt here to paraphrase these arguments.[72] It will be sufficient to mention one or two of the most important. One is the argument that Buchanan and Tullock's ideas rest on the dubious assumption that there is some *status quo* which all the individuals accept. Another is an argument against automatically accepting the validity of a 'second best' on the same grounds that the relevant ideal is accepted. Buchanan and Tullock acknowledge that given the 'costs' (time, energy, etc.) of bargaining, complete unanimity is impracticable. Nonetheless, they argue, an approach to it—in the form of qualified majority voting—is a desirable second best. Barry seeks to show that even if the unanimity principle were acceptable (which it is not) under conditions of 'costless' bargaining, this does not mean that the qualified majority principle is to be accepted when costs are taken into account.

One of the most damaging arguments that can be brought against Buchanan and Tullock, however (and one that is developed by Barry),[73] is to point out the incredible amount of information that would be required by voters if they were to engage in the kind of bargaining envisaged. It would be quite irrational for voters to attempt to achieve this level of knowledge. Buchanan and Tullock could reply that they modify their account by recognizing that a representative, rather than a direct, system of democracy would be necessary. And they say that representatives (or, presumably, candidates organized as political parties) could organize and greatly simplify the bargaining process (the possible role of parties in bargaining has already been mentioned). However, although there is something in this argument, it really does involve too great a departure from the idea of autonomously bargaining individuals for the rest of the theory to be properly relevant. The authors themselves half acknowledge this, but leave the matter in the air : 'The result [of bargaining organized by candidates] is not precisely equivalent to that which would be expected under direct bargaining, but we do not propose to consider the differences in this work.'[74]

The analysis contained in *The Calculus of Consent* must, it seems, be rejected. Nonetheless, we are left with the important idea of the mutual interaction of individual viewpoints. This is to be contrasted with the ideas of the theories considered earlier in this chapter—which involved the measuring, and weighing against each other, of the inviolable and discrete entities that their conception of individual preferences implied. Bargaining is often an important part of the process of interaction. But there is also another and more illuminating idea to be found in democratic theory that should be considered here. This is an idea—or set of ideas—concerning the role of a process of discussion in collective decision-making. Kendall and Carey saw this sort of idea of the discussion process as contributing to a 'solution' of the intensity problem : intensities can be weighed and accommodated by means of discussion (or dialogue). And the discussion process produces 'the "sense" (*not* the will) of the people as a whole'.[75] This notion of the role of discussion they associated with the idea of decisions by 'consensus'[76] rather than decisions by majorities. The idea of consensus will be taken up again in the consideration of necessary conditions in Chapter 7. At this point it is sufficient to note that the idea, as it appears here, is similar to Lindsay's conception of a 'spirit of the common life'. And—as we saw in Chapter 3—it is in neo-Idealist democratic theory that the 'theory of discussion' is most typically developed.

Kendall and Carey related these remarks on the role of discussion to what they saw as a Madisonian model of democracy. Hence the discussion process was conceived to occur primarily where most (but not the most basic) decision-making occurred : in the representative assembly. In neo-Idealist theory, on the other hand, discussion plays an important role in the electoral process itself. This is most clearly formulated by Barker.[77] We have already seen that, in neo-Idealist theory, discussion is thought of as the very essence of democracy. And we saw that, for Barker, the electorate has a vital part to play in the discussion process. 'The electorate discusses and selects the men who are to continue political discussion in the following stage . . . as well as the programmes that are to be discussed. . . .'[78] But although the electorate as such has a vital part to play, it is only a part. The archetype for the discussion process is really the small group. In the case of the modern electorate the interchange and the give and take which the process involves is, to a significant extent, performed 'for' the electorate by the party system. (Barker sees the functions of parties as best performed by a two-party system.)

The general object of discussion—as we saw in Chapter 3—is to discover 'the spirit of the common life'. Discussion is conceived to achieve this by revealing what the different opinions and interests are, and, by the clarification, interchange and intermeshing of views that it involves, bringing them together to form some sort of collective view. One idea that seems to be involved here is that of wisdom (or 'the truth') being crystallized out of the many separate—and very imperfect, because incomplete—perceptions of it. 'Truth dwells in more than one habitation, and . . . its elements have to be collected, and not only collected but reconciled, before it can be enthroned.'[79] But, more specifically, there is of course the derivation from the Rousseauist and Idealist notions of the general or common will. (As was pointed out earlier, on

p. 99, the notion of a collective decision is in the end inseparable from the notion of the common interest.) Discussion brings together and reconciles differing interests and views; and because of the context in which it takes places, the common denominator will be found in policies which benefit all—the common good.

All this means that collective views are seen as being generated out of the many and divergent original individual views[80] rather than being equated with a particular set of preferences—held by some rather than all the individuals. And this is surely the only sensible way to conceive a relationship between collective and individual views. It is not necessary for the process to be on quite such a high plane as that portrayed in neo-Idealist theory. Bargaining and testing of strength—strength of feeling (the intensity issue again), and political strength generally—can also be fitted into this general scheme. Such 'down-to-earth' processes also involve accommodation and compromise between differing views[81] rather than starkly recording and counting them. But the essential point is that discussion be involved as well, and that the whole process be structured by the requirement that a common interest be arrived at. (It is, of course, entirely possible that views will be such —and/or society be so structured—that such a process cannot occur.)

But how does the making of decisions fit into this analysis? It will be recalled that it was by virtue of the recognition of decision-making by the people that we viewed neo-Idealist (as distinct from Idealist) political theory as democratic. The important point here is the one raised earlier (p. 108 above): there comes a point where a decision on some proposal is taken. But the questions of what proposal, and of the process that preceded its submission, are of crucial significance. On page 108 it was pointed out that there can be many differing views that relate to an issue before these are structured in relation to a specific proposal. And the point here is that neo-Idealist theory sees the discussion process as important in the pre-decision structuring of views, and in determining what proposal is (or proposals are) actually put. It should be noticed that one feature of this structuring is that it is a process not unduly affected by gradations of alternative views held by individuals ('ranking of preferences'). The interchange and testing of ideas help here in two ways. The individuals' views themselves are modified and become more integrated; and the proposals finally submitted are based on these modified views so that there is less likelihood of their provoking distinct, ranked responses. In fact, one of the aims of the discussion process is so to integrate and reduce differences of view that only one choice need finally be made on each issue. (In the case of electorates, rather than small groups, the position is more complicated : here series of choices are made at one time by the electorate. One of the functions of parties, however, is to integrate alternatives in such a way that the electorate is presented in effect with a reduced number of proposals (two in the case of a two-party system).)

When it actually comes to voting on proposals, we are apparently brought back to the difficulties we started out with. There will be a majority for one response and a minority for the other : how can it then be said that there has been a decision by 'all'? The answer to this is that the proposals submitted have already emerged from a process of integration of views, so that although one response 'wins', this still means that the views of all are reflected to an important extent in the outcome (the British 'consensus' and the similarity of party programmes, for example, has often been commented upon). In so far as there remains a difference of view which appears in the form of a majority and a minority response, the only rationale (apart from the 'moral justifications' of the majority principle) for selecting the majority as the winner is, after all, that it is more nearly equivalent to all than is the minority.[82] But it must be remembered that the integrative process which precedes the voting is supposed to prevent the submission of proposals which will divide a majority from a minority too deeply. Barker discusses the case where there is a fairly stable majority and minority. We cannot do better than to end this look at the role of discussion with Barker's own words :

Discussion is not only like war: it is also like love. It is not only a battle of ideas; it is also a marriage of minds. If a majority engages in discussion with a minority, and if that discussion is conducted in a spirit of giving and taking, the result will be that the ideas of the majority are widened to include some of the ideas of the minority which have established their truth in the give and take of debate. When this happens, the will of the majority will not be the abstract or isolated will of a mere majority, considered in itself and as standing by itself in opposition to the similar will of a mere minority. Some fusion will have taken place: some accommodation will have been attained. The majority-will, when discussion is finished and the final vote is taken, will have assumed a new quality. It will not, indeed, have become the agreed and active will of all. But it may have accommodated itself so much to other wills, and absorbed so much of the elements of truth which they contain, that it has become a will which is tolerated by all and resented by none. It has assumed a certain quality, and attained a certain value. It is in this sense that discussion produces, if not unanimity, at any rate something so near it that we may speak of common consent. It is in this way that the will of a majority can become something of the nature of the will of all.[83]

In conclusion, then, we can say that what is perhaps the central problem within strictly individualist democratic theory is insoluble. To make sense of the notion of a decision by all the people it is necessary to move away from the narrowly individualist assumptions and recognize the ways in which common views can arise which are attributable to no particular individuals as such. (Other, alleged, solutions are to be found in 'modern' democratic theory. These will be covered in Chapter 6.)

In Chapter 5 we shall move on to look at certain problems that arise from the application of democratic theory—problems arising from the relationship between theory and empirical reality.

NOTES AND REFERENCES

1 See p. 89 above for a reference to the relationship between 'collectivist' conceptions of the people and this 'minimal individualism'.

2 It should be noticed that the basic issue here is whether, and how, a collective decision as such is possible. For the sake of clarity this issue is often discussed in its simplest form—by reference to small groups. The intention is for any conclusions to be applied to large modern electorates. However, such application sometimes strains credibility a little. In what follows, references will sometimes be made to this difficulty (in particular, the role of political parties in organizing the electoral decision will be mentioned). It should also be noticed that the question of what sort (and what proportion) of decisions are made by the people is largely by-passed here (for a discussion of these issues refer to Chapter 3). Suffice it to say that most of the following discussion applies most clearly to decisions on policy, rather than merely on who should hold office. However, as has previously been pointed out, in any model of *democracy* it is policy decisions—basic ones at least—that are central (see also Chapter 6). It could be argued that the quasi-mathematical treatments of voting often assume a detailed decision-making by the people of the type postulated by RDT.

3 The assumption of the diversity of preferences tended to be counter-balanced in RDT by the influence of Rousseau: there is a strand in RDT according to which it is presumed that individuals achieve unity of view (if only a consensus on fundamentals). '[For the Radical], ideally, "the people" act as one; yet they achieve that unity by a series of individual acts of mind. . . . Presumably by discussion the ultimate atoms will be led to discover their general will and thus to unity of action'—S. H. Beer, *Modern British Politics*, p. 43.

4 See Chapter 3 for a discussion of the representative-constituents–national-interest relationship in traditional democratic theory.

5 It is, of course, a decision (or set of decisions) *to the same effect* as the individual decisions which is meant here. There is also a sense in which a 'decision is made by all' merely by virtue of all sharing in the process by which the decision is arrived at. This may be a condition that is important in its own way, but it is importantly different from a 'decision made by all' in the sense in which we are here interested.

6 Dahl, *A Preface to Democratic Theory*, pp. 124–31.

7 ibid., p. 132.

8 These points are well made by Willmoore Kendall in his *John Locke and the Doctrine of Majority-Rule*, Chapter 1 (this also contains a useful general introduction to the majority principle).

9 This can also work 'in reverse'. Some of the justifications of democracy (e.g. the Utilitarian) are of the form 'majority rule is desirable for reason x, democracy involves majority rule, therefore democracy is desirable for reason x'.

10 The argument that the majority would get their way in any case is also used to buttress the 'majority-approximates-to-the-whole' argument (see p. 102 below).

11 This argument is related to the idea (discussed below) that majority decision-making allows everyone 'a turn' in the winning group. Of course, arguments for majority rule can be challenged by disputing the account(s) of the nature and implications of majority rule that they presume. Differing analyses of what majority rule involves are dealt with later in this chapter. For general discussions of the majority principle, see, for example (besides Kendall, *John Locke and the Doctrine of Majority-Rule*): E. Berg, *Democracy and the Majority Principle*, Goteberg, Akedemiforlaget (Scandinavian University Books), 1965 (Berg bases his discussion on an examination of twentieth-century theorists, but this leads into a general analysis); H. E. Commager, *Majority Rule and Minority Rights*, New York, Oxford University Press, 1943; H. B. Mayo, *An Introduction to Democratic Theory*, Chapter 8.

12 There are two rather important points to note here. First, the idea of *counting as* 'all' a number which is near to being so is also used in democratic theory—and in common sense—to cover the occurrence of abstentions. A unanimous decision by all participants would be regarded as the decision of all the people even if a few had abstained from voting (and in cases of non-unanimity the whole people would be said to have voted, despite a few abstentions). There is, of course, a problem here: it is only if 'a few' are involved that this way of regarding things remains obviously reasonable. Similarly with majority decision-making: minorities are frequently too large to be dismissed as 'a few'. This problem is discussed later in the text. The second point is in some ways related to the first. This is that, although it is traditional democratic theory's individualist conception of the people that is involved here, there is sometimes a tendency to slip—at a point where it is inconsistent to do so—into a conception of the people as a corporate entity. The majority difficulty is 'resolved' since there is no obvious number—not even *all* the present adult population—that have to make decisions before it can be said that the corporate entity has 'decided'. But a *purely* corporate conception of the people is not compatible with the idea of a *decision* by the people (see pp. 89–90 above). See the text below for further discussion of the ambiguities and confusions arising from slipping back and forth between different conceptions of the people.

13 Locke, *Second Treatise of Government*, section 96, Laslett edition, pp. 375–6. This is a good example of the slipping between conceptions mentioned in the previous note.

14 The idea of natural law has been of great importance in political philosophy. The idea has taken different forms, but one of its bases is the notion that there is a natural moral order (divinely ordained or occurring naturally in some other way) which is, or should be, the basis of the political order. In the present context, however, it is not (or not only) the moral aspect of natural law that is being invoked (it is not only a justification, but

a demonstration of the logic, of majority rule that Locke is giving here). Part of the power of the natural law concept was that it often purported to combine the (what would now be regarded as separate) ideas of moral and scientific law. On natural law in general, see, for example, A. P. D'Entreves, *Natural Law*, London, Hutchinson, 1967; on natural law in Locke, in particular see, for example, M. Seliger, *The Liberal Politics of John Locke*, Chapter 2.

15 S. K. Padover (ed.), *Thomas Jefferson on Democracy*, p. 15.

16 'When we consider the decision of a political body, what appears desirable in the first place, is to obtain the unanimous wish of its members: what is desirable in the second place, is the will which most nearly approaches it. This leads us to be contented with the will of the simple majority; since, how far soever this may be from the really universal will, it is nearer to it than the contrary will'—'An Essay on Political Tactics', in *Works*, ed. J. Bowring, Edinburgh, Tait, 1838–48, Vol. 2, p. 306. The majority principle can also be seen to accord with the general theory of Utilitarianism: 'The majority . . . is the least fallible of masters: for since each individual is the best judge of his interests, it is the majority of individuals which will be able to estimate the interests of the greater number'—Halévy, *The Growth of Philosophical Radicalism*, p. 491. The whole paragraph is well worth reading.

17 *First Inaugural Address*, 4 March 1861.

18 Even this is doubtful. It is not necessarily the case that the majority is stronger. Even accepting that systems in which the régime is clearly one of minority rule are here excluded, it still cannot be said that majorities are never dominated by, say, well-armed and well-organized minorities.

19 It is only by virtue of the combination of the individualist conception of the people with the corporate conception of the state that difficulties about the idea of the people *acting* are avoided in individualist democratic thought.

20 cf. '. . . The closer a group approaches to an equal division, the more any rule seems to be a mere matter of convenience . . .'—Dahl, *A Preface to Democratic Theory*, p. 41.

21 Even this formulation by-passes an ambiguity. Berg states it in the following way: '. . . the "majority principle" is a generic term covering two different decisional rules. One is the "absolute majority rule", which prescribes that in case of disagreement . . . that policy alternative should be chosen which is favoured by more than half of all those members who express a preference on the matter; the other—and this is the rule defined in Dahl's theory—is the "plurality rule" (relative majority rule), which prescribes that in the case of . . . disagreement . . . that policy alternative should be chosen which is favoured by more of those members who express a preference than is any other alternative'—E. Berg, *Democracy and the Majority Principle*, p. 128; i.e. even though more people favour a certain alternative than favour any other, this number may not amount to more than half of the membership (or half of those with preferences) of the relevant group—in our case 'the people'.

22 cf. S. I. Benn and R. S. Peters, *Social Principles and the Democratic State*, London, Allen & Unwin, 1959, pp. 336–7.

23 See below, pp. 108–15, for a discussion of some further difficulties regarding the combining of preferences.

24 The multi-party case is rather different. It could be argued that the bargaining and the shifting coalitions among the various parties approximated to the 'equal-turns' ideal model of majority decision-making—with the parties taking the places of individuals (the more parties there were, the closer the approximation). However, such activities would occur in the legislature after the election, rather than being a characteristic of the election itself. They could, therefore, only be part of a 'decision by the electorate' in a very indirect sense.

25 This argument should not be confused with those asserting that a group of 'top men' (a power elite) *rather than* the electorate control the government (see next two chapters). The presumption at this point is that government is specifically controlled by electoral decisions, and we are here talking about groups of *voters* who might control government by means of these decisions—rather than groups who might control government despite, or in defiance of (or in the absence of meaningful), electoral decisions.

26 Dahl, *A Preface to Democratic Theory*, p. 28. However, see C. J. Friedrich for an opposite viewpoint—summarized in E. Berg, *Democracy and the Majority Principle*, pp. 59–60 (but see also Berg's criticism of Friedrich's position, pp. 63–4).

27 Quoted in Birch, *Representation*, p. 85.

28 There could also, of course, be abstentions. Throughout this discussion it has, for the sake of simplification, been assumed that all the electors actually vote. This ignoring of abstentions does not significantly alter any of the conclusions (the main effect of recognizing the existence of abstention would be to make the majority principle even more difficult to uphold).

29 Most discussions of this subject have focused particularly on groups smaller than a modern electorate (legislatures, committees, etc.). Indeed, the relevant logical points can be exemplified most conveniently with a group of only three individuals. However, in the literature, these are often explicitly said to be applicable to larger groups such as electorates (although it is arguable that there are also relevant differences between small groups and electorates). It should also be noticed that the following discussion relates specifically to voting upon policy alternatives, etc., and not the election of representatives as such (although in many cases it is applicable to both).

30 Jean Charles de Borda (1733–99) pointed out that attention to single (first) preferences only could produce the 'wrong' result (see D. Black *The Theory of Committees and Elections*, Cambridge, Cambridge University Press, 1958, p. 157). He was the first to argue that 'a rational voting scheme requires knowledge of all preferences among the candidates and not only the first choice'—K. J. Arrow, 'Values and Collective Decision Making', in P. Laslett and W. G. Runciman (eds.), *Philosophy, Politics and Society* (Third Series), p. 227.

31 op cit. This book contains a general history of the 'logical theory' of social choice.

32 W. H. Riker, 'Voting and the Summation of Preferences: An Interpretive Bibliographical Review of Selected Developments During the Last Decade',

in *American Political Science Review*, Vol. 55 (1961), p. 900. This article is one of the best introductions to this whole area of analysis.

33 New York, John Wiley, 2nd edition, 1963 (1st edition, 1951). A concise outline by Arrow of some important aspects of his argument can be found in K. J. Arrow, 'Values and Collective Decision-Making'.

34 W. H. Riker, 'Voting and the Summation of Preferences . . .', p. 901.

35 See, for example, ibid., p. 909. If individual's preferences are not transitive, then 'the chance of a transitive social ordering declines still further' (ibid.). However, in one way this would matter less: the 'arbitrariness' of the social ordering would be a 'true reflection' of individuals' preferences in that their preference orderings would be arbitrary in the same sense.

36 ibid., p. 901.

37 ibid.

38 K. J. Arrow, 'Values and Collective Decision-Making', p. 228.

39 See the works by Arrow already cited; a convenient summary is to be found in the article by Riker already quoted. This article also contains a review of some of the subsequent discussions of Arrow's theorem. Besides being relevant to democratic theory, the theorem is of great importance for economics—indeed, it seemed to destroy the foundations of welfare economics—and it is in this field that most of the relevant literature is to be found.

40 W. G. Runciman, *Social Science and Political Theory*, Cambridge, Cambridge University Press, 2nd edition, 1969, p. 133. See also R. P. Wolff, *In Defense of Anarchism*, New York, Harper & Row, 1970, pp. 58–63.

41 This is Pattanaik's description of an argument by Graaf (P. K. Pattanaik, *Voting and Collective Choice*, Cambridge, Cambridge University Press, 1971, p. 46. The article referred to is J. de V. Graaf, 'On Making a Recommendation in a Democracy', in *Economic Journal*, Vol. 72 (1962), pp. 293–8.)

42 See Pattanaik, *Voting and Collective Choice*, p. 46.

43 ibid., p. 171.

44 N. M. L. Nathan, 'On the Justification of Democracy', in *The Monist*, Vol. 55 (January 1971), p. 95. For further defence of democracy against the 'Theory of Social choice', see E. Mates, 'Paradox Lost—Majority Rule Regained', in *Ethics*, Vol. 84, No. 1 (October 1973), pp. 48–50.

45 cf. ibid., p. 102. This constitutes a modification of the straightforward majority-decision principle. Nevertheless, it still leaves the problem that there are people who have in some sense voted against the 'social choice'.

46 Black, *The Theory of Committees and Elections*, pp. 59–66 and 156–9. See also, Arrow, *Social Choice and Individual Values*, pp. 27 and 94.

47 See Black, *The Theory of Committees and Elections*, pp. 182–3—where also comparisons are made with the 'Concorcet criterion' (see also pp. 57–66).

48 ibid., pp. 4–10.

49 Riker, 'Voting and the Summation of Preferences . . .', art. cit., p. 906.

50 Arrow, *Social Choice and Individual Values*, p. 76; Nathan, 'On the Justification of Democracy', p. 102. Riker ('Voting and the Summation of Preferences . . .', p. 907) epitomizes the existence of single-peaked preference curves among all members of society as a state of affairs in which 'some sort of inner harmony exists among the persons in the society'. There are connections

here with the notion of consensus, and with the idea of it being a necessary condition for the existence of democracy (see Chapter 7).

51 cf. the conclusion drawn by R. G. Niemi. He notes that for Black's 'single-peakedness argument' to work, the preference ordering of every individual must be singlepeaked, and that 'empirically this is most unlikely to happen'. Niemi concludes that this highlights 'the role of all those factors which contribute to the widespread adoption of a common standard of judgement [such a standard is implied by single-peakedness]. Systems of political parties are perhaps the most commonly cited factor. The two-party system is especially useful for this purpose, not only because the number of alternatives is sometimes limited to two (making the paradox impossible), but because judgements among several alternatives, such as presidential candidates within one party, are often structured along a dimension on which the parties are arrayed'—'Majority Decision-Making with Partial Unidimensionality', in *American Political Science Review*, Vol. 63, No. 2 (June 1969), pp. 488 and 494. The role of political parties will be discussed in the next chapter.

52 Oxford, Basil Blackwell, 1969. Martin Shubik says in the preface that 'Farquharson is concerned with the same problems dealt with by Kenneth Arrow in *Social Choice and Individual Values*, but Arrow limits his analysis of voting and preferences to nonstrategic, independent, direct optimizing behaviour by individuals' (p. ix).

53 There may be some complex behaviour by those who seek to organize and to attract blocks of voters. An argument of this kind is referred to below. Just as there is a literature of quasi-mathematical analyses of individual voting (which has just been discussed), there is also a literature of quasi-mathematical analyses of the behaviour of political parties in seeking to obtain votes. The best-known, and most influential, of the works in this field is *An Economic Theory of Democracy* by Anthony Downs (New York, Harper & Row, 1957); for a critical review of some of this work, including Downs's book, see B. M. Barry, *Sociologists, Economists and Democracy* (London, Collier-Macmillan, 1970). Work in this field is not directly relevant for us here since it is not concerned with the very concept or possibility of a social decision. It can also be argued that, interesting as it is, it has but a limited contribution to make to an understanding of the processes of democracy. For an estimation of its contribution, see ibid.).

54 Pattanaik, *Voting and Collective Choice*, p. 147.

55 Dahl points out that crucial problems are by-passed 'by making "most preferred" equivalent to "preferred by most" . . .'—*Preface to Democratic Theory*, p. 90.

56 Nathan, 'On the Justification of Democracy', art. cit., pp. 106–7.

57 cf. Dahl, *Preface to Democratic Theory*, pp. 90–102 and 118–23. Dahl also relates the question of intensities to the question of the stability of democracies.

58 ibid., p. 92.

59 ibid., p. 119. Pattanaik similarly concludes that there is no 'satisfactory solution to the problem of introducing preference intensities into the social decision process' by the use of formal models (*Voting and Collective Choice*, p. 149.)

60 Willmoore Kendall and an associate have dealt with the intensity problem from broadly within the terms in which it is posed by Dahl (W. Kendall and G. W. Carey, 'The "Intensity" Problem and Democratic Theory', in *American Political Science Review*, Vol. 62 (1968), pp. 5–24). However, they move towards conclusions similar to those suggested by 'neo-Idealist' democratic theory, and so their ideas are more properly referred to below when this latter type of theory's contribution is indicated.

61 This is argued, for example, in the article cited in the previous footnote.

62 Subtitled 'Logical Foundations of Constitutional Democracy', Ann Arbor, University of Michigan Press, 1962 (Ann Arbor Paperback, 1965); see pp. 126–8.

63 ibid., p. 126.

64 It is, of course, at best a drastic oversimplification to talk of preferences here at all. As we shall see below, the essential point is that the interaction between individuals that can occur in collective decision-making involves a process in which views are generated: the 'raw' preferences of an individual are but one of the elements out of which his view is generated.

65 *The Calculus of Consent*, p. 131.

66 An American expression for the process of vote-trading to be found in Congress: x will agree to vote for a measure favoured by y (typically, because it benefits his constituents), if y will vote for a measure favoured by x.

67 *The Calculus of Consent*, pp. 125 and 128.

68 ibid., p. 145.

69 ibid., pp. 134–5.

70 An associated feature is the assumption that all relevant behaviour is characterized by narrow and unmitigated self-interest.

71 London, Routledge & Kegan Paul, 1965.

72 They can be found in Chapters 14 and 15, and Notes R, S and T of *Political Argument*.

73 ibid., pp. 268ff.

74 *The Calculus of Consent*, p. 222.

75 Kendall and Carey, 'The "Intensity" Problem and Democratic Theory', p. 21.

76 ibid., p. 22.

77 A useful summary of Barker's ideas can be found in Berg, *Democracy and the Majority Principle*, pp. 48–57.

78 ibid., p. 49.

79 Barker, *Reflections on Government*, p. 70.

80 This is an oversimplification: it will be remembered (as we note in a moment) that in this tradition of thought the primary individual views themselves owe a great deal to previous discussions—and, more generally, to the society and polity in which the individuals find themselves.

81 'Views' here covers both 'opinions' and 'interests'.

82 There is a sense in which the justification for majority decision-making here is that *a* rule (which is not clearly unreasonable) is needed, rather than that the difference—which may be relatively very small—between the sizes of the majority and minority is deemed important (cf. Morris Cohen's view that coming to a decision is often more important than waiting for

adequate reasons on which to base a right decision—quoted in Kendall, *John Locke and the Doctrine of Majority Rule*, p. 29). After all, due to quirks in electoral systems, the *minority* sometimes 'wins'—1951 in Britain, for example. (And in any case, even where the winning party has more votes than the other main party, it does not necessarily have a majority of all those voting, let alone of the whole electorate. This is usually the case in Britain, for example.) Although there is adverse comment in such cases, the result is nonetheless accepted. (One of the factors here is that another important function of the electoral system is not necessarily impaired: the reflection of movements of opinion in the *replacing* of one party in power by another.) All this is not to deny that there will, in reality, be occasions when sufficient integration of views is lacking (perhaps because it would be impossible to attain). Depending on the nature of the particular case, there may be justification for still using the majority principle (most people would use some form of Utilitarian justification), but this is not the same as saying that in such a case a decision is made by all. A further point of importance is that although majority decision-making itself is not equivalent to the expression of the will of all, it may well be that an institutional system that provides majority decision-making is a necessary condition for that integration of views that does go to make up the will of all.

83 ibid., p. 67.

CHAPTER 5

Problems in Applying Democratic Theory

Chapter 4 was concerned with some problems 'inside' democratic theory; in this chapter we shall be concerned with some problems that arise even if these internal ones can be solved—difficulties that arise from the application of democratic theory to the real world of politics. It is, then, the confrontation between theory and empirical reality that will be at issue : the confrontation between democratic theory's model of a political system and the actual nature of the Western political systems which are called democracies.

Because there are different democratic *theories* rather than any single *theory*, there is not only a single confrontation of this kind. It will, however, be a common RDT model that is singled out for initial consideration. The outline of the difficulties encountered by RDT will be followed in Chapter 6 by a consideration of other democratic theories[1] in the light of these difficulties (in fact, it was in part as a response to the difficulties encountered by RDT that 'modern democratic theory' arose). The nature of the difficulties themselves will also be reassessed.

RDT is of primary importance in the sense that it is the fundamental or archetypal democratic theory of the Western democracies. It is the theory against which other democratic theories are compared or offered as alternatives, and it is the type of theory initially referred to when the empirical adequacy of democratic theory is called into question.

Part of the reason for this primacy of RDT is that it is the 'most democratic' of democratic theories. That is to say, it ascribes the largest and most positive role to the people. It is also, in a real sense, the original Western democratic theory. It was the influence of Rousseau and the thought of such people as Paine, Bentham, James Mill and Jefferson that produced the first specifically democratic theory of the Western world. LDT developed more uncertainly and took time to become specifically democratic. It is only with J. S. Mill—and then somewhat hesitantly—that the type of theory, with its circumscribed role for the people, associated with Locke's *Second Treatise* and with

The Federalist, really became acknowledged as democratic.[2] For both these reasons—its 'democraticness' and its historical priority—RDT has assumed a central and fundamental role in the democratic political culture of the West.[3] To the extent that the Western democracies think of themselves as democratic, they view themselves in terms of the model provided by RDT. The editors of *Democracy Today*, for example, see the 'focal problem' of the book as stemming from 'an apparent sense of discrepancy between ideal and practice'. But the ideal, which is the RDT ('classical') model, still binds our thinking : '. . . Louis Hartz [one of the contributors to the book] finds us bound by a classical "image" of democracy . . . an ideal derived from revolutionary-democratic thinkers like Locke and Rousseau, or the Jeffersonian dream.'[4] Schumpeter is another who makes a similar point : although, he says, the 'classical' theory of democracy has been 'blown to pieces', it has nonetheless 'survived to this day and continue[s] to hold its place in the hearts of the people and in the official language of governments'.[5] Finer asserts that 'it is still very commonly held that the constitution expresses a sort of Tom Painite or Rousseauean dependency on the "will of the people" '.[6] Finally, we might note an article by L. Tivey in which he argues that what is in effect the RDT model 'represents the received or standard theory of how democracy works in Britain' (and he goes on to distinguish degrees of belief in this theory in different circles).[7]

It is certainly arguable, then, that RDT has a predominant role in the Western democracies. But this predominance does not just mean that these political systems are *pictured* in this way : they are also actually patterned on the RDT model to a significant extent. Of course, this does not necessarily mean that the political systems actually accord with the model—indeed, the present chapter is concerned with the possible extent of *non*-accordance with the RDT model. It does, however, mean that institutions and patterns of behaviour are, to a significant extent, moulded by the ideas of RDT.[8] RDT shapes political reality as well as images of that reality (there is also often a reciprocal influence between political reality and the images of it).[9] The question is whether, despite this shaping, political reality accords with the RDT model. A model can, after all, be said to be shaping reality without the intended shape being achieved. An unsuccessful traffic-control system is an example.

The problems outlined in this chapter, then, arise from the discrepancy between the RDT model and political reality. Such a discrepancy is widely recognized, and when it is specifically outlined or pointed out, this is often regarded as an attack on RDT. But there are some complications here, and such attacks can be seen as taking different forms. Quite often—especially when studies of voting behaviour are being discussed—the attack takes the form of showing that the type of political system portrayed by the RDT model is undesirable. This is done, in effect, by reasserting some traditional criticisms of democracy concerning the unfitness of the mass of the people for political power. The other form of the attack asserts that the discrepancy is such that the type of political system depicted by the RDT model does not exist. The relationship between these two kinds of attack is somewhat complicated. However, it is mainly in the context of considerations of the voting behaviour studies that the first sort of attack has occurred, and further analysis of this relationship will be left until our look at the implications of these studies.

What has given rise to these attacks? In part it has been developments within the Western democracies and in part developments in the study of those democracies—although there is no very clear-cut distinction here since, to some extent, changes in the democracies have been reflected in (or have been exaggerated by) developments in the study of them. Roughly speaking, developments in the first category—changes in the actual systems—have included the growth of political parties and the demise of 'individual representation';[10] the growth of pressure groups and the threat to the will of the electorate; and the growth in the scale, scope and complexity of governmental activity—often viewed as part of a general crushing of the individual by the ever-growing state. Of what can be regarded as developments in the second category—those occurring in the study of democracies—the main relevant ones have been the increasing concern with the nature and role of elites, and the studies of voting behaviour that have yielded a picture of the electorate as ignorant and apathetic.

Let us now take a look at these developments and the associated attacks on RDT (initially at those attacks concerned with showing the non-existence of what is portrayed by the RDT model). First, then, there is the growth of political parties. This was often held to have involved the extinction (or attenuation) of democracy.[11] But this view is not so common now as it was in the nineteenth, and the earlier years of the present, century: indeed, a view of the functions of political parties has been virtually grafted on to RDT. However, doubts about the compatibility of parties with democracy are still often reflected in aspects of arguments used against two-party systems and in support of multi-party systems and proportional representation.

There were two, interrelated, bases for the hostile view of parties.[12] First, there was the idea of parties as subverting the pursuit of the general interest. Parties originally tended to be viewed as factions (with partial or particular interests), and doubts about their role sprang from a concern with the effects of faction as outlined by Madison in the famous Tenth Paper of *The Federalist*. It was Rousseau who had most explicitly linked the pursuit of the general interest with the notion of the popular will in his conception of the general will. However, there are in RDT reflections of, or analogues to, this view (the basis of Bentham's idea of 'sinister interests', for example), so that factions were viewed as also subverting the popular will. In time, however, this view tended to be supplanted by Burke's conception of a political party : 'a body of men united, for promoting by their joint endeavours the national interest, upon some particular principle in which they are all agreed'.[13] Despite their other possible faults, parties became accepted as at least being concerned with a view of the general interest.[14] In more recent times, the concern with 'faction' has become part of a concern with pressure groups rather than with parties (see below).

The second main way in which political parties could be seen as challenging the validity of the RDT model consisted in a perception of them as subverting the individualist character of the political system. As we have seen, in the model the political system is portrayed primarily as a collection of individuals, with little attention being given to the importance of corporate entities, or to social forces and the autonomy of political culture and its role. In the model, then, collective decisions consist simply of some sort of summation of autonomous individual decisions—the notion of a decision of the people only having meaning as the separate decisions of the individual persons somehow being added together (the problems arising here were discussed in Chapter 4). But this decision of the people has full authority because it *is* the embodiment of the authentic decisions of all the individuals.

The radical would make government the instrument of 'the will of the people', a unified and authoritative force in which he found the only sovereign of the polity and for which the majority spoke. Toward any lesser grouping, toward those influences that divide the community and create partial goals, he was supremely hostile: there should be only individual 'atoms' . . . and the state. Lesser groupings were the 'special interests' or, in Bentham's phrase, the 'sinister interests' against which 'the people' and their champions fought.[15]

In the model, representation—as a means of coping with the impracticability of assembling all the people for the continuous making and aggregating of their decisions—is seen as a matter of numbers of individuals having a particular individual to act on their behalf. Each such person (representative) has to transmit the opinions and decisions of the individuals who elected him. To do this he must be under the control of no one but his electors. In the legislative assembly, therefore, each representative is autonomous in relation to the executive and to other representatives. The object is to reproduce as faithfully as possible the views of all the individual electors, and for the representatives to make the decisions their electors would have made had they been present.[16] The essence, then, of this view of representation, is in important respects, of autonomous individuals acting in the place of other autonomous individuals. The absence of this means the absence of decisions by the people, i.e. the absence of democracy.

Political parties can be seen as subverting this individualist system in three ways. — extra parliamentary parties -

First, mass political parties can be conceived of as destroying or as interfering with the individualist character of the electorate. Instead of existing as separate and autonomous individuals, electors become, as is were, merged together into parties. Individual opinions are submerged by but a few party programmes, and electoral behaviour becomes party—not individual—behaviour. Even electors who are not actually members of a party usually show by their voting behaviour that they are in a real sense tied to a party (see below).

Secondly, political parties can be viewed as putting constraints upon individuals' voting behaviour, thereby replacing what could properly be regarded as the making of individual decisions by acquiescence to a whole set of decision made elsewhere—the party programme. Moreover, even such choices as party programmes provide have a restricted range since voting options are effectively limited to the number of effective parties. This means that very often individuals cannot make even the oversimplified 'decisions' that they might wish to make, thereby again limiting their individual autonomy. And this applies even to those who are not tied to a party. In short, what both these arguments allegedly show is that the existence of parties means that authentic individual decisions are replaced by artificially restricted choices of options.

Thirdly, political parties have been fairly widely regarded as destroying the individual autonomy of representatives. Modern party systems have often involved what has been seen as the replacement of an absence of constraints upon representatives by a necessity for them to accord with their party. The U.S.A. is something of an exception here. Party cohesion in Congress is so weak that the autonomy of congressmen and senators is restricted but little by the parties—although it is often argued that they are too much influenced by pressure groups (pressure groups as a threat to democracy are discussed below).

In these ways, then, modern political parties have been viewed as destroying the individualist—and hence democratic—character of the Western 'democracies'. Even where this view is not fully accepted—even where political parties as such are accepted as constituents of democracy—elements of it are frequently echoed in arguments against two-party systems. In such arguments, multi-party systems are seen as more democratic because they allow a greater variety of voting and legislative behaviour, thereby allowing a greater expression and representation of views. In other words, a multi-party system is seen as more democratic than a two-party system because it more nearly approximates to a non-party system.

Despite the occasional or modified appearance of this view of political parties as undemocratic, it has, in fact, been largely replaced by an understanding of them as properly democratic. A conception of parties and their role has, indeed, almost been incorporated into RDT—grafted on, as it were. According to this conception, the party takes the place, in a sense, of the representative. That is to say, the party is seen as the vehicle which transmits or promulgates the electors' views in the legislature, and which is removable by them should it cease to advance their views—whether because of the perverseness of the party or a change of mind by the electors. The individual representative is thus not required for this function, and hence the prevention of his performance of it by the destruction of his autonomy no longer matters. The individualist nature of the electorate is maintained by emphasizing the element of individual rational choice that can be involved in belonging to or voting for a party.[17] The idea that the range of voting options is limited is either disregarded or is countered by emphasizing the effectiveness of the choice rather than its range—parties being regarded as a more effective means of presenting their electors' views in the legislature than are individual representatives. A party gives to a view the weight of numbers. But, more importantly, it provides the organization not only to achieve the coherent and effective presentation of this view, but also—because of this—the possibility of at least its partial implementation. This idea is carried further in the case of a two-party system, where the winning party is seen as a highly effective mechanism for directly translating its voters' views into governmental actions. The two-party system is viewed as a particularly effective electoral choice system for this reason. From this point of view, the two-party system is the most, rather than the least, democratic of party systems.[18] This idea of the democratic character of parties became part of the doctrine of the mandate : the doctrine—particularly espoused by the left—that a (party) government should, and should only, pursue such policies as is was elected to carry out.[19] This view rests on the notion that at elections the voters decide on—and authorize—a policy programme put forward by a party.

Mass political parties—those with a large membership from amongst the mass of the electorate—came also to be viewed as providing a valuable additional dimension for popular participation. Left-wing parties particularly were seen in this way by theorists of the left.[20] Mass parties were, then, viewed as mobilizing the electorate and involving it in policy-making; and as acting as important 'transmission belts' between the people and the government. Political parties conceived of in this way are vital elements in the process by which the popular will is generated, manifested and made effective. Far from subverting democracy, parties are a crucial constituent of it.

The idea that parties are anti-democratic has therefore largely been replaced by conceptions of their democratic functions, and parties are now regarded as a vital and integral part of the democratic process (besides the role they play in other models of democracy—see Chapter 6).

Worries about parties and their role were, however, superseded by doubts about another typical feature of the political process in the Western democracies—pressure groups.

Pressure groups[21] are organized groups that seek to influence public policy—primarily by influencing governments—but which, unlike parties, do not seek to become (or become part of) a government. Typical examples of pressure groups are the Confederation of British Industries (C.B.I.), the Transport and General Workers' Union (T. & G.W.U.), the Trades Union Congress (T.U.C.), the British Medical Association (B.M.A.), the R.S.P.C.A., the Campaign for Nuclear Disarmament (C.N.D.) and Shelter. These are British examples, but similar groups abound in other Western democracies. The absence of the objective of taking over government has, as its corollary, the restriction of the primary aims of pressure groups to the inducing of fairly particular governmental activity, rather than the implementation of wide-ranging policies (although some pressure groups—such as the T.U.C.—have general views as well as particular concerns). This difference between the particular and limited aims of pressure groups and the wide-ranging and general aims of parties is extremely significant in assessing the place of pressure groups in democracy (see Chapter 6).

Pressure groups have always been an important element in the political process of the Western democracies, but a concern about their role has had a shorter history. This concern has been manifest since the turn of the century in the U.S.A., where there is a more thorough acceptance of a relatively unadulterated RDT than there is in Britain. In Britain, also, the structure of politics is different : the strong party system to some extent modifies and disguises the role of pressure groups by providing a counteracting influence on political behaviour. Moreover, not only is RDT less pervasive in the way previously indicated, but there is also a strong element in British political culture legitimizing the idea of group representation. This, as S. H. Beer points out, is very much alive in the modern collectivist era.[22] However, RDT does still have *an* important role, and concern about pressure groups in Britain accompanied the full recognition of their role. This recognition really began in the 1950s with the 'discovery' of pressure groups in Britain by British political scientists[23] (who also began demonstrating that pressure groups did have democratic functions as well; see Chapter 6).

The relative newness of the concern about pressure groups is due in part to the relative recency of the interest which political studies have taken in the 'extra-institutional' aspects of the political system. But this, in itself, was partly the result of changes in the importance, nature and functioning of pressure groups. While pressure groups have always been significant, it has only been with the growth in the complexity of the economy—and with governments' involvement in it—that interest groups have grown to a position of such importance. Interest groups are those groups whose object is to perform services for their members and to promote their interests (e.g. the C.B.I. and T. & G.W.U.). They are frequently contrasted with 'cause' or 'promotional' groups—groups that promote some cause and/or the interests of some grouping other than that formed by their members (e.g. C.N.D. or the Howard League for Penal Reform).[24] And it is, on the whole, interest rather than cause groups that have the most influence—although a new type of 'participatory' pressure group, such as Shelter and the community action groups, is nowadays becoming increasingly important (for a discussion of 'community groups', see Chapter 9). Moreover, it is, typically, interest groups which pose the problems for RDT mentioned below. Cause groups do not raise all—although they do raise some—of the issues concerning the relationship between 'particular' wills and the 'will of the people'.

It has already been suggested that pressure groups could be said to have 'inherited' from political parties the odium of the mischiefs of faction. The basic idea in this view of pressure groups as subverting democracy[25] is that of the prosecution of the people's policy being interfered with or replaced by the pursuit of the particular interests promoted by pressure groups (as we have just indicated, cause groups escape some of this censure).

This notion that the activities of pressure groups thwart the proper pursuit of policy has two forms, although, under the influence of Rousseau, they can be united for radical democrats into one complex idea. The first form consists of the perception of the general interest as distinct from, and as essentially incompatible with, particular or partial interests.[25a] Wage claims, for example, often conflict with what is for the general good of the economy. It is true that, on this view, the general interest is also that which is in everyone's *real* or long-term interest (even those who seek higher wages would benefit more in the longer term from a sound economy). Therefore, there is a sense in which the alleged particular interests are spurious : that which is thought to be in the particular interest of an individual or group is not really so. However, that which is in the general interest is not always easy to perceive, while particular interests usually are—besides which, they encompass that which is more immediately beneficial. The general interest is frequently obscure,[26] particular interests are frequently very clear. Moreover, the relevant particular interests here are group interests. Membership in a group of like-minded people will reinforce and encourage the individual's pursuit of these particular interests. Furthermore, involvement with a group and its interests means that groups will appear as important to their members. Groups will appear as the salient features of the social environment. 'Society', or the overall community, will, on the other hand, appear as shadowy, unreal and possibly unimportant—not really an entity with a discernible interest. Groups, then, can be seen as solidifying, accentuating and, to some extent, legitimizing particular interests.

In its second form, the idea of interference with the prosecution of the people's policy focuses on the conception of the will of the people and of its incompatibility with particular group 'wills'. If the group wills are effective, it is at the expense of the implementation of the will of the people. The argument here is that the government is elected to carry out the will of the people (as manifested at the election which produced the government) and that attempts by pressure groups to influence the government are nothing less than attempts to divert it from implementing the will of the people. If, for example, a government elected to introduce a prices and incomes policy were thwarted by the non-co-operation of the unions and/or employers' organizations, then this would be said to be a case of particular interests frustrating the will of the people.

Rousseau united these two forms of the basic idea in the conception of the general will—and that by which it is subverted. This conception refers to the real will of the people—which is for the general interest. Pursuit of particular interests by groups thus frustrates the general interest and the popular will at one and the same time.

Group activity is also incompatible with the individualist nature of the RDT model.[27] Reliance on groups by the individual for his dealings with the government renders less necessary, and therefore less likely, the making of his own individual political decisions. He will tend merely to take his opinions from, and leave activity to, the group. This is part of what is involved in the individual's losing sight of the general interest. It also means the dilution or the elimination of the popular will, since in the RDT model this consists of the combination of the political decisions of individuals. Rousseau himself said : 'It is therefore essential, if the general will is to be able to express itself, that there should be no partial society within the State, and that each citizen should think only his own thoughts. . . .'[28] According to this view, then, pressure groups not only frustrate the implementation of the popular will, they also interfere with its formation.

In so far, then, as pressure groups are effective in influencing political decisions—and according to many analyses they are very influential—the democracy of RDT is threatened or extinguished. In Chapter 6, however, we shall have a look at an alternative type of democratic theory which sees group activity not as a threat to, but as the very essence of, democracy.

The third of the developments mentioned earlier as sometimes associated with the demise of democracy was the growth in the scope, scale and complexity of governmental activity. Basically, the argument is that the sheer quantity and difficulty of decision-making that occurs and is required in the modern state makes it impossible for a mass of necessarily poorly informed people to engage in the relevant detailed and/or complicated decision-making. The development of science and technology; the complexity of modern economies; the involvement of governments in attempts to regulate them; the modern responsibility of the state for social welfare—these are some of the factors that have given rise to the complexity of the structure and process of modern government. Partridge has expressed a similar point well :

The states with which we must concern ourselves are characterized by their great geographical extent, the size of their populations and other qualities which are at first sight just as unpromising to the idea of government by consent [and even more so to the more positive ideas of RDT]. Their complexity includes the enormous variety of organizations, groups, activities, aspirations and interests that divide their populations. And there is the speed with which conditions within these states develop and change, the rapidity with which problems needing the attention of governments emerge and the need for incessant activity and continuous decision to cope with them.[29]

According to such views, not only are the people incapable of playing an adequate role in political decision-making, but it is also often—argued—this, plus the overpowering scale and remoteness of modern government, has lead to a feeling of helplessness and alienation on the part of individuals. And because this turns the individual away from political participation and thereby further reduces it, the amount, and desire for, involvement by the people in political decision-making is further diminished.

This argument about the impossibility of popular rule in the modern state sometimes appears also in a slightly different form. The answer of RDT, after all, to the impossibility of direct popular rule has been the system of representation and government by—or the control of the government by—the representative assembly (see Chapter 2). But those who point to the scale and complexity of government also argue that this makes government by assembly—or the adequate control of the executive by the assembly—impracticable. Hence, even indirect government by the people is not possible. It might be answered that, in a two-party system at least, the assembly is anyway by-passed since the government is under the direct control of the electorate.[30] But this apparently brings us back to the points about the impotence of the electorate in the modern state.

These arguments concerning the reasons why the electorate must be inadequate are obviously tied in with the arguments derived from the voting behaviour studies demonstrating that the electorate actually is inadequate (see below). They also become part of the elitist attack on democratic theory—political elites being seen as the inevitable and/or desirable response to the incapacity of the masses to cope with ruling complex modern societies. It is to this elitist attack that we now turn.

The RDT model has, then, also been challenged by the increased concern of political science with the nature and role of elites.[31] During the twentieth century, students of politics have become ever more aware of what they see as the widespread or universal existence of elites and the crucial role they play in political systems—including the 'democracies'. This has, of course, given rise to ideas about their desirability or otherwise.[32] Anti-democrats were in favour of elites, and democrats were opposed to them (although now—with the advent of modern democratic theory—many democrats take a favourable view of elites). Although not our direct concern, this question of the value of elites is involved in the central issue arising here : the compatibility of political elites with the existence of democracy. Democrats who are against elites see them as subverting or negating democracy, while those in favour of them see elites as compatible with—indeed as a vital element in—democracy. The favourable view, however, involves a different form of democratic theory ('elitist democratic theory')—which will be discussed in Chapter 6. Here it will simply be pointed out that democracy of the kind portrayed by RDT is incompatible with elites having an important political role : the democracy of the RDT model does not exist if political elites do.

'Elite' is a term difficult to define satisfactorily since it has been given many overlapping—but also, to some extent, conflicting—uses. And this reflects the difficulties and ambiguities inherent in the concept and some of the theories with which it has been associated. Nevertheless, a rough working definition may be given : the term 'elite' is usually used to mean a minority group distinguished from the mass of the people by some factor or factors that put it in a more advantageous position than the mass with regard to certain important aspects of social life.[33] The kinds of elites with which we are here concerned are often referred to as political power elites (though sometimes more precise meanings make these terms not quite synonymous). Such elites have as one of their distinguishing features the possession of, especial access to, or especial ability to gain, political power.[34] In short, a political elite is an elite that holds, or is especially likely to hold, political power—perhaps because it *is* an elite. Some elite theorists see power as held by one elite; others see circulating or competing elites. But, even in the latter case, political power is always in the hands of some elite or elites. The question of what is here meant by 'political power' is rather important. It should be noted that the meaning may vary from complete political power to power simply in the sense of having the constitutional (and constitutionally limited) authority to issue commands that even the government in the RDT model has. In the RDT model, however, the use of this authority is specifically governed by the policy decisions expressed in elections, whereas elites—even those with power only in the weak sense—are not closely regulated in this way. Nonetheless, these elites have considerably less than complete power since they are removable. In theories such as these, there is a plurality of elites and the elite in the position of power at any one time can, in certain circumstances, lose this position to another elite. This, indeed, becomes an important part of 'elitist democratic theory' (see Chapter 6).

The elitist tradition of political thought has, of course, a long history.[35] In a sense, Plato was an elitist. But modern 'organizational elitism' has arisen in the last 150 years or so,[36] achieving its most notorious expression in more recent times in the works of the 'classic' elitists, Mosca and Pareto, and of Mosca's disciple, Michels, with his famous 'iron law of oligarchy'. As already indicated, there tended at first to be concern in many circles over the alleged existence of political elites. But their existence has become less lamented as it has come to be more widely recognized. Today, many would consider the existence of political elites as axiomatic[37]—as an inevitable phenomenon of modern political life. Those democrats who now welcome instead of deploring this have, in effect, evolved what they see as an elitist democratic theory in which elites are seen 'as the bulwarks of democracy, protecting it from the dangers of totalitarianism'.[38] The nature of this kind of theory, and the extent to which it actually is a *democratic* theory, are matters which will be taken up in Chapter 6. But, for many, elitist theories clearly imply the non-existence of democracy, quite simply because political power—disproportionate if not complete—is held not by the people but by elites.[39] As Parry says, 'elites which have exceptional access to "key positions" in the society, or which appear to wield control over crucial policies disproportionate to their numbers, can understandably seem to be living contradictions of the notion of "government by the people" '.[40] In other words, the existence of political elites is incompatible with the existence of democracy of the kind depicted by the RDT model. Whether this means that elites are incompatible with democracy of other kinds—and in what way there can be other kinds of democracy—are the issues to be discussed in Chapter 6.

The elitist challenges to democratic theory obviously tie in with those derived from the studies of voting behaviour. The idea that there are and/or ought to be political elites is a concomitant of the idea that the mass of the electorate is too ignorant and apathetic to be capable of ruling, or of ruling properly.

Before turning to the attacks stemming from the voting studies, it is necessary to return to the issue of the relationship between the two broad kinds of attack on RDT indicated on page 129. It is in these attacks that the issue particularly arises since so many of them have, misleadingly, focused only on the question of the desirability of democracy. Other types of attack have, as we have seen, more often been explicitly concerned with the question of the existence of democracy. There has, in fact, been considerable confusion in attacks derived from voting behaviour studies owing to a failure to recognize the complications here.

The main complication is that, properly speaking, the argument that democracy is undesirable—the one in fact usually discussed in considerations of voting behaviour—simply does not arise *because of* the non-existence argument. The point is that the very features of voting behaviour which are used to show the undesirability of democracy, demonstrate, when more carefully considered, its non-existence. A similar point would be involved if it were arranged that all plants would disappear—victims of disease, perhaps—and hence that botanical gardens would become undesirable since they would lack plants.[41] We shall, however, begin with a look at the alleged undesirability argument, and then see how this really turns into the non-existence argument. But first there is yet another clarification to be made.

The demonstration that what is portrayed by the RDT *model* does not exist can provoke the argument that the *theory* (RDT) is *undesirable*. A political theory concerned with a political system that does not exist would be condemned by many as unrealistic and utopian. Some, however, argue that one of the functions of a political theory can be to guide and inspire rather than reflect reality—and that this is the proper function of democratic theory. G. Duncan and S. Lukes argued, in an influential article,[42] that those who have criticized traditional democratic theory as being unrealistic have missed the point that such theory does not have the function of reflecting, describing or explaining reality. On the contrary, 'most of the traditional theories of democracy were largely, if not primarily, normative, and critical of the societies in which they were conceived'.[43] However, it may be doubted whether this argument applies when the theory is *greatly* at odds with reality. Even Duncan and Lukes acknowledge that 'if such a theory seems intolerably remote from reality, it may be charged with utopianism'.[44] And it can be pointed out that, if the RDT model is inaccurate even now when the institutional requirements exist which were lacking when RDT was formulated, then it would seem that RDT is *too* unrealistic—and that it has failed in its normative guidance function. Moreover, many would argue that modern political science has shown not just that the RDT model has not been actualized, but also that such an actualization is impossible[45] (although Duncan and Lukes deny this[46]). Others, however, have maintained that even a model impossible to realize in practice has a desirable role to play in inspiring action and attempts to bring reality as *close* as possible to the model. G. Sartori, for example, argues that the function of democratic theory is to exert 'deontological pressure' : 'ideals are not made to be converted into facts, but to challenge them'.[47] But, for most people, the gap between theory and reality—if there ought to be one at all—should only be small, and certainly not insuperable. Apart from anything else, too large a gap leads to disillusionment. As Robert Presthus has said : 'While idealized conceptions of our system may inspire both higher aspirations and performance in the real world, it is also true that too great a gap between democratic ideals and reality may inspire fanciful expectations whose frustration breeds cynicism.'[48] And even Sartori modifies his account of the role of unattainable ideals.[49]

But let us return to the studies of voting behaviour and the alleged attacks on the desirability of democracy—or, rather, on the desirability of the kind of political system portrayed by the RDT model. It is important to remind ourselves here of this qualification, as the attacks take two forms : those which attack the desirability of RDT's democracy, but which still defend democracy, albeit of a different kind; and those which challenge the desirability of democracy as such—mainly a reaffirmation of certain traditional criticisms of democracy. The explicit concern here is with the latter type only—since the former will, in effect, be covered in the examination of modern theories of democracy in Chapter 6. This will, moreover, show that the two types of attack are not, after all, so different, some modern theories of 'democracy' amounting to a defence of a minimized role for the people in part *because of* the reassertion of traditional criticisms of democracy.

Studies of voting behaviour were originally limited to statistical analyses of voting figures : turnout, numbers voting for each party, geographical breakdown of such statistics, etc. But during the last three decades or so studies have been made more sophisticated by the development of the sample-survey method. This may be used to gain additional and often more accurate information about correlations between voting behaviour and the socio-economic and other characteristics of the electors. But, more importantly, it may also be used to obtain direct—and therefore more—information about the electors' perception of politics, and, in particular, about their knowledge of, and their interest in, matters up for decision at elections. General political participation—emphasized particularly in some varieties of RDT (see Chapter 3)—may also be 'measured'.

The main point is that what these studies have apparently overwhelmingly shown is that the electors are largely ignorant of, and uninterested in, the issues at an election and the policies put forward by the parties for their considerations; and that, more generally, they participate little in politics.

Beginning with *The People's Choice*[50] in America in 1940, this sort of conclusion has been documented in a long series of studies,[51] mainly, though not only, in Britain and the U.S.A. The ignorance and apathy have been indirectly suggested by the correlations between voting and social characteristics. The argument has been that the elector's voting behaviour is a reaction to his social position (or, more particularly, the correlated aspects of it) rather than a response to the issues and policies. In Britain the main 'social determinant' has, of course, been seen as class, or as class mediated by family background. Even Butler and Stokes, who emphasize the variety and complexity of factors influencing voting behaviour, say that their 'findings on the strength of links between class and partisanship in Britain echo broadly those of every other opinion poll or voting study'. And, they add, 'there were strong enough cross-currents in each class for partisanship not to have been determined entirely by class. Yet its pre-eminent role can hardly be questioned.'[52] In the U.S.A. the main determinants have been seen as ethnic group, class, religion and place of residence (urban or rural). Indeed, the authors of *The People's Choice* went so far as to construct an 'index of political predisposition' which could be used to 'explain' political preferences : 'a person thinks, politically, as he is, socially. Social characteristics determine political preference'.[53] Later studies drew back from such oversimplifications, but most of them still implied a large measure of 'social determinism'.

As already indicated, it was not only, or primarily, this indirect evidence that was involved : the voting studies also provided more direct and positive evidence of the electorate's ignorance and lack of interest. Not only was it shown that 'the conveyors of political information are massively ignored, except by a small nucleus of partisans',[54] but it was also confirmed that this contributes to a massive ignorance of issues and policies. For example, in the Bristol North-East constituency during the 1955 general election a sample of electors was presented with statements expressing typical party views on issues, but without party labels attached. It was found that 'voters were not very successful in attributing the propositions to the right parties. Even if an elector had given the name of a single party in answer to all four questions, or if he had given Labour and non-Labour answers at random, he would still have scored 50 per cent. The actual scores were not much higher.'[55] Similarly, in the 1952 American Presidential election it was estimated that roughly two-thirds of the electorate did not know, or did not see, the differences between the policies of the Democratic and Republican parties.[56] The authors of *The American Voter* said that 'many people know the existence of few, if any, of the major issues of policy', and concluded that there is little 'evidence of the kind of structural political thinking that we might expect to characterize a well-informed electorate'.[57] And writing of Congressional (rather than Presidential) elections, two of these authors reported that 'of detailed information about policy stands not more than a chemical trace was found'.[58] The voting studies' picture of the electorate's ignorance was well summed up by Abrams and Rose : 'The electorate is uninformed. . . . The number who are well informed is probably no more than one-tenth of the electorate on the great majority of issues.'[59]

Straightforward lack of information has not been the only relevant finding here. Even such beliefs as electors do have are said to have little coherence or meaning. 'Large portions of an electorate do not have meaningful beliefs, even on issues that have formed the basis of intense political controversy among elites for some time.'[60] Moreover, even where political views can be discerned, they often do not 'correspond' with electoral choice : apparently people often vote for parties whose policies they do not support.[61] Alternatively, it has also been found that such 'knowledge' as electors do have, rather than forming a basis for their voting decisions, serves to bolster preferences already formed and 'decisions' already made. The conception of 'social determinism' has already been mentioned, but there is also direct evidence that the electors' perception and information is highly biased :

Voters cannot have contact with the whole world of people and ideas; they must *sample* them. And the sampling is biassed. People pick the people and ideas that suit their personal equilibrium and then project that sample upon the universe. First, selective perception, then misperception, then the strengthening of opinion and then, in turn, more selective perception.[62]

This view on voting behaviour as resulting from a process in which such knowledge as there is of issues and policies is used to reinforce political attachments rather than forming the basis upon which voting decisions are made, was supported by the findings on the stability of party loyalty. Studies of voting behaviour revealed that a great majority of voters (about three quarters) always voted for the same party; later work has shown a greater volatility in voting behaviour, but the normally high proportion of 'constant' voters remained a very striking feature of the electorate. Moreover, even where voting changes occur, they are often but 'deviations' from an underlying and constant partisan loyalty which normally determines the direction of voting.[63] This is now a commonplace, but it came as a surprise to the authors of *The People's Choice* who approached their investigation of the 1940 election with a model of the voter as one who changes his mind according to his current perception of the issues and policies. However, 'the model turned out to be wrong at several crucial points. . . . It was discovered that on the electoral "market" there are a large number of voters with strong "brand loyalties", most of them had long-standing attachments to one or the other political party.'[64] And, as just indicated, this finding has been confirmed by numerous other studies.

The election studies also painted a dismal picture of the electors' interest—or, rather, lack of it—in the issues and policies. As measured by their own rating of their level of interest,[65] only between a third and a tenth of electors during an election campaign were shown to be 'interested' or 'very interested' in politics.

According to Abrams and Rose, the position could be summed up by saying that 'the electorate is not only uninformed, it is also uninterested'.[66] This lack of interest in the issues and policies at elections is also suggested by—and reflected in—the low level of general political participation.[67] (Apart from voting, the rather 'weak' concept of 'participation' here includes such activities as discussing politics, seeking information and joining political organizations.)[68]

The electorate, then, has been depicted as ignorant and apathetic. 'There seem to be widespread ignorance and indifference over many matters of policy. And even when opinions are held, many persons are not motivated to discover or are unable to sort out the relevant positions adopted by the parties.'[69] Voting behaviour, it would appear, is not motivated by a concern with and knowledge of the issues and policies. In a word, this amounts to a characterization of voting behaviour as irrational. As we saw earlier (Chapter 3), the concept of 'rationality' is somewhat fluid and a difficult one to define. However, the idea of rational behaviour was roughly summed up by saying that it is behaviour that results from the possession and use of adequate relevant knowledge. In this context, then, rational voting behaviour could be said to exist where votes are the outcome of reflection by the voters upon what they know of the issues and policies. But this is precisely what does *not* occur according to the voting behaviour studies. This lack of rationality has been commented upon many times. To quote but two examples: 'he [the American voter] most surely acts unrationally [*sic*] in his political choices. . . . ';[70] and, 'the rational nature of electoral choice is much more akin to a legal fiction than to a psychological reality'.[71]

It might also be thought that irrationality of this kind could mean that the electorate did not make decisions so much as yield to 'manipulation' by political leaders (and survey analysis itself might increase the leaders' manipulative skill). The authors of one election study, for example, felt that the findings (at least in respect of those who, in one sense, 'determined' the result by voting differently from the previous election) suggested a proneness to yield to manipulative pressure.[72] However, the control of the communication media necessary for uni-directional manipulation is lacking. Moreover, the very apathy, ignorance, resistance to change and biased perception which constitutes the electors' irrationality makes them highly resistant to manipulation of their attitudes, opinions and voting behaviour.[73] And, in view of this, and of the resistance of such crucial relevant factors as economic circumstances to adequate 'manipulation', there is little that sample-survey information can do to increase political leaders' capacity to manipulate the electorate.[74]

However, the argument, and its implications, that the electorate is irrational remains. But, at this point, it might be argued that it does not matter that the bulk of the electorate is irrational, for elections are decided by the floating voters. Most voters normally vote the same way, thus they can, in a sense, be discounted. The outcome of an election, it has been argued, is decided by the decisions of the floating voters, in the same sense that one person standing in the middle of a see-saw—rather than the large immobile groups at each end—decides which end shall go down. The idea is that it is precisely this minority of floating voters which votes rationally—indeed, this rationality is thought to be suggested by the very fact that these individuals do change their votes rather than being bound by social position or unreflecting habit. But this kind of argument is not acceptable. Apart from the fact that the change in votes between elections only partly results from the actions of the floating voters,[75] the findings of election studies were apparently that the floating voters were, if anything, *less* rational than other voters. 'Far from conforming to the "rational independent voter", the favourite of the political seer, changers were characterized by a rela-tively low exposure to campaign propaganda : they were closer in characteristics to the apathetic citizen.'[76] In fact, 'party changers [in this case those who changed voting intention during the campaign] were considerably *less* concerned with the election than were the "constant" voters';[77] they 'are likely to be less interested in the election and less exposed to propaganda than other voters'.[78] It is true that the con-clusion that the floating voters are *less* rational was powerfully chal-lenged.[79] But even granting this, there was no evidence that they are any *more* rational than the rest of the electorate—and so the idea that elections express rational decisions cannot be saved by pointing to the floating voters.

Owing to the irrationality of voting behaviour, then, elections do not constitute or express rational decisions by the electorate. Elections are, of course, the mechanism through which the people make decisions. Some alternative formulations of democratic theory give a different function to elections, and some of them see 'decisions by the people' as occurring—in part at least—in ways other than through elections (see Chapter 6). However, the concern here is with RDT, and in the RDT model it is through—and almost exclusively through—elections that decisions are made by the people.

In the context of RDT, then, this irrational voting behaviour constitutes irrational decision-making by the people. A democracy is shown to be a political system in which political decision-making is in irrational hands. And this is the nub of the undesirability argument. It amounts to a reassertion and confirmation of the traditional anti-democratic arguments, which say that democracy is an undesirable political system because it is one which gives power to the irrational mass of the people. Such a fear of power being in the hands of the irrational mass has been a persistent theme in political thought. This fear and disapproval have been evoked by a perception of the tendency of the masses to violence and foolishness. Irrationality has been viewed as involving or producing both a lack of restraint and a lack of wisdom—symptoms or aspects of the absence of adequate relevant knowledge or its use. From Socrates to the Victorian critics of democracy,[80] foolish policies and/or the breakdown of order have been widely seen as the result of power being in the hands of the people—'the mass' or 'multitude'. Popular rule was viewed as, or as tending towards, mob rule.

Studies of voting behaviour, then, give rise to the argument that democracy is undesirable since the people are irrational and unfit to rule. To be more precise, the argument at this point is that a democracy of the kind portrayed by RDT is undesirable. But, as indicated earlier, these same findings of the voting studies may more properly be seen as showing the *non-existence* of the system depicted by the RDT model.

Though it has not been sufficiently realized, the findings have only to be viewed in a slightly different way for this non-existence to be demonstrated—and this does seem to be a correct view. The point is that a democracy is a system in which the people make decisions on public policy, and in the RDT model the decisions are fairly definite and specific. And since they are made through the mechanism of elections, voting is seen in the RDT model as expressing fairly definite and specific decisions—which means decisions on the issues and policies before the electors.[81] But this is precisely what has been shown not to occur. It has just been indicated how the voter is shown as someone who has little or no knowledge of, or interest in, the issues and policies, and who reacts or responds habitually to his social position. Whatever it does express, a vote does not, on this account, express a decision on the issues and policies. Therefore the democracy of the RDT model does not exist.

It is true that there is a sense in which matters are *decided by the actions* of the voters, even though they cannot be said to make *decisions upon* them. That is to say, the outcome[82] of an election is, of course, determined by the way the electors cast their votes. This does not, however, mean that it can be said that the voters have decided they want the public policies whose implementation will supposedly result from the outcome. Similarly, it cannot be said that the arrival of a rambler at a particular village as the result of his choosing a path because it looked pretty shows that he decided to go to that village.

It is also true that the unimportance of elections is not necessarily demonstrated by this sort of attack. The fact that elections take place; the fact that important events occur because they take place (such as the substitution of one set of government personnel for another)— these would still be very important features of a political system even if elections were not decisions by the people. But the crucial point still remains : if the attack we have been outlining in this chapter is valid, the democracy of the RDT model does not exist, because elections are not, in fact, decisions by the people of the kind outlined in the model.

In Chapter 6 some possible responses to this, and other, attacks on RDT will be examined. This will involve looking at other possible democratic theories and a reassessment of some of the attacks themselves.

NOTES AND REFERENCES

1 Including LDT and neo-Idealist democratic theory.
2 For the nature of RDT and LDT, see Chapter 3 (as we saw, Locke's thought can also be developed in the direction of RDT).
3 This is not to deny that there are also other elements—those that derive from LDT—in these democratic political cultures. This is particularly true of Britain. In Britain also there are important pre-democratic aspects of the political culture: those emphasizing the independent authority and initiating role of the executive—the modern expression of the traditional role of the Crown (see, for example, G. A. Almond and S. Verba, *The Civic Culture*, Princeton, Princeton University Press, 1963, e.g. p. 493). LDT—with its emphasis on the independent role of representatives—tends to get tied in with these pre-democratic aspects, leaving the RDT elements as the most clearly democratic aspects of the political culture.
4 W. N. Chambers and R. H. Salisbury (eds.), *Democracy Today* (originally published as *Democracy in the Mid-Twentieth Century*), New York, Collier Books, 1962, p. 12.
5 *Capitalism, Socialism and Democracy*, pp. 249 and 264–5.
6 S. E. Finer, *Anonymous Empire*, London, Pall Mall, 2nd edition, 1966, p. 112.

7 'The System of Democracy in Britain', in *The Sociological Review* (New Series), Vol. 8 (1958), pp. 110–11.

8 Social phenomena are, to a crucial extent, actually constituted by the concepts used by the participants, according to one important view of the nature of social reality. See, for example, P. Winch, *The Idea of a Social Science*, London, Routledge & Kegan Paul, 1958.

9 Analyses of ideology have often been concerned with this point. G. Parry reminds us of its importance when considering the power structure of democracies: see *Political Elites*, London, Allen & Unwin, 1969, pp. 123–4.

10 The growth of political parties (in their modern form, at least) in fact largely coincided with the growth of the suffrage. It would seem, therefore, that developed political parties have existed for as long as there have been democracies, and consequently that the growth of parties cannot be considered as a *development within* the democracies. However, the essential point is that this was a development within political systems that were seen as democratic in terms of a model—the RDT model—with which an important role for political parties did not accord (see pp. 129–33 below— where it is also pointed out that later the RDT model came to accommodate the role of parties).

11 Phrases such as 'the extinction of democracy' or 'the non-existence of democracy' are, unless the context clearly indicates otherwise, used as shorthand for 'the extinction (non-existence, etc.) of democracy of the kind portrayed in the RDT model'.

12 Some early hostile views were, in effect, directed against majority-rule democracy, rather than party as such (see A. Ranney and Willmoore Kendall, pp. 116–38, esp. p. 137). Our concern, however, is with the hostility that arises from conceiving parties as subverting democracy (see, for example, ibid., pp. 150–1, and A. Ranney, *The Doctrine of Responsible Party Government*, Urbana, Ill., The University of Illinois Press, 1954 (paperback, 1962), Chapters 7 and 8).

13 'Thoughts on the Cause of the Present Discontents', in *The Works of Edmund Burke*, London, Henry G. Bohn, 1861, Vol. I, p. 530.

14 Some of the other charges brought against parties have been that participation 'becomes impossible . . . to the extent that parties interpose themselves between the sovereign citizen and his government' (*Democracy and the American Party System*, p. 151); that they 'obscure the responsibility of the individual Members of Parliament'; that they 'discourage the country's able men from entering public life', and that they 'crush dissent and promote a slavish orthodoxy and truckling to the majority . . .'—*The Doctrine of Responsible Party Government*, p. 119. The latter four statements refer to the views of I. Ostrogorski, whose *Democracy and the Organisation of Political Parties* (London, Macmillan, 1902), was one of the best-known books on the undemocratic tendencies of political parties. One of Ostrogorski's arguments was that the internal structure of parties was undemocratic. This was also the theme of another famous work: R. Michels, *Political Parties* (Glencoe, Free Press, 1915—first published in German in 1911). This becomes part of the general argument concerning the significance of elites, which is taken up below. In general, views concerning the

undemocratic implications of the *existence* of parties merge into those that see undemocratic implications in aspects, or particular characteristics, of modern political parties—such as their elitist internal structure or the rigidity of their discipline.

15 S. H. Beer, 'New Structures of Democracy: Britain and America', in *Democracy Today*, p. 48.

16 Proportional representation has often been advocated to avoid the problem of the representative somehow having to reflect and make decisions in accordance with the probably differing opinions of his individual constituents.

17 That rational choice is not *in fact* involved is, however, precisely what is apparently shown by the voting behaviour studies (see below).

18 A one-party system might be said to secure implementation of views even more effectively, but would not be counted as democratic from this general viewpoint since it provides for no electoral choice at all (see Chapter 2).

19 For the doctrine of the mandate and its validity, see, for example, A. H. Birch, *Representative and Responsible Government*, pp. 116–22. Chapter 9 of this book contains a useful discussion of 'party democracy'.

20 Not all socialist ideas of democracy are specifically Marxist. Non-Marxist varieties tend to be closely connected with 'party-modified RDT': there is the same view of parties as instruments for the implementation of popular initiatives. However, there is a departure from individualist conceptions. It tends to be classes rather than (the views of) collections of individuals that are seen as represented by parties. See S. H. Beer, 'New Structures of Democracy', and *Modern British Politics*, esp. Chapter 3. The main burden of Beer's work here is to show that individualism has been replaced by a collectivism of the type exemplified in such socialist ideas of party democracy. In so far as classes are types of groups, then these ideas overlap those contained in 'pluralist democratic theory'—see Chapter 6, where the nature and validity of 'group democracy' is discussed. If, and in so far as classes are seen as groups which are more important than, rather than as groups within, the overall community, then there ceases to be a theory of democracy. Democracy involves decision-making by and for a community.

21 The term 'pressure group' is sometimes viewed with disfavour on the grounds that actual pressure is by no means always a feature of the operations of the groups referred to. However, there is often potential (even where there is no actual) pressure. Moreover, 'pressure group' is a widely accepted and understood term. See G. C. Moodie and G. Studdert-Kennedy, *Opinions, Publics and Pressure Groups*, London, Allen & Unwin, 1970, pp. 61–2. On pressure groups generally, see also, for example, D. Truman, *The Governmental Process*, New York, Knopf, 1951; A. Potter, *Organised Groups in British National Politics*, London, Faber & Faber, 1961; S. E. Finer, *Anonymous Empire*, London, Pall Mall, 2nd edition, 1966, and G. Wootton, *Interest Groups*, Englewood Cliffs, Prentice-Hall, 1970 (pp. 103–8 of this book—'To Explore Further'—contains a useful bibliography).

22 S. H. Beer, *Modern British Politics*; see also Beer, 'New Structures of Democracy: Britain and America', and 'The Representation of Interests in British Government: Historical Background', art. cit.

23 Generally reckoned to have been begun by W. J. M. Mackenzie's article: 'Pressure Groups in British Government', *British Journal of Sociology*, Vol. 6, (1955), pp. 133–48. The book by S. E. Finer first appeared in 1958 (as did J. D. Stewart's *British Pressure Groups* (Oxford, Clarendon Press).

24 See, for example, Finer, *Anonymous Empire*, pp. 3–4, where it is also pointed out that some groups share both characteristics and could be called 'hybrid' groups (e.g. the Roads Campaign Council). In a sense the 'participatory' groups mentioned in the text are hybrid groups. There are also groups that come into existence to defend or to promote some interest(s), but which are not permanent or service groups (e.g. the commercial television lobby, which brought about the establishment of ITV—see H. H. Wilson, *Pressure Group: the Campaign for Commercial Television*, London, Secker & Warburg, 1961).

25 Depending upon the particular analysis of the power of pressure groups that is made, this subversion may be seen as a dilution, or as the potential or actual elimination, of the democratic character of the system.

25ᵃ We are here focusing upon the simplified model of RDT usually utilized, rather than RDT in all its diversity—see Chapter 3 for the varying theories of the general interest/particular interests relationship in RDT.

26 And this is to leave aside the whole problem of differing and incompatible genuine views (i.e. not rationalizations of particular interests) of what is in the general interest.

27 See, for example, pp. 31–4 of L. Hartz 'Democracy: Image and Reality' in *Democracy Today*.

28 *The Social Contract*, ed. cit., p. 23.

29 *Consent and Consensus*, p. 24.

30 See above, p. 132.

31 For a good short discussion and review of the work on political elites, see Parry, *Political Elites*.

32 Even 'value-free' analyses—which many studies of elites claim to be—are, in fact, usually characterized by implicit value judgements about the existence and function of elites. Anyway, even where the studies themselves refrain from explicit evaluation, the readers of the studies probably will not.

33 One of the difficulties concerning the use of the concept of 'elite' is that it often becomes 'watered down' in use so that a grouping rather than a group is referred to. In other words, what apparently start as significant statements about actions by an integrated group, often dissolve away into not so significant statements about numbers of individuals who merely have certain attributes in common.

34 There is often a crucial difficulty here—when possession of, or access to power is taken as the only feature distinguishing the 'power elite' as an elite. If this is linked with the muddle noted in n. 33, the notion of a power elite degenerates into a catalogue of those individuals who have power. In the extreme case, this can refer to little more than those who hold positions of constitutional authority, and what apparently purport to be interesting assertions about the existence of a group that wields great political power, can turn out to be tautologies of the form 'power is held by those who hold the positions of power'.

35 The reference here is both to theories of the desirability and of the existence of political elites—although the former (unless entirely utopian) are more or less directly tied to some variety of the latter.

36 'St Simon was the first to proclaim a new elitism in the name of organizational needs of science and industry . . .'—S. Wolin, Foreword to the American edition of P. Bachrach, *The Theory of Democratic Elitism* (Wolin's Foreword is not reprinted in the English edition).

37 D. Germino, for example, exclaims in a footnote (p. 172) in his *Beyond Ideology*: 'As if there can be any science of politics without a theory of elites.' There are those who challenge this, however (see next chapter). But it is not too clear whether 'pluralism' is a challenge to, or a variety of, elitism; see, for example, Parry, *Political Elites*, Chapter 3.

38 ibid., p. 13.

39 For the classic elitists one of the objects was to expose the 'myth' that in the so-called democracies government was by the people (see ibid., p. 25).

40 ibid., p. 13.

41 The position is complicated by the existence of another argument, which just possibly *is* valid. This is of the form: *this* democracy is undesirable because in it the people do not govern. This would be like arguing that a particular botanical garden was undesirable because it had no plants. A little reflection shows, however, that the statement 'this is an undesirable democracy (botanical garden)' is totally different from the statement 'democracy is (botanical gardens are) undesirable'.

42 'The New Democracy', *Political Studies*, Vol. 11, No. 2 (June 1963), pp. 156–77 (reprinted in H. S. Kariel (ed.) *Frontiers of Democratic Theory*, New York, Random House, 1970).

43 ibid., p. 164. (For further statements of views on the relationship between a democratic ideal and a reality that does not accord with it, see, for example, *Democracy Today*, pp. 13–29, and G. A. Almond and S. Verba, *The Civic Culture*, pp. 486, 487, and 481.)

44 'The New Democracy', p. 165.

45 This question is again touched on in Chapters 6 and 9.

46 'The New Democracy', p. 166.

47 *Democratic Theory*, pp. 64–5.

48 I. R. Presthus, *Men at the Top*, a Study in Community Power, New York, Oxford University Press, 1964, Preface.

49 *Democratic Theory*, pp. 65–8.

50 P. F. Lazarsfeld, B. Berelson and H. Gaudet, *The People's Choice*, New York, Duell, Sloan & Pearce, 1944 (2nd and 3rd editions: New York, Columbia University Press, 1948 and 1968).

51 Some of the more important have been: B. Berelson, P. F. Lazarsfeld and W. McPhee, *Voting*, Chicago, University of Chicago Press, 1954; M. Benney, R. H. Pear and A. P. Gray, *How People Vote*, London, Routledge & Kegan Paul, 1956; R. S. Milne and H. C. Mackenzie, *Marginal Seat 1955*, London, Hansard Society for Parliamentary Government, 1958; A. Campbell *et al.*, *The American Voter*, New York, John Wiley, 1960; D. Butler and D. Stokes, *Political Change in Britain*, London, Macmillan, 1969 (Penguin Books, 1971).

Collections of articles etc. can be found in, for example, E. Burdick and

A. J. Brodbeck (eds.), *American Voting Behaviour*, Glencoe, Illionois, The Free Press, 1959; and W. J. Crotty (ed.) *Public Opinion and Politics*, New York, Holt, Rinehart & Winston, 1970. Useful general analyses and surveys are: S. M. Lipset, *Political Man*, London, Heinemann, 1959; J. Blondel, *Voters, Parties and Leaders*, Harmondsworth, Penguin Books, first published 1963 with revisions in later reprints); R. R. Alford, *Party and Society*, London, John Murray, 1964; and P. G. J. Pulzer, *Political Representation and Elections*, London, Allen & Unwin, 1972.

On political participation generally, see, for example, L. W. Milbraith, *Political Participation*, Chicago, Rand McNally, 1965; and G. Di Palma, *Apathy and Participation*, New York, The Free Press, 1970.

52 *Political Change in Britain*, p. 76.

53 Lazarsfeld *et al.*, *The People's Choice*, p. 27 (page numbering of the original text is the same in the different editions).

54 E. Burdick, 'Political Theory and the Voting Studies', in Burdick and Brodbeck, *American Voting Behaviour*, p. 140. There are two points here. First, that the electors fail to receive the political information that is conveyed (by the mass media, campaign literature, etc.); and second, that if information is received it is not utilized in forming the decision on how to vote (see text below).

The first of these assertions appears to have been invalidated by studies of the effects of television, and doubt has even been cast on the second. (See next chapter. Other findings presented in this chapter will also be critically assessed in the next.) On the effects of television, see, for example, the articles by I. Pool and K. and G. E. Lang in *American Voting Behaviour*; J. Treneman and D. McQuail, *Television and the Political Image*, London, Methuen, 1961; J. G. Blumler and D. McQuail, *Television in Politics*, London, Faber & Faber, 1968; K. and G. E. Lang, *Politics and Television*, Chicago, Quadrangle Books, 1968; and J. G. Blumler 'The Political Effects of Television', in J. Halloran (ed.), *The Effects of Television*, London, Panther Books, 1970. See also the useful discussion in D. F. Thomson, *The Democratic Citizen*, pp. 107–14, and the references he gives.

55 Milne and Mackenzie, *Marginal Seat*, p. 120.

56 A. Campbell, G. Gurin and W. E. Miller, *The Voter Decides*, Evanston, Illinois, Row Peterson, 1954, p. 125.

57 *The American Voter*, pp. 170 and 542.

58 W. E. Miller and D. E. Stokes, 'Constituency Influence in Congress', in A. Campbell *et al.*, *Elections and the Political Order*, New York, John Wiley, 1966, p. 367 (reprinted from *American Political Science Review*, Vol. 57, No. 1 (March 1963), pp. 45–56; also reprinted in Cnudde and Neubauer, *Empirical Democratic Theory*).

59 M. Abrams and R. Rose, *Must Labour Lose?*, Harmondsworth, Penguin Books, 1960.

60 P. E. Converse, 'The Nature of Belief Systems in Mass Publics' in D. E. Apter (ed.), *Ideology and Discontent*, New York, The Free Press, 1964, p. 245 (reprinted in part (this statement is a part of the text that is not retained) in Crotty (ed.), *Public Opinion and Politics*).

61 See, e.g., Benney, Gray and Pear, *How People Vote*, pp. 140–1; Milne and

Mackenzie, *Marginal Seat*, p. 119; J. Blondel, *Voters, Parties and Leaders*, pp. 75–81. Of course, this lack of congruence between opinions and policy of the party voted for can also be due to inability to discern party policy— see, e.g., *The American Voter*, pp. 179–87.

62 Berelson, Lazarfeld and McPhee, *Voting*, p. 232.

63 See, for example, Campbell *et al.*, *Elections and the Political Order*, particularly Chapters 2, 3, 4, 5 and 7; and P. Converse *et al.*, 'Continuity and Change in American Politics: Parties and Issues in the 1968 Election', in *American Political Science Review*, Vol. 63, No. 4 (December 1969), pp. 1083–1105 (esp. p. 1085). Butler and Stokes find the British pattern a little different, but that nonetheless 'the elector's long-established habits of looking at politics can be a powerful influence restoring him to a traditional voting pattern'—*Political Change in Britain*, p. 299.

64 P. Rossi, 'Four Landmarks in Voting Research', in Burdick and Brodbeck, *American Voting Behaviour*, p. 17.

65 It would seem probable that this is a fairly meaningful and reliable measure; see, for example, *Marginal Seat*, pp. 66–7, where it is argued that this can be confirmed by correlating self-rating with some 'objective indicators'.

66 *Must Labour Lose?*, p. 73.

67 See, for example, Milbraith, *Political Participation* (esp. p. 142), and Di Palma, *Apathy and Participation* (esp. p. 32).

68 *Apathy and Participation*, p. 3. (In the United States even the number merely voting can fall to about half the electorate.)

69 *The American Voter*, p. 186.

70 E. Burdick, 'Political Theory and the Voting Studies', in *American Voting Behaviour*, p. 138.

71 J. Stoetzel, 'Voting Behaviour in France', *British Journal of Sociology*, 1955, p. 98.

72 M. Janowitz and D. Marvick, *Competitive Pressure and Democratic Consent*, 2nd edition, Chicago, Quandrangle Books, 1964, p. 34.

73 See the argument put forward by Thomson, and the evidence he quotes: *The Democratic Citizen*, pp. 92–7. This would not refute a Marxist-inspired argument to the effect that the masses were indoctrinated with the ideology of the ruling class. This is not the place to assess this argument (which anyway seems self-defeating: the argument itself would be 'invalid' ideology if the argument were correct, since it is not clear how one could escape the conclusion that all thought was ideological). Here it will merely be remarked that either the 'ruling ideology' permeates all aspects of society and hence equally controls all (leaders as well as the mass)—in which case the leaders (the present ones, at least) are not manipulating the mass; or else the previous argument showing that the mass are not manipulated remains relevant.

74 See Butler and Stokes, *Political Change in Britain*, pp. 443–4.

75 A large proportion of it is made up of a 'turnover' in the composition of the electorate: the electoral register changes to a significant extent between elections, owing to deaths, people reaching voting age and changes of residence. It is also the case that by no means all the electors who change their votes change from one party to another—many changes are from abstention to voting or vice versa. Moreover, even the party changers do

not *all* change in the same direction. The 'floating vote', then, is not simply made up of floating voters. For an exhaustive analysis of these points, see H. Daudt, *Floating Voters and the Floating Vote*, Leiden, Netherlands, H. E. Stenfert Krose, N. V., 1961. See also Butler and Stokes, *Political Change in Britain*, Part III.

76 Rossi, 'Four Landmarks in Voting Research', p. 18.

77 *The People's Choice*, Preface to 2nd edition (reprinted in 3rd edition), p. xxx.

78 R. S. Milne, 'Voting in Wellington Central, 1957', *Political Science*, Vol. 10, No. 2 (September 1958), p. 61.

79 See *Floating Voters and the Floating Vote*. See also Chapter 6.

80 For example, Maine, Stephen, and Lecky (see B. E. Lippincott, *Victorian Critics of Democracy*, Minneapolis, University of Minnesota Press, 1938), and, more generally, those who reacted against the extension of the suffrage in the nineteenth century. Even J. S. Mill had doubts and favoured weighted voting to give the better educated (the more rational) more influence.

81 More precisely, the RDT model as modified by the conceptions of the democratic functions of parties.

82 'Outcome' here means the direct result (e.g. the number of seats obtained by each party).

CHAPTER 6

Modern Democratic Theory

In Chapter 5 we saw how RDT can be shown as unsatisfactory in the face of political reality. One response to this is to consider the adequacy of other democratic theories : the 'failure' of RDT does not necessarily mean the 'failure' of all democratic theories. An obvious candidate for such consideration is LDT. Although it shares important features with RDT, we saw in Chapter 3 that it also differs from it in important— and highly relevant—respects. However, modern theorists often misperceive the nature of LDT. As we have already noted (p. 71 above), there is a tendency to lump LDT together with RDT and refer only to 'traditional' or 'classical' democratic theory. In fact such 'traditional democratic theory' usually turns out to be very like RDT, and is found unsatisfactory in the same way as RDT. Modern democratic theory is then formulated as a replacement for the unsatisfactory 'traditional theory'. For this reason we shall at this point look at modern democratic theory. LDT will, later in the chapter, be released from the invalid union and premature dismissal with RDT. The question of its adequacy can then be assessed in the light of the whole previous analysis of the viability of democratic theories. Neo-Idealist democratic theory will similarly be discussed later in the chapter.

Let us, then, turn now to an analysis of the nature and viability of modern democratic theory. The term 'modern democratic theory' is usually used to refer to theories of the last three decades or so that have sought, by diminishing or modifying the role of the people, to be 'realistic' replacements for 'traditional democratic theory'. However, beside these there is another, and very different, type of democratic theory that has been developed fairly recently—and which could therefore also be described as modern. This will be discussed in Chapter 9. To avoid confusion, this latter type of theory will be referred to as 'new democratic theory' (there is, indeed, a book on the subject entitled *The New Democratic Theory*[1]). There are also the quasi-mathematical analyses of democratic processes of the type referred to in Chapter 4, including the work of Arrow, Downs, and Buchanan and Tullock.

These are comparatively recent and therefore also describable as 'modern'. Not only have we already indicated the nature of at least some of these, however, but they are also hardly describable as democratic theories in their own right. Rather, they are new ways of dealing with certain ideas and issues as formulated by existing democratic theory. Such theories (or analyses) will therefore not be discussed in this chapter.

What, then, is contained in this chapter under the label of 'modern democratic theory'? Basically, two types of theory are referred to. These may be described as 'elitist' and 'pluralist democratic theory'. They are discernible as two types, but there are important interconnections, and the writings of some theorists contain an amalgam of both. Some might also discern a third category, which might be termed 'the democratic theory of apathy'. This is a corpus of analyses concerned with showing that the widespread existence of apathy in the electorate is not, after all, to be deplored since it has important beneficial consequences for those political systems called democracies.[2] However, we shall not make use of such a category in the present discussion, in part because such theories about the function of apathy tend to be theories about the necessary conditions of democracy[3] rather that democratic theories as such. Consequently, they fall within the subject-matter of Chapter 7. They do, moreover, also overlap very considerably with theories in the other two categories.[4] In fact, 'the democratic theory of apathy' often becomes a part of (or, at least, an adjunct to) elitist democratic theory: the relative apathy of the mass is a concomitant of an important role for elites. Thus the relevant points raised by the theory of apathy will be covered in our consideration of pluralist and (especially) elitist democratic theory (hereinafter referred to as PDT and EDT respectively).

As suggested just now, EDT and PDT can become closely related. Nonetheless, there are enough differences for it to be helpful to outline them as two separate types of theory. We shall start with EDT.

EDT—or the theory of democratic elitism (and there are other variations in the terminology)—is itself not so much a theory as a category containing theories with differences as well as similarities.[5] Nonetheless, it is often referred to as a theory—the focus being upon the similarities—and one finds discussions of the nature and standing of EDT as such. And such discussions indicate that, today, EDT is the generally accepted (or orthodox) theory of democracy, at least among students of politics.[6] Sartori suggests 'that the democratic theory of elites is in the light of present-day factual knowledge the core of democratic theory itself'.[7]

EDT—as is characteristic of modern democratic theory—aims to be primarily descriptive rather than prescriptive. It sets out to provide

a model of political systems (the Western democracies) as they are
rather than as they ought to be. It has been argued, however, that this
implies approval of, and helps to bolster, the *status quo* (moreover,
particular examples of EDT—as in the case of Sartori—may have as
part of their avowed purpose the demonstration of the value, indeed
the necessity, of elite leadership).[8] But whatever might be the prescriptive content of EDT, in *aiming* to be primarily descriptive it is seeking
to provide (or is treated as being) a 'realistic' replacement for traditional
democratic theory.[9] Where traditional theory is seen as unsatisfactory
in the manner depicted in Chapter 5, EDT is seen as according with
political reality.

One of the ways, of course, in which EDT is 'realistic' is in its
recognition of the existence of elites. Where the RDT model is incompatible with elites having an important role (see Chapter 5), the EDT
model includes such a role as one of its defining features. By definition,
EDT delineates an important role for elites in the political systems that
are called democracies. Hence EDT is specifically a democratic theory
that is not harmed if elites are shown to exist. It thereby disposes of
what is, for RDT, one of the principal difficulties. And also, since
elites are seen as a response to the complexity of modern society,
EDT does not, like RDT, suffer from the 'complexity-of-the-modern-
state' argument (see Chapter 5). The relationship of EDT to the findings
of voting behaviour studies will be discussed later, but again the essential
point is that EDT can be,[10] in part, specifically a response to these
findings and their implications.

EDT is obviously elitist, but in what sense is it alleged to be democratic? (In terms of the RDT model, after all, we saw that the existence
of elites demonstrated the *non*-existence of democracy.) The key point
is that a plurality of elites is postulated in the EDT model; and while
power is always held by an elite (or elites), the choice of *which* elite(s)
shall hold political power for a certain period remains in the hands
of the whole people. It is by virtue of this decision-making by the
people (deciding who shall hold power), together with the dynamic
relationship between elites and the mass of the people which this
involves, that the EDT model is seen as democratic (although the
'definitional fallacy' is sometimes involved as well—see below).

Before looking at EDT in a little more detail, it should be noticed
how the line between EDT and PDT can become blurred or non-
existent. The greater the emphasis on the importance of the *plurality*
of elites, and the dispersal of power that this involves, the nearer EDT
comes to PDT. Indeed, the two sometimes merge (as in the case of
Dahl), and one finds references to 'pluralist-elitists'.[11] The relationship
between EDT and PDT is further discussed below.

But let us return to EDT. We can see that starting from an acceptance of the inevitability of the existence of elites in modern political systems, it seeks to reconcile this (or simply assumes it to be compatible) with the existence of democracy. Sheldon Wolin has provided a succinct statement of the character of this response to elitism by democratic theorists. Elitist democratic theorists acknowledged

... that democratic politics, in varying degrees, was dominated by elites; they sought to escape the consequences of this admission by arguing that the sufficient condition of democracy was fulfilled if (a) the electorate were able to choose between competing elites, (b) the elites did not succeed in rendering their power hereditary or in preventing new social groups from gaining access to elite positions, (c) the elites had to draw support from shifting coalitions which would mean that no single form of power would become dominant, and (d) the elites dominating various areas of society, such as business, education, and the arts, did not form a common alliance.[12]

Let us now amplify some of these general statements a little. First, the simple but important point that EDT postulates, or discerns, a plurality of elites. The existence of choice by the people of which elite(s) shall hold political power—the key 'democratic feature' of EDT —involves the existence of more than one elite. 'It would be very helpful', Sartori writes, 'if the term "elite" were consistently expressed in the plural when we refer to democratic *elites*—a reason for this being that *'ex hypothesi*, if there is *one* elite of the *ruling* kind, this already means that there is no democracy'.[13] In the EDT model, then, there is at any one time rule by a minority (an elite, or combination of elites); but over time there is an alternation, or some other form of changing-about, of elites in power. There is, as Dahl says, 'not minority rule but minorities rule'.[14]

This process of moving in and out of power involves the elites in competition : they compete for the positions of power. And this gives to the people their ultimate power. '*The people are powerless if the political enterprise is not competitive.* It is the competition of political organizations that provides the people with an opportunity to make a choice. Without this opportunity popular sovereignty amounts to nothing.'[15] The competition is for the favour of the mass and involves the promising of benefits to sections of the people. 'The result of the competition between [elites] is democracy. And this is because the power of deciding between the competitors is in the hands of the *demos*—the onlooker who benefits from a quarrel between other people.'[16] This central idea of EDT is summed up in the definition of democracy given by Joseph Schumpeter, the 'founding father' of EDT, in his well-known book *Capitalism, Socialism and Democracy* : 'The democratic method is that institutional arrangement for arriving at political decisions in which individuals acquire the power to decide by means of a competitive struggle for the people's vote.'[17] It should be added that the people's ultimate power consists in the capacity to *remove* elites from power as well as to appoint them to it : '. . . in making the primary function of the electorate to produce a government . . . I intend to include in this phrase also the function of evicting it'.[18] This feature of EDT ties in with the general idea, fundamental to all theories of liberal-democracy, that there should be meaningful choice at elections. It also connects up with another important thread in modern commentaries upon democracy : the importance of opposition.[19] The presence of an active and legitimized opposition to the government of the day is held to safeguard and to make more salient the choice presented to the electorate (besides being an example of what liberals see as desirable checks upon government).

The capacity of the electorate to appoint and remove elites reinforces, and is reinforced by, the 'operative ideal' of accountability on the part of the ruling elite(s).[20] The elite(s) in power have a duty to give an account of themselves and their actions to the people—who have a right to remove them if this account is thought unsatisfactory.

The choice and removal of elites by the mass is effected by means of elections. Thus the electoral process holds a key place in EDT[21]—as it does in traditional democratic theory. It is the mechanism which gives the people the ultimate control over the elites—but whether this implies policy decision-making by the people is an issue both crucial and difficult to resolve; and it is one that is discussed later. However, whether or not elections are deemed to provide policy choices by the people, EDT does stress their importance. 'I am inclined to think,' writes Dahl, 'that the radical democrats . . . who insist upon the decisive importance of the election process in the whole grand strategy of democracy are essentially correct.'[22] And even if we come to the conclusion that EDT sometimes gets itself into a muddle and invalidly argues that such elections provide democracy even if they have no policy content, we can still agree on their importance in the EDT model : as was argued in Chapter 5, elections have functions that are of profound importance whether or not they may be deemed democratic. The existence, for example, of peaceful removal and appointment of rulers is a feature of a political system that has very great value.

Although the above are the main relevant features of EDT, there are others that should just be mentioned—one an aspect of the 'elitist' side', as it were, and the other of the 'democratic side'. The elitist element is the stress on the importance of leadership. The special need in a democracy for *some* measure of wise overall guidance, combined with a degree of initiation of thought and action, has often been stressed : 'the truth is that democracies depend—as the most thoughtful scholars have observed—on the quality of their leadership'.[23] EDT has, built into it, the notion of guidance by the governing elite of the day—and most conceptions of elites include the idea that their members have relevant intellectual qualities significantly superior to those of the politically less competent masses.

The remaining—and democratic—feature of EDT to be noted is the 'openness' of elites in the EDT model.[24] Not only is an 'external' popular influence postulated, via the external relationships of the elites with the mass (and each other), but so also is an 'internal' influence. The latter results from the openness of membership of elites : some members of the mass can—and do—become members of elites (there is also the possibility of the rise of new elites from out of the masses). Hence, there is an added responsiveness of elites to the mass of the people.

We shall shortly consider the viability of EDT as a theory of democracy. But this will be linked with a similar consideration of PDT, and so it is to an outline sketch of the nature of PDT than we now turn.

It was remarked earlier that the distinction between PDT and EDT often breaks down. Both point to the power of groups other than the people as a whole, and both thereby run counter to traditional democratic theory. Both PDT and EDT see the 'democraticness' of their models as consisting in the plurality of power-holding groups and in their relationship to one another and to the mass of the people. As we shall see, there can in fact be a very considerable interpenetration of PDT and EDT. Nonetheless, this may be regarded as the intermixing of separate tendencies, and two more or less distinct models do appear at times. Initially, then, we shall sketch in a model of 'democracy' that is different from that found in EDT.

PDT may be contrasted with EDT (in so far as it *is* different) by virtue of the types of groups—and their functions—that it focuses upon.[25] In EDT, the concern is with groups that control, or seek to control, government (the elites). In PDT, the focus is upon groups that seek to influence rather than control the government. This distinction roughly parallels that usually drawn between political parties and pressure groups (see Chapter 5); and, indeed, EDT tends to be combined with analyses of the roles of parties in democracies, while PDT is associated with corresponding analyses of pressure groups and their functions. An aspect of this difference is the different role given to the electoral process in the two types of theory. As we have seen, in EDT the democratic process is still centred upon elections : it is by virtue of the competition for the people's vote that the EDT model is held to be democratic. In PDT, on the other hand, although elections may be seen as a necessary condition for the existence of the democratic process,[26] that process is itself constituted primarily by the inter-election activity of groups.

In PDT, then, the power of the people is exercised *through* groups rather than, as in EDT, by influence upon groups. Indeed, there can here be quite a stark contrast between the two types of theory. This is a reflection of the fact that, to an important extent, PDT was a reaction against (non-democratic) elitism, whereas EDT represented a 'coming to terms' with elitism. PDT was formulated as part of a rejection of elitist analyses of politics; EDT incorporated elitist analyses *into* a reformulation of democratic theory. Many of the conflicting analyses of political reality—elitist and pluralist—are to be found in the field of community power studies. These are studies, mostly in America, of the power structures of local communities. Detailed studies of such communities (mainly in medium-sized towns) were possible when corresponding analyses of the nation as a whole clearly would not have been. Nonetheless, the findings and theories have often been extrapolated to, or combined with, analyses of the national power structure, so that they become much more than theories of local politics.[27] The general pattern was that an oversimple pluralism, associated with the names of Bentley and Truman (see below), was countered by an elitist analysis of community power (essentially begun by Floyd Hunter's *Community Power Structure*)[28]. This, in turn, was challenged by Dahl's sophisticated pluralism (which is, properly speaking, a combination of PDT and EDT).[29]

It was the group theories of politics associated with Bentley and Truman[30] that provided the immediate intellectual bases of PDT (Dahl's response to the elitist critique really constitutes 'pluralist-elitist' democracy theory—see below). Truman 'rediscovered' Bentley, and during the 1950s group analyses of politics became the orthodoxy in political science. Owing to 'the increasing complexity and the quickening pace of change in modern society', there has been 'an increase in both penetration of society by government and co-operation among individuals on behalf of their shared interests'.[31] This, it is argued, has led to an increasing tendency for organized groups to arise and to act politically, both to promote and to protect their interests. Group theory, then, 'attempts to explain the formulation of public policy and the maintenance of public order in terms of the interplay among the contending group forces of society'.[32]

Group theory enters into PDT in two main ways. First, it provides the view of the polity as composed basically of groups (as distinct from atomic individuals or a monolithic society-state) upon which PDT is based. This group basis is not merely discerned, it is also greatly valued : it is seen as the embodiment and the guarantee of individual liberty in the modern world (hence, when it is acknowledged as more than a purely explanatory theory, pluralism is seen by its adherents as liberalism updated). William Kornhauser's *The Politics of Mass Society*,[33] for example, argues the importance of the existence of 'intermediary groups' as a means of safeguarding liberty. Such autonomous groups engage the interests of the populace and act as a buffer between the masses and the elites. In this way, they prevent the formation of an apathetic and 'atomized' mass, and the takeover by a totalitarian elite for which such a mass would be ripe.

Secondly, group theory provides the foundation for what amounts to a 'pressure-group theory of democracy'. We saw in Chapter 5 that pressure groups and their activities have been viewed as subverting democracy. But we also saw that political scientists developed a different view of pressure groups.[34] In this alternative view, the guiding idea is that 'the general interest' and 'the popular will' (and hence 'the general will') are intolerably vague conceptions—if, indeed, such phrases have any meaning at all. Partly because of this—and also because of the incapacity of the electorate in specific policy decision-making—political parties are said to 'represent' the voters' wishes, if they do so at all, in a way so vague that performance of such a function is of little practical importance.[35] Pressure groups, on the other hand, are conceived to represent people in a meaningful way. They articulate, and make effective, the specific demands of the citizenry upon government. The groups themselves may be somewhat oligarchical in structure,[36] but they do provide for some real participation.[37] Moreover, whether or not many actually participate in pressure-group activity, the groups do actively advance the perceived interests of a great many people. This means that there is a direct and meaningful identification with their activity.

The fundamental idea behind the pressure-group theory of democracy, however, is that the general interest and the popular will *consist in* the outcome of the pressure-group process. Far from subverting it—as was suggested in Chapter 5—pressure groups are seen as embodying the particular interests that go to make up the general interest. The argument is that the only meaning that can be given to 'the general interest' is 'the sum total of particular interests' (either this, or else that there is no such thing as a general interest).[38] This is a Benthamite notion of the general interest—but with groups substituted for individuals. Similarly, with regard to the idea of the popular will, pressure groups are conceived to constitute it rather than to subvert it. The vacuous 'electoral decision on policy' is dismissed, to be replaced by the conception of the will of the people as consisting in the sum total of their particular—and meaningfully precise—demands (and the basic group theory provides the notion that it is group demands that embody the relevant wishes of individuals). 'The sum total' of particular interests is not a notion that is examined too closely. The tendency is for such a summation to be viewed, somewhat optimistically, as that which results from the 'interaction'—or clash—of pressure groups.[39] It is true that such a conception is supplemented by an idea of the 'rules of the game' or 'democratic mold' (to use Truman's terminology).[40] However, such rules merely structure the group conflict; they are not themselves seen as components of the general interest or the popular will.[41]

Two important assumptions behind, or corollaries to, this type of analysis should be noticed. First, since the desired outcome results merely from the interplay of groups, there is really no need for government at all (at most, the government is needed to 'hold the ring' and uphold the rules of the game). This ties in with the fundamental pluralist notion of the dispersal of power and the consequential weakening of the power of government.[42] Secondly, the electoral process is downgraded. Elections may still be regarded as very important (see p. 159 above), but they are no longer seen as embodying the democratic process. The will of the people is manifested in the pressure-group process rather than at elections. (And, if this were a viable idea, it would mean that PDT contained a solution to some of the important problems for democratic theory examined in the previous two chapters. Democratic theory's difficulties concerning the combining of individual divisions, and those arising from the findings of the voting-behaviour studies, stem from a questioning of the workings of the electoral process. If the idea is dropped that the function of elections is to embody virtually the whole, or at least a crucial part, of the democratic process, then it no longer matters if elections are deficient in the performance of such a function.)

We may now sum up PDT by focusing on those features which are alleged to make it a democratic theory. First, there is the emphasis on the dispersal and clash of power. 'Because one centre of power is set against another, power itself will be tamed. . . .'[43] This ties in with the liberal notion that the power of the people is manifested when the power of the government is limited ('tamed').[44] But there is also a link with the idea of processes for achieving something more general than majority decisions (see Chapter 4) : 'Because even minorities are provided with opportunities to veto solutions they strongly object to, the consent of all will be won in the long run.'[45] Secondly, there are the ideas involved in 'pressure-group theory'. These could be summarized by saying that the will of the people is the outcome of a process in which the demands of all sections of society[46] (and therefore of all individuals) are combined.

We have outlined EDT and PDT as separate democratic theories. But, as was suggested earlier, they in fact often become merged. This is most notably the case in the work of Dahl. The general model of 'pluralist-elitist' democratic theory is one in which the EDT conception of elite government and electoral competition is combined with the PDT stress on the dispersal of power. The plurality of elites is regarded in the same light as (or, indeed, as an instance of) the plurality of groups in PDT. Moreover, the intermediate as well as the elite groups are usually retained in the model. The people act through both the electoral system and the group process. In the case of Dahl, and his type of theory of democracy (or 'polyarchy'[47]), one should mention two more features. First, the dispersal of power concept includes the idea of 'noncumulative or *dispersed inequalities* in political resources'.[48] One may have a state of affairs in which 'nearly every adult may vote but where knowledge, wealth, social position, access to officials, and other resources are unequally distributed'.[49] Nonetheless, this is to be contrasted with *cumulative* inequalities,[50] and the key notion is that although resources may not be dispersed equally, they *are* dispersed : they do not all collect in the same hands. Secondly, there is the idea of categorizing citizens into two strata : the political and the apolitical. The political stratum is populated by *homo politicus* —the type of individual who is more highly involved in political thought and action; the apolitical stratum contains the apathetic (or non-involved) citizens—*homo civicus*.[51] The members of the political stratum, rather small in number, staff the politically active groups and/or exercise a fairly sophisticated check upon leaders via elections. It is thus *homo politicus* who has the direct influence on political decisions. But *homo civicus* does have an indirect influence.[52] His passivity can disappear if he becomes too dissatisfied, and his voting strength may then be mobilized. In other words, the apolitical stratum has 'slack' or potential power—which can become actual.[53] Moreover, leaders anticipate the reactions of the apolitical, whose influence is thus indirectly exerted(the 'rule of anticipated reactions' has already been mentioned, and will be discussed again below).

Now that we have had a look at EDT and PDT, can we say that they measure up to the challenge to democratic theory presented in Chapter 5? Do they succeed where RDT has failed? There is a sense in which the answer to such questions is obvious. As has already been pointed out, these modern theories of democracy were often developed specifically as responses to the kind of undermining of RDT outlined in Chapter 5. Indeed, in some instances the very factors used in a challenge to RDT actually become a part of modern democratic theory : this is so with both elites and pressure groups.

What was a challenge to RDT, then, simply becomes absorbed into the structure—or into the reasoning behind—modern democratic theory. Elites and pressure groups were just mentioned. The complexity of modern society and of the issues with which the state is concerned are factors that are part of the rationale of EDT : they not only help to explain the existence of elites, but also provide reasons for judging them to be desirable. Group theory is also, in part, a response to the recognition of the complexity of modern society and government. The findings of voting-behaviour studies have a similar relationship to modern democratic theory. EDT is, to an important extent, a reaction to the acknowledgement that the mass of electors are unfit for, or are incapable of, making decisions on issues and policies. PDT, recognizing the inadequacy of the electoral process for the purpose, postulates other processes as eliciting the will of the people.

It thus seems clear that modern democratic theory is, in one sense, left unscathed by the factors that entered into the challenge to RDT. Whether this is so in another sense, however, is not so clear. This is an issue of some complexity, involving a general assessment of modern democratic theory, but the central question may be stated simply : in meeting the challenge to RDT, does modern 'democratic' theory in fact remain democratic?

One of the complications is that just as there are different strands and emphases within modern democratic theory, so there can be different answers to this question. But then another complication arises : in so far as some varieties of modern theory *are* democratic, the question of their 'empirical viability' re-emerges. We shall now attempt to outline some kind of an answer to these questions.

First there is one complication which *can* be cleared out of the way —that caused by occurrences of 'the definitional fallacy' (see Chapter 1). It is quite often assumed that EDT and PDT are democratic theories simply because they are theories about political systems (often the American and the British—but most often the American) that are commonly called democracies.[54] However, as we saw in Chapter 1, this is a fallacy. Moreover, there is also an implicit tendency to rely on a circular argument : 'the theory is democratic because it is about systems that are democratic, the systems are democratic because the theory says they are'. There is, of course, no escaping the fact that to determine whether modern 'democratic' theory *is* democratic, we must break out of the circle and apply criteria derived from the definition of 'democracy'.

When we apply such criteria, what do we find? Let us look first at EDT. Whether or not EDT is to be judged a democratic theory depends upon what strands or emphases are focused upon within the theory. Regarded from one angle, it is not democratic. The appointment and removal of elites by means of elections is held to be the key democratic process. But if this means that the electorate *only* appoint (and remove) governors, and do not decide upon issues and policies,[55] then this is not an instance of democracy. It will be remembered that the definition of democracy outlined in Chapter 1 specified the making of political decisions by the electorate. And it was argued in Chapter 5 that—given the central role of elections (retained in EDT)—this entailed electors making decisions on the issues and proposed policies (this can include indirect decisions via evaluation of past governmental performance— see below). If the electorate were to choose only the representatives (with *no* implications concerning the policies they were to follow when elected),[56] then this would mean the electors had no voice in the running of the country. It is true that elections would still affect policy—but this would not imply that the electors were in any sense choosing or deciding on policies (see Chapter 5, p. 146).

It is also possible to regard PDT as failing to be a democratic theory. We saw just now that PDT in effect rejects the argument used in Chapter 5 concerning the subversion of the general interest and the popular will by pressure groups. But is this rejection valid? It is PDT's argument that, far from subverting them, the group process and its outcome constitute the popular will and the general interest. But such an argument rests upon a basic fallacy—a fallacy that has often been exemplified in political thought (in Utilitarianism for example)—since that which results from the pursuit of particular interests may be that which is desired by nobody. There is, in fact, a double fallacy here. First, there is the mistake of supposing that the outcome of the clash (or 'interaction') of particular interests will necessarily bear a relevant relationship to those particular interests. The result of a clash between, say, groups representing property developers, inhabitants, architects, local authorities and environmentalists[57] over a policy for slum clearance might well be that nothing was done. This would be an outcome greatly at odds with what each one of the groups wanted. The second misconception is to suppose that individuals want only what is incorporated in their various special interests. Indeed, what an individual *as such* wants may run counter to what is involved in the pursuit of one or more of the various special interests he has as a result of membership in various groups. As a member of the Automobile Association, 'he' would have an interest in more roads, but as an individual he might wish for a greater protection of the environment against the motor-car. And the point here is this : it is as individuals—or, at least, as citizens— that people have views on what the state should do. It is necessary, as Rousseau would say, to ask people the right question. And the 'right question' is, 'What do you think the state—the community—should do?' (i.e. what is for the public good, or the general interest?). As wage earners—as trade unionists—many people might want higher wages. But, if 'asked' at an election, they might well say that as individuals they wanted a sound economy and an end to inflation, even if this meant wage restraint.[58]

It follows from these lines of reasoning that for it to be said that the people are making decisions on matters of public policy, citizens must be specifically considering and making decisions upon possible lines of public policy. The interaction of group pressures and interests does not achieve this. Group activity may well have a part to play (see below, p. 172), but it is necessary at some point to ask all individuals to give their verdict on the policy alternatives—i.e. by voting. Hence, the central role of elections in the democratic process is reaffirmed. (It can still be recognized that pressure-group activity is desirable as, for example, a safeguard for individual liberty. And since it also has a part to play in the democratic process—provided it is kept within limits determined by the electorate—such activity is widely regarded as an aspect of the pluralist structure which many see as a necessary condition for the existence of a liberal-democracy.)

These are the fundamental ways in which it may be argued that modern 'democratic' theory fails to be democratic. There are other arguments to this effect, and these are touched on in Chapter 9 when we consider 'new democratic theory'. However, it is those just outlined that are the arguments that go to the conceptual heart of modern theory.[59]

Modern democratic theory, however, cannot be dismissed as undemocratic quite so readily. If attention is paid to elements within the theory other than those just examined, the picture is rather different. These are elements that are emphasized more in some instances than in others (or which do not occur in some theories).

One important point here is that although the electoral process must remain as central, attention should also be paid to the ways in which 'questions are put'. After all, as was pointed out in Chapter 4, the process that precedes the voting decisions is absolutely crucial. And here we should remember that EDT postulates 'open' elites. This means that there is a continual, if indirect, mass influence on the elites. Such an influence will affect the behaviour of elites, including the way they compete for power at elections. Hence, the content of the issues and policies involved in such electoral competition will also be influenced. Moreover, the argument of Chapter 4 stressed the importance of issues to be voted upon emerging from a broad consensus. And in modern democratic theory, the operations of elites and other groups are often seen as occurring within, and as being greatly influenced by, such a consensus.[60] This consensus both integrates the people's views and helps to keep the operations of groups (elites included) in line with those views.

The points made in the previous paragraph are important, but they fail to overcome the lack of policy decision-making that we earlier saw as characterizing the electoral process in EDT (and we have seen that PDT—in so far as it is distinct from EDT—ignores or rejects the electoral process but fails to substitute another popular decision-making process). Without such decision-making at elections, EDT would remain 'at best' a theory of 'responsive oligarchy' : decisions would not be made by the people, although they might have *some* influence upon them. Modern 'democratic' theory would, therefore, fail to be democratic. However, our previous outright dismissal of the idea of policy decision-making at elections was an oversimplification. Even if some varieties of EDT really do exclude decision-making of this kind at elections,[61] there are others which do not. Dahl, for example, points to the policy decision-making content of elections when he refers to them as key mechanisms 'for insuring that governmental leaders will be relatively responsive to non-leaders'.[62] Plamenatz may be taken as expressing this line of thought in EDT when he characterizes elections as deciding 'who shall have power *and roughly on what terms*'.[63] And because elections are, at least sometimes, recognized in EDT as linking elites' continuance in power with policy views (albeit diffuse) of the electorate, a further dimension of influence by the electors arises. This is the effect, mentioned earlier, that has been conceptualized as 'the rule of anticipated reactions'. Sartori, for example, refers to the behaviour of elites being 'guided by "the rule of anticipated reactions", that is, by the expectation of how the voters will react at the next elections'.[64]

It may be said, then, that EDT does not exclude a policy decision-making role for the electorate. That this implies that EDT can after all be treated as democratic is confirmed by Sartori's forthright statement : 'In full, our definition says that democracy is a procedure that produces a polyarchy in which competition on the electoral market results in the attribution of power to the people.'[65]

Now that we can see, however, that at least some modern democratic theory *is* democratic, we are back with the problem which helped to give rise to the theory in the first place. By showing it to be democratic, it would seem that we have shown it to be unrealistic : in Chapter 5 we saw how it can be argued that the electorate do not, in fact, make policy decisions. In so far as it is democratic, modern theory would seem to suffer the fate of the RDT it sought to replace; in so far as it escapes this fate, it ceases to be democratic theory. This is the impasse at which we have now arrived.

Is there a way out of this impasse? It would seem that there is. Up until now we have accepted the kind of interpretation of the studies of voting behaviour exemplified in Chapter 5. But this interpretation can be powerfully challenged. It may be that such a challenge would be insufficient to reinstate RDT, but modern democratic theory would be another matter. The broader, negative, popular decision-making of the kind postulated in EDT might exist even if the specific and positive decisions characteristic of RDT do not. This, of course, raises another point. Earlier in this chapter it was pointed out that modern discussions of the validity of 'traditional democratic theory' have often, misleadingly, lumped LDT together with RDT under this label. But, as we saw in Chapter 3, LDT is in crucial respects similar to EDT—the relevant point being that, in both types of theory, the electoral decision is seen as negative and as relatively unspecific in policy content. It follows that a demonstration of the viability of EDT in the face of the studies of voting behaviour would imply a similar kind of viability for LDT (other factors relating to the question of the adequacy of LDT will be commented upon below).

Let us now look at the nature of this challenge to the previous treatment of the voting-behaviour studies. There is here quite a body of material, and a number of lines of argument, but to keep our discussion within reasonable bounds, it will be necessary to do no more than indicate the main outlines.

The general nature of the challenge, then, consists in questioning (explicitly or implicitly) the idea that the electorate can be shown as an ignorant and apathetic mass moved not by perceptions of politics but by social pressures and/or blind habit. The Foreword to an influential book by Key, the purpose of which was to mount just such a challenge, picks out the author's assertion that 'the perverse and unorthodox argument of this little book is that voters are not fools'. Instead of 'fools', Key discerns 'an electorate moved by concern about central and relevant questions of public policy, of governmental performance, and of executive personality'.[66]

One aspect of this general type of challenge to the former orthodoxy consists in assertions of a different view of the extent of the electorate's knowledge. Not only can one find a different picture of the amount of information possessed by electors,[67] but also a different account of the 'quality' of their knowledge. Biased perception—selective perception of facts and opinions to reinforce existing prejudices—'is probably much less universal than had previously been supposed'.[68] Moreover, Converse's demonstration of a lack of meaning and coherence in political beliefs (see Chapter 5, p. 142) may well be 'artificial' : if attention is paid only to the issues that people deem important (about which they have a 'genuine' opinion), it could well be that their belief patterns would appear a great deal more coherent.[69] But even if the electors' knowledge of issues and particular policy proposals is judged to be scanty and/or somewhat lacking in coherence, it does not follow that relevant or meaningful knowledge is wholly absent. The voting-behaviour studies themselves implied this by their use of the concept of a party image.[70] Such a concept included at least a general belief about what the parties stood for—and unless a fairly systematic misperception at this *general* level was postulated (which on the whole was not), then this implied at least a general knowledge of a relevant kind. Moreover, it has been argued that *The American Voter*, for example, was not above using just such knowledge in explanations of voting behaviour. In the course of a searching analysis of the American and English voting behaviour studies then published, H. Daudt wrote of *The American Voter* :

. . . it is apparent that, despite the lack of any detailed knowledge, a global view of politically significant matters generally exists and that this, according to the authors, determines the political choice. . . . They set against the voter's lack of detailed knowledge his insight into the 'broad objectives of government', with which one or other of the parties has managed to identify itself.[71]

Interest and participation in politics may also be a good deal higher than the 'orthodox' picture of the electorate suggests. R. E. Lane, in an analysis of people's involvement in politics, commented upon findings that 'suggest[ed] a much more *actively* interested public than has been supposed to exist'.[72] Analysis of television viewing during an election campaign revealed widespread and genuine interest in obtaining information about the political environment.[73] Moreover, interest in politics rises when great issues are at stake (witness Britain in 1974) : 'When a nation faces a crisis—major changes in its social, economic, or political system or in its international position—the electorate as a whole takes a greater interest in politics'[74]—as in the U.S.A. during the 1930s.

It may be argued, then, that the electorate's knowledge and interest are considerably greater than the orthodox interpretation would have us believe. But such a contention is of little use in arguing that the electorate do, after all, make political decisions unless it can be further shown that voters make their decisions *on the basis of* their perception of issues and policies (or the broad choices encompassing these). If it is the case that voters habitually vote the same way, and/or that they react to social pressures, then they cannot be said to be making the relevant decisions (if they can be said to be making decisions at all). However, it is in just this area that there has been the most concerted attack on the former orthodox view of voting behaviour.

One of the points made here is that long-standing attachment to a party need not imply unreflecting habit—it may, after all, mean that such voters 'are satisfied with the way in which their party approaches the political problems'.[75] This point 'should', says G. M. Pomper, 'be remembered by all electoral researchers, lest they again treat American party loyalists as unthinking prisoners of tradition and habit'.[76] But the main thrust of the challenge here has consisted in a frontal attack on the idea that the voters' perception of politics does not guide their voting behaviour. We have already noted *The American Voter*'s use of 'political explanation', and Key's important book in which he asserts a consistency (among both those who change their vote and those who do not) between voting behaviour and policy preferences—and the consequent guidance of the former by the latter.[77] But there has in fact recently been quite an extensive literature on this theme. The best introduction to it, and some recent contributions, will be found in the *American Political Science Review* for June 1972.[78] One of the mistakes of the earlier election studies was, it seems, to mistake analyses of features of voting behaviour in the rather apolitical 1950s for a picture of the permanent nature of the electorate. If voting behaviour is, however, properly analysed over time, it can be argued that voters respond to broad issues and that they vote accordingly. Hence it may be said that 'parties can now meaningfully stand as "groups of like-minded men" offering particular stances toward public issues. Their victories in elections can now reasonably be interpreted as related to the mass choice of one set of issue positions over another.'[79] And even if voters were still judged to fall short of requirements in respect of choice of future policies, there is still the effect of the electorate's retrospective judgement of government performance to take into account. Many studies of elections have noted that voters respond to what the previous government has done more than to other political factors (for one thing, governmental performance—particularly its handling of economic matters—can be an especially tangible object of perception). Then there is the rule of anticipated reactions to consider. Thus, 'after a policy is enacted, voters make a retrospective evaluation of its success. The electorate's influence over such a policy is the leaders' anticipation of voters' reactions in the following election.'[80]

If all this is not enough to convince the sceptic, one can try adding new conclusions about the floating voter. It is now argued 'that a substantial proportion of the floating voters [are] well-informed and interested in politics'.[81]

It follows from this kind of analysis that it is no longer possible to dismiss the electorate as irrational. 'In the large the electorate behaves about as rationally and responsibly as we should expect, given the character of the alternatives presented to it and the character of the information available to it.'[82] It is true that it does not follow that, because electoral decisions are made by a rational electorate, such decisions necessarily control public policy. The decisions of a rational electorate can still be somewhat diffuse, and perhaps because of this, those elected to power might ignore the decisions. However, the latter assertion overlooks the real influence of a political culture that requires that leaders should pay attention to electoral decisions (even if there are conflicting strands within the culture).[83] It also ignores the point made above concerning the rule of anticipated reactions.

The diffuseness of at least some election results—owing to the difficulty of interpreting voter reaction to a multiplicity of issues and concerns[84]—is, however, a genuine difficulty. Nonetheless, it is a difficulty for, rather than an argument against, democratic theory. And even as such it can be exaggerated. The point already made about anticipated reactions should be remembered here : those in government will often anticipate definite reactions, even if they may not be able to discern them in actual election results (an election result may even be diffuse *because* possible definite reactions had been forestalled by anticipatory action).[85] But in any case, election results are not always unreadable. And the existence of a fairly coherent two-party system, as is usually exhibited in Britain, makes it possible to say, without gross violation of the truth, that an election often constitutes a broad choice between different lines of policy (the differences will be greater on some occasions than on others).[86] The whole question of the extent of popular control is summed up by Boyd in these words :

On some issues the electorate exercises no effective constraints on leaders' policy choices. On others, the electorate permits political leaders a wide array of options at the time of the adoption of policy, while passing a retrospective judgement on such choices in subsequent elections. . . . Finally there may be issues on which the public rather severely limits the options of leaders at the time of the adoption of policy.[87]

It should be remembered that we are here discussing the extent to which types of democratic theory are realistic, and not whether actual political events accord with the theory on *every* occasion. To an extent even a 'realistic' theory of democracy can have a prescriptive as well as a descriptive element. Thus the argument that it is realistic to expect elections to broadly control government activity does not imply or presume that government activity in Britain and America is *always* controlled in this way. It may well be that there are important instances of basic policy choices that do not flow from decisions by the electorate —but these would then be condemned, even by a 'realistic' theory, as undemocratic. The British decision to join the Common Market could be said to be an example. The essential point is that the theory is not systematically at odds with the facts.

It is now clear, then, that the argument indicated in Chapter 5 is mistaken. We do not have to accept the complete dismissal of decision-making by the electorate. But what are the implications of this? Does it follow that RDT is reinstated? This is surely not the case. There are still the difficulties just alluded to concerning the diffuseness of electoral decisions. But apart from this, even those who challenge the earlier orthodoxy usually agree that it is upon a broad appraisal of kinds of policy, and of performance, that votes are based, rather than upon a detailed knowledge of issues and policies. (And there are also the fundamental points concerning the relative infrequency of elections, the role of leaders in initiating policy proposals, and the scale and complexity of modern society and its government.) However, even if RDT is not supported by the new picture of the electorate, EDT is. Indeed, the above analysis of the nature and role of the electorate is very similar to that portrayed in the EDT model.

As we saw earlier, if EDT is shown to be empirically viable, so is LDT. But neither EDT nor LDT contain a satisfactory account of the nature of a collective decision. In LDT, the individualism is such that there is no adequate conception of the manner in which the implications of the many and various policy preferences can be combined into coherent programmes of action upon which the electorate can pass judgement (both before and after enactment). EDT does have such a conception. It could be argued that the elites performed this function. However, this is most clearly the case where the 'elites' are the political party leaderships. And given the difficulties and ramifications of the general concept of 'elite'—plus the additional channels of popular influence contained in mass parties—it does seem that the 'party variant' of EDT is the most satisfactory form of this type of democratic theory. However, even EDT contains no satisfactory account of the way in which the individual views expressed in votes can be combined into a decision by the people.

A satisfactory democratic theory, then, would contain an important element of neo-Idealist theory. We saw in Chapter 4 how the sort of democratic theory associated with Barker and Lindsay came to grips with the problem of the collective decision. And in so far as groups express more than purely sectional interests,[88] and in so far as their 'interplay' involves some measure of rational discourse and interaction, PDT can to some extent complement neo-Idealist theory. In such a combination of theories—as in neo-Idealist theory itself—the inter-election political process helps in the crucial integration of views that precedes the electoral decision. (We have already referred in this chapter to the importance of the manner in which 'questions are put'.) But, of course, the electoral decision itself remains as the central element —as the mechanism by which a choice is made among or between the options developed by the integrative process.[89] And it will be remembered that neo-Idealist democratic theory has a conception of the nature of electoral decisions like that found in EDT : they are seen, to an important extent, as judgements on results, as well as being viewed as of a broad and general nature (see Chapter 3). Thus, like EDT and LDT, neo-Idealist theory accords very well with the nature of voting behaviour as it is now discerned by many political scientists.[90]

It would seem, then, that a satisfactory theory of democracy can be developed out of a judicious combination of elements of EDT, PDT and neo-Idealist democratic theory. And this is broadly the kind of democratic theory to which the present writer would subscribe. However, there are criticisms of modern democratic theory which have not been considered in this chapter. Such criticisms vary from pointing to groups that are excluded from the pluralist system of power to Marxist or neo-Marxist critiques asserting the irrelevance of the political structures and processes that we have so far focused upon. Some criticisms assert that reality is such that the model of democracy to be found in modern democratic theory is inapplicable, while others amount to a critique of the model itself. The latter stress the value of extensive participation and positive decision-making by the people, and form a 'new democratic theory' which is, to a significant extent, a reassertion of RDT. To the objection that reality does not conform to such a model of democracy, the reply is that it is the function of theory to change reality. We are back to some of the issues raised in Chapter 5, but with some new perspectives introduced. The issues now become extremely wide-ranging and lead outside the province of the present book. However, the new theory and some of these issues will be briefly discussed in Chapter 9. For the moment we turn to another aspect of the analysis of democracy: Chapter 7 will look at some questions concerning the necessary conditions of democracy.

NOTES AND REFERENCES

1 By K. A. Megill.
2 This type of analysis is exemplified in the following: W. H. Morris Jones, 'In Defence of Apathy: Some Doubts on the Duty to Vote', in *Political Studies*, Vol. 2 (1954), pp. 25–37; B. Berelson, 'Democratic Theory and Public Opinion', in *Public Opinion Quarterly*, Vol. 16 (1952), pp. 313–30 (reprinted in H. Eulau, S. S. Eldersveld and M. Janowitz (eds.), *Political Behaviour*, Glencoe, Illinois, The Free Press, 1956); Berelson, Lazarsfeld and McPhee, *Voting*, Chapter 14, and L. W. Milbraith, *Political Participation*, Chapter 6. Excerpts from the latter two appear in H. S. Kariel (ed.), *Frontiers of Democratic Theory*, (this book contains a very useful collection cf material on the general theme of the nature and critique of modern democratic theory). Further references will be found in Chapter 7.
3 Strictly speaking, this should be phrased more cautiously. There is insufficient consideration of whether the systems as portrayed in such theories *are* democracies in anything more than name. There is, indeed, a persistent tendency for the 'definitional fallacy' to be committed (see above, pp. 5–8). This issue is further discussed below.
4 See, for example, Almond and Verba, *The Civic Culture*, Chapter 15 (excerpts reprinted in *Frontiers of Democratic Theory*).
5 See, for example, R. A. Dahl, 'Further Reflections on the Elitist Theory of Democracy' in *American Political Science Review*, Vol. 55, No. 2 (June 1966), p. 297; Dahl strenuously objects to the impression, given by the article to which he is replying, that there is *an* elitist theory of democracy (although this is also an objection to what he sees as an inclusion of non-elitist theories —labelled PDT here—in the category of elitist theories). J. L. Walker, the

subject of Dahl's attack, conceded that it might be better to talk of an 'attitude' rather than something as precise as a theory ('A Reply to "Further Reflections on the Elitist Theory of Democracy"' in the same issue of the *American Political Science Review*, p. 391. This issue also contains the original article by Walker: 'A Critique of the Elitist Theory of Democracy', pp. 285–95.)

6 See, for example, Walker, 'A Critique of the Elitist Theory of Democracy', pp. 285–6, and P. Bachrach, *The Theory of Democratic Elitism*, p. 93. According to D. M. Ricci, EDT 'developed into the conventional academic wisdom' although 'it did not penetrate to the folk level of society' (*Community Power and Democratic Theory*, New York, Random House, 1971, p. 51. This book contains a good account of the decline of traditional democratic theory and the factors giving rise to modern democratic theory.) Sartori contrasts EDT with the orthodox traditional theory, but sees EDT as *the* new theory of democracy (*Democratic Theory*, p. 126—and see quotation that follows in the present text).

7 Sartori, *Democratic Theory*, p. 128.

8 On this question of the extent to which EDT is prescriptive, see, for example, Lane Davis, 'The Cost of the New Realism', in Kariel (ed.), *Frontiers of Democratic Theory* (reprinted from 'The Cost of Realism: Contemporary Restatements of Democracy' in *Western Political Quarterly*, Vol. 17 (1964), pp. 37–46), and the controversy between Walker and Dahl already cited. (Dahl argues that Walker greatly exaggerates the extent to which EDT is prescriptive and asserts that it is mainly empirical.) See also Q. Skinner, 'The Empirical Theorists of Democracy and Their Critics', art. cit.

9 It should be remembered that, as already explained, in such contexts 'traditional democratic theory' in practice usually means RDT.

10 See, for example, Sartori, *Democratic Theory*, particularly Chapters 5 and 6, and J. Plamenatz, 'Electoral Studies and Democratic Theory', in *Political Studies*, Vol. 6 (1958), pp. 1–9. See also Ricci, *Community Power and Democratic Theory*, pp. 60–1, for the historical connection between the rise of empirical studies of the electoral process and the rise of EDT.

11 For example, Parry, *Political Elites*, p. 67 (it should also be noted here that Parry's last chapter contains an excellent succinct discussion of the nature of EDT—and of its relationship with empirical political studies and 'classical' democratic theory).

12 Foreword to American edition of Bachrach, *The Theory of Democratic Elitism*, p. ix.

13 Sartori, *Democratic Theory*, p. 113.

14 *A Preface to Democratic Theory*, p. 132.

15 E. E. Schattschneider, *The Semisovereign People*, 1960, p. 140.

16 Sartori, *Democratic Theory*, p. 124.

17 p. 269.

18 ibid., p. 272.

19 See, for example, R. A. Dahl (ed.), *Political Oppositions in Western Democracies*, New Haven and London, Yale University Press, 1966; and Dahl, *Polyarchy* (subtitled 'Participation and Opposition'), New Haven and London, Yale University Press, 1971.

20 The effect of removeability is also enhanced by the 'rule of anticipated reactions'—see below.

21 Ricci points out how this provides a methodological simplification for research, concerning the location of power, that had been complicated by an earlier pluralist analysis (see below for further discussion of issues raised here): 'By stressing the importance of the "competitive struggle for the people's vote", what [EDT] said, in effect, was that a very narrow realm of power—electoral politics—constitutes the critical field of human behaviour that can prove whether or not we practice democracy'—*Community Power and Democratic Theory*, p. 60.

22 *A Preface to Democratic Theory*, p. 125.

23 Sartori, *Democratic Theory*, p. 118; and see Chapter 6 ('Democracy, Leadership and Elites') generally—including the interesting discussion of the difficulty of translating the English language's distinction between 'leadership' and 'rulership' or 'headship' (p. 110). For a more general discussion of democracy and leadership (but one in which it is suggested that the role of elites may amount to more than leadership), see J. R. Pennock, 'Democracy and Leadership', in Chambers and Salisbury, *Democracy Today*.

24 See, for example, Sartori, *Democratic Theory*, p. 116, and Bachrach, *The Theory of Democratic Elitism*, p. 8.

25 The term 'pluralist' democratic theory derives from PDT's place in a general theory, or outlook, concerning politics known as pluralism or pluralist theory. This is, loosely speaking, a body of thought, some general ideas behind which go back a long way, but which in a more specific form is manifested in the political thought of Madison and Calhoun (and in the early twentieth century by the 'philosophical pluralism' of thinkers such as Harold Laski, G. D. H. Cole and R. H. Tawney). Pluralism can be characterized by its view that power is, or ought to be, 'pluralized': decentralized and scattered (i.e. amongst numbers of groups). Burtenshaw writes of the 'belief that power is not centralized, [but] is scattered around in pellets or small pieces throughout society, or even is "sort of lying around the streets to be had for the asking" '—C. J. Burtenshaw, 'The Political Theory of Pluralist Democracy', in *The Western Political Quarterly*, Vol. 21, No. 4 (December 1968), p. 586 (Burtenshaw's quotation is from A. Wildavsky, *Leadership in a Small Town*, Totawa, New Jersey, Bedminster Press, 1964, p. 358). On the background to pluralism, see D. Baskin, *American Pluralist Democracy: A Critique*, New York, Van Nostrand Reinhold, 1971, esp. Chapter 1. Since about the 1950s pluralism has manifested itself especially in the 'group theory of politics' (see below in the text). Some, indeed, would treat 'group theory of politics' and 'pluralism' as synonymous.

26 See, for example, Plamenatz, 'Electoral Studies and Democratic Theory', p. 9 (final sentence).

27 See, for example, N. W. Polsby, *Community Power and Political Theory*, New Haven and London, Yale University Press, 1963; and R. A. Dahl, *Pluralist Democracy in the United States*, Chicago, Rand McNally, 1967.

28 New York, Anchor Books, 1963 (first published in 1953). Also published in the 1950s was an immensely influential elitist analysis of national

politics in America: C. Wright Mills, *The Power Elite*, New York, Galaxy Books, 1959 (original edition, 1956).

29 The literature on community power analysis is now vast, but an excellent guide, and analysis of the subject, is to be found in Ricci, *Community Power and Democratic Theory*. Dahl's classic pluralist-elitist (see below) analysis of community power must also be mentioned here: R. A. Dahl, *Who Governs?*, New Haven and London, Yale University Press, 1961. Two relevant collections of readings concerning the analysis of power, but which are not concerned only with local community power studies, are: W. V. D'Antonio and H. J. Ehrlich (eds.), *Power and Democracy in America*, Notre Dame, Ind., University of Notre Dame Press, 1961; and R. Bell, D. V. Edwards and R. H. Wagner (eds.), *Political Power*, New York, The Free Press, 1969.

30 A. F. Bentley, *The Process of Government*, Evanston, Ill., Principia Press, 1935 (first published, 1908); D. Truman, *The Governmental Process*, New York, Knopf, first published 1951.

31 D. Baskin, 'American Pluralism: Theory, Practice and Ideology', in *The Journal of Politics*, Vol. 32, No. 1 (February 1970), p. 73.

32 ibid. On the general background to group theory, and the philosophical setting of pluralism, see also D. Baskin, *American Pluralist Democracy: A Critique*, Chapter 4.

33 London, Routledge & Kegan Paul, 1960.

34 See, for example, Finer, *Anonymous Empire*, Chapters 8 and 9 (this is not a 'one-sided' view: arguments both for and against the view that pressure groups are democratic are assessed).

35 See R. T. Mackenzie, 'Parties, Pressure Groups, and the British Political Process', in *The Political Quarterly*, Vol. 29 (1958), pp. 5–16, reprinted in a slightly amended and abridged form in W. J. Stankiewicz, *Crisis in British Government*, London, Collier-Macmillan, 1967 (Mackenzie sees the parties' function as that of the elites in EDT—to provide competing teams of leaders).

36 See, for example, *Anonymous Empire*, pp. 124–8.

37 Parry, *Political Elites*, p. 147; Kornhauser, *The Politics of Mass Society*, p. 77.

38 Truman had said that '. . . we do not need to account for a totally inclusive interest, because one does not exist' (*The Governmental Process*, p. 51). Baskin says that 'pluralists simply reject' the conception of a 'public interest', and contend that 'the social interest can be little more than the sum, often conflicting, of . . . group-desired outcomes' ('American Pluralism . . .', p. 77).

39 Somewhat in the manner of Calhoun, some see this as essentially a negative process—one in which groups are concerned to veto attempts to interfere with their position and interests. See D. Riesman, *The Lonely Crowd*, New York, Doubleday Anchor, 1953; and W. Kornhauser's article comparing Wright Mills and Riesman: ' "Power Elite" or "Veto Groups"?', in S. M. Lipset and L. Lowenthal (eds.), *Culture and Social Character*, New York, Free Press, 1961 (reprinted in Bell *et al.* (eds.), *Power and Democracy in America*).

40 *The Governmental Process*, pp. 129–39 ('democratic mold'), 348–50, 448–49, 486–7 ('rules of the game'); Ricci, *Community Power and Democratic Theory*, p. 71. There is also the notion of 'multiple group memberships' ('over-

lapping memberships')—which is conceived to moderate the sectional demands of groups (for a summary, see Ricci, op. cit., pp. 69–70).

41 It could well be argued that some crucial questions are ignored here, and that notions such as 'rules of the game' admit too much—that they let in the idea of the general interest (and possibly the popular will) by the back door. (See, for example, Ricci, *Community Power and Democratic Theory*, p. 73; the discussion in Finer, *Anonymous Empire*, explores some of the issues here.)

42 This is one of the elements which is seen as placing pluralism in the tradition of liberalism. On occasion, however, some pluralists imply that this lack of government has gone too far: 'I would contend that in most American communities there isn't a single centre of power. There is even a sense in which *nobody* runs the community. In fact, perhaps this is the most distressing discovery of all: typically a community is run by many different people, in many different ways, at many different times'—R. A. Dahl, 'Equality and Power in American Society', in D'Antonio and Erlich, *Power and Democracy in America*, p. 75. (Dahl is here using a pluralist-elitist analysis rather than pure pressure-group theory, but the point about the lack of government is the underlying idea to which pressure-group theory is linked.)

43 Dahl, *Pluralist Democracy in the United States*, p. 24.

44 See pp. 38 and 41 above.

45 Dahl, *Pluralist Democracy in the United States*, p. 24.

46 Truman accommodated the lack of organized group representation for some sections with the notion of 'potential groups'—those not in organized groups could always form one (and the rules of the game would ensure an appropriate place in the group process). The 'interests [of potential groups] are usually weak and dispersed. . . . Nonetheless, in the last analysis "if those wide, weak interests are too flagrantly ignored, they may be stimulated to organize for aggressive counter-action" '—Ricci, p. 69 (his quotation comes from *The Governmental Process*, p. 114). Some criticisms of group theory have, however, contended that this is too complacent an analysis.

47 Roughly speaking, by 'a polyarchy' Dahl means 'a political system that is towards that end of a scale of classification at which democracy is the extremity'. Dahl coined the term in order to categorize systems that approached what he regarded as the unattainable ideal of democracy. See, *A Preface to Democratic Theory*, Chapter 3, and also *Polyarchy*.

48 Dahl, *Who Governs?*, p. 228.

49 ibid., p. 1.

50 The contrast is with elitist analyses (not to be confused with EDT: it will be remembered that elitist analyses postulate one elite in whose hands power is permanently concentrated, whereas in EDT elites have to compete for temporary power).

51 Dahl, *Who Governs?*, esp. Chapters 8 and 19; Ricci, *Community Power and Democratic Theory*, pp. 135–7.

52 Dahl, *Who Governs?*, pp. 102–3 and 163–5.

53 Ricci, *Community Power and Democratic Theory*, pp. 137–8.

54 'Schumpeter . . . explicitly defined democracy in terms of what Liberal states had managed to create. . . . Labelling the procedures of the United States and Great Britain democratic, however, has not convinced all men

that such is the case. Indeed, it can be argued that the process theory begged the very question it presumed to answer—that is, what is democracy?—by calling what is, democracy.' 'Truman presumed that what existed in the United States was actually democratic, and that it only remained to explain how the system operated . . .' (ibid., pp. 62 and 67).

55 Schumpeter explicitly stated that his theory would reverse the precedence which RDT gave to the deciding of policy over the selection of representatives: 'Suppose we reverse the roles of these two elements and make the deciding of issues by the electorate secondary to the election of the men who are to do the deciding'—*Capitalism, Socialism and Democracy*, p. 269.

56 It will be remembered that, in Chapter 2, we examined different concepts of representation—and their relationship to the concept of democracy. Although no single means of electors influencing policy through the election of representatives was specified, it was common to all democratic varieties of the concept that representation should function as a means of giving the electors some say in political decisions. Elites in EDT have a function similar in crucial respects to that of representatives—see below.

57 As this example indicates, it is usual for some of the groups involved to be different from those concerned only with the promotion or protection of *interests* (in the usual sense). Some varieties of 'new democratic theory' focus upon participatory groups that promote local communal—rather than economic sectional—interests (see Chapter 9).

58 For the sake of simplification and clarity, this discussion ignores some of the complications. Chief amongst these is the fact that people often do prefer their particular interests. But particular interests do not always conflict with the general interest. And, if this is their response even when asked the right question, then it is because they conceive (or persuade themselves) that what is in their particular interests does not seriously conflict with— or is actually also in—the general interest. After all, that which is against the general interest must, in the long run at least, be against the various particular interests (e.g. wage increases in the end become useless if there is continuing inflation). Where this is not true, it is either because of the small scale of the particular interests (e.g. the building of a motorway at the bottom of some individuals' gardens), in which case what the affected individuals desire is minor administrative action rather than political decisions; or else because the community is breaking down (as in Northern Ireland), in which case democracy is not possible anyway. This is not to deny, of course, that *within certain limits* it could well be in the general interest for people (or groups) to be left to pursue particular interests. And, indeed, rather than viewing group activity as somehow constituting the general interest, it is more meaningful to regard it as interaction between (governmental action resting on a diagnosis of) the general interest and (the to an important extent legitimate promotion of) particular interests.

59 It might be said that arguments derived from Marxist analyses are equally —if not more—'fundamental'. It is not at all clear, however, how far these can be regarded simply as arguments against modern democratic theory— rather than as against all Western democratic theory (or as against the possibility of democracy as such). Again, some of the issues involved here will be touched on later, in our reference to new democratic theory.

60 See, for example, Dahl, *A Preface to Democratic Theory*, pp. 132–3.

61 It is difficult to believe that theorists would accept the implications of *total* exclusion of policy decision-making at elections. Such total exclusion would imply either that (a) voters were acting completely habitually (or were totally 'socially determined')—in which case they would not be making 'decisions' at all; or else, (b) they were making decisions on the basis of factors totally irrelevant to politics (such as colour of candidates' hair, and so on). It would not be clear why elections of this kind should be given any importance in a theory. In any case, such an account would not really give much sense to the idea of elite competition for electoral support. It would be difficult to envisage the nature or point to such competition in these circumstances!

62 *Preface*, p. 125.

63 'Electoral Studies and Democratic Theory', art. cit., p. 9 (italics added). But, in a later work on modern democratic theory, Plamenatz more or less denies that the electorate have a policy-deciding role: *Democracy and Illusion*, London, Longmans, Green, 1973, esp. p. 191.

64 Sartori, *Democratic Theory*, p. 125. On the role of anticipated reactions, see, for example, R. G. Gregory, 'Local Elections and the "Rule of Anticipated Reactions" ', in *Political Studies*, Vol. 17, No. 1 (March 1969), pp. 30–47. Gregory's references include: Dahl, *Who Governs?*, pp. 89–90, 101, 163–4, and R. V. Presthus, *Men at the Top*, p. 39. See also *The American Voter*, p. 5. (R. Bell *et al.*, *Political Power*, is dedicated '. . . to The Rule of Anticipated Reactions' (p. v).

65 Sartori, *Democratic Theory*, p. 126.

66 Foreword by Arthur Maas to V. O. Key, *The Responsible Electorate*, Cambridge, Mass., Harvard University Press, 1966, p. vii. Key 'was working with intense urgency on' this important book before he died 'in part, as his close friends have testified, because he knew that' this 'perverse' argument was 'of basic importance for both the theory and practice of democracy in America' (p. viii). Key's argument would not be so widely regarded as perverse and unorthodox today.

67 As mentioned in Chapter 5, an important factor here has been the impact of television (really beginning in the mid-1950s). See, for example, Trenaman and McQuail, *Television and the Political Image*, Chapter 9; Blumler, 'The Political Effects of Television', art. cit. Trenaman and McQuail speak of 'the majority of the electorate' as having 'a fairly soundly based and well-informed view of what at any particular moment are the main problems facing society' (p. 176). It should also be noted that information purveyed by television reaches especially the less educated and the otherwise least well-informed.

68 Blumler, 'The Political Effects of Television', art. cit., p. 84.

69 Barry, *Sociologists, Economists and Democracy*, pp. 127–9. Similarly, greater 'rationality' could be ascribed to any apparent lack of congruence between voters' policy preferences and the policies of the parties for which they vote (see Chapter 5, p. 142). Moreover, there is some evidence of an increasing congruity: in the 1964 and 1968 American elections voters aligned 'their partisan loyalties far closer to their policy preferences' (G. M. Pomper,

'From Confusion to Clarity: Issues and American Voters, 1956–68', in *American Political Science Review*, Vol. 66, No. 2 (June 1972), p. 425.

70 The concept was introduced by Graham Wallace in his *Human Nature and Politics* in 1908. On the nature and role of party images, see, for example, Butler and Stokes, *Political Change in Britain*, Chapter 16 and the references given therein.

71 *Floating Voters and the Floating Vote*, pp. 165–6. The challenge to the former orthodoxy concerning the nature of voting behaviour has had two bases: new empirical analyses of voting behaviour and re-analyses of existing evidence. Daudt's book is the prime example of the latter.

72 *Political Life*, Glencoe, Ill., The Free Press, 1959, p. 54 (italics in the original).

73 *Television and Politics*, Chapter 4, esp. pp. 81–5.

74 Lipset, *Political Man*, p. 189. This relates to the argument, referred to in the text below, that illegitimate generalizations about the nature of the electorate were made from what were 'time-bound' studies of voting behaviour.

75 Daudt, *Floating Voters and the Floating Vote*, p. 161. In any case, the extent of the stability of voting behaviour has been exaggerated—see also R. J. Benewick, *et al.*, 'The Floating Voter and the Liberal View of Representation', in *Political Studies*, Vol. 17, No. 2 (June 1969), pp. 177–95. Stability has also actually declined—witness the 1974 British general election.

76 'Rejoinder . . .' in *American Political Science Review*, June 1972 (see n. 78), p. 467.

77 Key, *The Responsible Electorate*. It has been objected that a consistency between stated policy preferences and voting behaviour may merely mean that voters are 'rationalizing' their behaviour by pretending to have the policy preferences appropriate for the way in which they voted. This, however, seems unlikely—see R. Boyd, 'Rejoinder . . .', in *American Political Science Review*, June 1972 (see n. 78).

78 Vol. 66, No. 2, pp. 415–70. G. M. Pomper, 'From Confusion to Clarity: Issues and American Voters, 1956–68'; R. W. Boyd, 'Popular Control of Public Policy: A Normal Vote Analysis of the 1968 Election'; 'Comments' by R. A. Brody and J. H. Kessel, and Rejoinders to 'Comments' by Pomper and Boyd. Kessel lists 'some thirty books, articles, and convention papers [that] have appeared in recent years, all suggesting that issues, in one way or another, have had consequences with respect to presidential voting choice' (p. 459). A similar argument about the importance of issues (or, at least, broad perceptions of politics) is extended to British voting behaviour in *The Floating Voter and the Floating Vote*; and 'The Floating Voter and the Liberal View of Representation', art. cit., also gives a similar picture of British voting behaviour. See also Butler and Stokes, *Political Change in Britain*, Chapters 9 and 15.

79 Pomper, 'From Confusion to Clarity . . .', art. cit., p. 426.

80 Boyd, 'Popular Control of Public Policy . . .', art. cit., p. 442. Boyd adds that 'an archetypal example is Humphrey's loss of support [in the 1968 election] among voters who ranked Johnson's presidential performance as poor'.

81 'The Floating Voter and the Liberal View of Representation', art. cit.,

p. 195. It was pointed out in Chapter 5 that Daudt, *The Floating Voter and the Floating Vote*, came to the conclusion that at least the floating voters are not less well-informed and interested than the rest of the voters.

82 Key, *The Responsible Electorate*, p. 7.

83 See n. 3, Chapter 5, p. 146.

84 See, for example, Dahl, *A Preface to Democratic Theory*, pp. 125–30. Some of the problems to which Dahl alludes, however, were covered in our discussion in Chapter 4. We are not here concerned with the logical possibility of an electoral decision, but with its empirical character. Moreover, we have just dealt with what is often seen as the major 'empirical difficulty'— the (alleged) non-existence of votes that can be said to express policy preferences.

85 A range of complex and interesting problems opens up here concerning the possibility—and its implications—of the anticipation of non-existent reactions (or, at least, of mistakes concerning the character of the reactions). However, even if mistakes are made, it is still significant that leaders are influenced by *a perception* of popular opinion. But it is unlikely that mistakes could systematically be made: whatever the failings of elections as devices for registering popular opinion they can at least correct systematic errors of this kind. (At least the problem highlighted by Gregory does not—in the light of the challenge to the orthodox view of the electorate—appear to exist at the national level. Gregory pointed out that if politicians anticipate what turn out to be non-existent reactions then 'the [popular] control mechanism is precariously supported, for it rests upon little more than a bubble that must sooner or later be pricked by the passage of time and greater sophistication'—'Local Elections and the Rule of Anticipated Reactions', p. 47.

86 The argument that the party policies are too much alike must be set against the requirements of broad consensus preceding choice that was outlined in Chapter 4.

87 'Popular Control of Public Policy . . .', p. 446. On this issue, besides Boyd's article, see, for example, V. O. Key, *Public Opinion and American Democracy*, Chapter 18; G. M. Pomper, *Elections in America: Control and Influence in Democratic Politics*, New York, Dodd, Mead, 1968 (Pomper gives convincing examples of popular control of public policy (see pp. 97, 170, 180–81, 184–5, 202–3, 257, 259; writing of the electoral impact on the Vietnam war in 1968 he says 'these astounding events demonstrated the influence of elections (p. 257)); W. E. Miller and D. E. Stokes, 'Constituency Influence in Congress', in *American Political Science Review*, Vol. 57 (1963), pp. 45–56 (reprinted in Campbell *et al.*, *Elections and the Political Order*, and in Cnudde and Neubauer, *Empirical Democratic Theory*); and K. Prewitt, 'Political Ambitions, Volunteerism, and Electoral Accountability', in *American Political Science Review*, Vol. 64, No. 1 (March 1970), pp. 5–17.

88 The role of 'non-interest groups' is referred to again in Chapter 9.

89 Elections also remain important as a vital test of the authenticity of the integrative process, as formal significations of the electorate's views and as a necessary condition for the existence, or continuance, of the rest of the

democratic process. But see n. 26, Chapter 7, p. 195, for a reference to a somewhat different view of elections.

90 As it is so important in neo-Idealist democratic theory, it is worth referring to evidence concerning the amount of discussion electors engage in, and the extent of their concern with the general interest. (Although it should be realized that the total democratic process—including the operations of parties and other groups—must be included in any proper evaluation of the correspondence between the neo-Idealist model and reality. The various interactions in these processes involve a considerable amount of discussion, while the institutional setting and the imperatives of government—which has to act on behalf of the whole community—demand at least some attention to the general interest). Thompson reviews the evidence concerning discussion in Chapter 4 of *The Democratic Citizen* and shows that discussion of politics during an election campaign is widespread and that 'opinion leaders' have an important role. (Most voting studies have pointed to the existence of a fair number of individuals—making up about a quarter of the electorate—who try to convince other people of their political ideas through argument. These are the opinion leaders.) Thompson also concludes that 'discussion . . . helps many citizens to become aware of the interests of people who have different interests from theirs, thus contributing to a sense of community . . .' (p. 118). And while he finds direct evidence of voter concern with a procedural rather than a substantive general interest (p. 138), he also acknowledges that 'the final test of the inclinations of citizens and leaders to consider the general interest must be sought not in voting behaviour but in the provision of adequate common benefits . . .' (p. 137). (Thompson is not impressed with the results of such a test, but this is because his criterion of evidence is too superficial.)

CHAPTER 7

The Necessary Conditions of Democracy

There are some types of analyses that might be said to constitute modern 'theories of democracy', but which are not of the same form as the modern democratic theory discussed in Chapter 6. The theories we looked at then had as their core the postulation, analysis and justification of a conception of democracy. But as well as theories of this form, there are those that fall into a category sometimes labelled 'empirical democratic theory'.[1] Empirical theory is concerned with explaining the existence and workings of the actually existing political systems that are called democracies. There are important overlaps between the two kinds of theory, but there is at least a difference in emphasis; put crudely, the difference is that the former type of theory explains what phenomena constitute a democracy, while the latter seeks to explain how such phenomena function and why they exist.[2]

This chapter will be concerned with the nature of one of the main branches of empirical democratic theory—the analysis of the necessary conditions of democracy.[3] But although analyses of the necessary conditions of democracy will be our subject, this does not mean that there will follow a survey of candidates for consideration as such conditions. Instead, a brief outline will be attempted of some conceptual issues involved in the postulation of necessary conditions for democracy—although this will, of course, involve looking at some conditions that have been suggested as necessary.

First of all, there is the question of the meaning here of 'necessary conditions'. To say that 'x' is a necessary condition for 'y' is to say that without 'x' there will be no 'y'. (A necessary condition differs from a sufficient condition : if 'x' were a sufficient condition of 'y', then the presence of 'x' would guarantee the presence of 'y'.) In statements of necessary conditions for democracy, there is some variation in 'the meaning given' to 'y'. The most obvious meaning is 'the existence of democracy'. And, indeed, 'a necessary condition of democracy' is very often taken to mean 'that without which democracy could not exist'. But this is not always so. Quite frequently 'the *continued* existence of democracy' appears in the place of simply 'the existence of democracy'. A necessary condition for democracy then becomes that without which democracy could not for long continue to exist. Other replacements for the simple 'existence of democracy' have included 'the existence of a stable democracy' and 'the existence of a desirable, or successful, democracy' (although many would see no distinctions here).

There is variation not only in that which the conditions are seen as being necessary for, but also in the character—or 'strength'—of the necessity. Sometimes 'necessary conditions' become watered down to conditions which are extremely helpful for, or which sustain, the (continued) existence of (stable, etc.) democracy. (These, of course, would be empirically necessary conditions—see below.) In such cases, 'weaker'—or less exact—terms, such as 'prerequisites', are often used.

With these two dimensions of variation there can be quite a variety of questions in this general area that analysts concern themselves with. The extent to which such questions can depart from our prototype ('What are the conditions necessary for the existence of democracy?') is illustrated by the title of an article in the *American Political Science Review*: 'Cultural Prerequisites to a Successfully Functioning Democracy: A Symposium'.[4] The prototype question is the one that is raised most often where democracy does not—or might very well cease to—exist: as in analyses of the prospects for democracy in the developing areas. The other questions tend to be asked in relation to well-established democracies.

This leads us on to a clarification concerning the kinds of democracies to which we are referring in the present chapter.[5] Primarily our reference is to democracy in large, modern, industrialized states (although mention will also be made of 'the developing areas'). But, as Plamenatz has pointed out, it should be remembered that the '. . . conditions of successful democracy in [for example] the United States are not the same as in the forest cantons of Switzerland, nor are they what they were in the Athens of Pericles.'[6]

As one would expect, a great variety of suggested necessary conditions can be found.[7] Some of these suggestions conflict with others, but, of course, many are complementary. Not only is it reasonable to suppose that there is a plurality of necessary conditions for democracy,[8] but such conditions also fall into different categories. Such categories include cultural, political, economic and general social conditions. Now, as has just been pointed out, we are concerned here with some conceptual issues regarding—rather than a survey of—democracy's necessary conditions. But one of the best ways of illustrating these issues involves the exemplification of suggested necessary conditions: i.e. discussion of the nature of the postulation of the conditions in the various categories.

First, we must remind ourselves of the general reasons for the existence of some of these conceptual questions. It will be remembered that, in Chapter 1, we indicated that confusion is frequently caused by a failure to distinguish between different kinds of questions about democracy. We were then primarily concerned with the difficulties this presented for the definition of democracy. But, at the same time, we saw how these were also difficulties that complicated the answering of questions about the necessary conditions for democracy. And, among other things, it is the particular forms these general difficulties can take that we shall now illustrate.

One of the confusions indicated in Chapter 1 was that between what we called logically and empirically necessary conditions.[9] And examples, in fact, of the character of logically necessary conditions were provided in Chapters 5 and 6. In particular, it was in effect argued that the existence of voting behaviour of a certain broad type was a logically necessary condition for the existence of democracy: i.e. it is not that there have been empirical demonstrations of the unlikelihood of democracy existing—or continuing to exist—where such voting behaviour does not exist; rather, it is that in the absence of such behaviour it would simply be incorrect to call a political system a democracy. Confusions can arise simply from a failure to attend to this distinction. But they are made worse by empirical democratic theory's insistence that it is dealing primarily with empirically necessary conditions, when in fact many of these turn out to be logically necessary conditions. (It must be realized, however, that in practice the dividing-line between the two can become very blurred. This in itself is not an imperfection of analysis so much as an aspect of the very nature of explanation in political analysis.)[10]

An example of the 'dual status' of possible necessary conditions is provided by postulated requirements concerning participation. It can be argued that, in this context, participation has the same logical status as the kind of voting behaviour which was referred to in the last paragraph and with which it is closely connected. That is to say, participation can be seen as a logically necessary condition for democracy—perhaps even a defining feature. Almond and Verba, for example, say that '. . . citizen competence and participation are at the heart of the definition of democracy. . . .'[11] However, there would be general agreement on this only if a certain minimum of participation were meant. Some proponents of EDT would include little more than voting itself as the participation necessary for it to be said that democracy exists—and might even resist the idea of further participation. 'The only means of participation open to the citizen in Schumpeter's theory are voting for leaders and discussion. He rules out such acceptable activity as "bombarding" representatives with letters because . . . this is a negation of the whole concept of leadership.'[12] On the other hand, in RDT (or, at least, some varieties of it) fairly extensive participation is, in effect, seen as a logically necessary condition for democracy. This is even more evident in the case of 'new democratic theory'.

Now, there are two, interconnected, sorts of confusion that arise from such differences of view regarding the status of participation. First, proponents of different theories tend to 'talk past' one another. Modern democratic theory discusses a greater than minimal participation as if the question were whether such participation is an *empirically* necessary condition for democracy. And the typical conclusion is that it is not. This is seen most specifically in the 'democratic theory of apathy' (see Chapter 6), where, in fact, it is argued that extensive participation is actually harmful.[13] But it is harmful, it turns out, for the stability of existing systems (in which there is a low level of participation). Whether such systems *are* democracies is a question that gets left on one side : it is simply assumed that they are. For participatory theorists, on the other hand—since extensive participation is a logically necessary condition of democracy—the *question* is whether such systems are democracies. To be told that extensive participation is not an empirically necessary condition for the existence or stability of systems called democracies does nothing to detract from their view that such participation is a logically necessary condition of democracy. Modern democratic theory is, of course, here guilty of the 'definitional fallacy'. Even Dahl comes very close to this kind of confusion when he writes that :

. . . The classic assumptions about the need for citizen participation in democracy were, at the very least, inadequate. If one regards political equality in the making of decisions as a kind of limit to be achieved, then it is axiomatic that this limit could only be arrived at with the complete participation of every adult citizen. Nevertheless, *what we call democracy*—that is, a system of decision-making in which the leaders are more or less responsive to the preferences of non-leaders—does seem to operate with a relatively low level of citizen participation. Hence it is inaccurate to say that one of the necessary conditions for 'democracy' is extensive citizen participation.[14]

The second confusion generated by differing conceptions of participation as a necessary condition arises from the persisting legacy of RDT. Modern theory, as we have seen, rejects the notion that extensive participation is a logically necessary condition of democracy (or even that it is an empirically necessary condition). However, owing to the continuing hold of the RDT model—despite its explicit rejection by modern theory—the idea of such participation as a logically necessary condition is difficult to banish entirely.[15] This means that there is a feeling of unease about rejecting participation of this kind as a necessary condition of democracy. Modern theorists would seek to account for—

and, in a sense, allay—such doubts by referring to the extensive participation requirement as a 'norm' or 'prescription' handed down by traditional democratic theory.[16]

Analogous confusions tend also to arise in assessments of consensus as a necessary condition for democracy. Again, modern theory tends to treat the question of the extent of consensus required by democracy as if it were a question about empirically necessary conditions. And some analysts come to the conclusion that an extensive consensus is not, after all, empirically necessary for the existence of democracy : '. . . contrary to the familiar claim, a democratic society can survive despite widespread popular misunderstanding of and disagreement about basic democratic and constitutional values'.[17] However, we argued earlier (Chapter 4) that a degree of integration and merging of views was necessary for it to be said that 'decisions by the people' existed. Now, the meaning of 'consensus' is somewhat vague and difficult to pin down, but it does seem that at its heart is the notion of broad agreement.[18] And such 'broad agreement' is very much what is conceived to result from the process of integration of views (moreover, there is the associated similarity that in both cases the diffuseness of the agreement is such that there is still the need for particular decisions to be made). 'Consensus' is, then, often very similar to what we earlier saw as a logically necessary condition for the existence of decisions by the people—and hence for democracy. And, indeed, discussions of the question of whether consensus is a necessary condition for democracy do sometimes shift from an empirical to a logical concept—but without a recognition of the implications and complexities involved in such a move.[19]

While it is correct to equate many accounts of consensus with the integration-of-views idea, it is an oversimplification to suggest that all accounts can be equated in this way. The truth is that there are differing ideas of consensus, and differing theories of the relationship of consensus to democracy (as has already been indicated). One way in which conceptions of consensus differ is in respect of the 'subject matter' of the broad agreement focused upon. In some cases, the subject matter is the kinds of policy to be pursued by government. This is sometimes referred to as 'substantive consensus'. It is substantive consensus that can be equated with the neo-Idealist account of integration of views. In other cases, the subject matter is the framework within which the policy decisions occur. Broad agreement concerning the nature and desirability of such a framework is sometimes referred to as 'procedural consensus'. Procedural consensus may be taken as a merely convenient measure of agreement to use one set of rules rather than another for conducting business (without it particularly mattering which set of rules is chosen). However, in discussions of democracy it is more often the case that the subject matter of procedural consensus, should it exist, is seen as the fundamental norms of the political system. After all, in a democracy 'the rules for conducting business' *are* the basic features of democracy itself. Procedural consensus of this kind is sometimes seen as underlying any substantive consensus. However, it has also been viewed as making the non-existence of substantive consensus possible.[20] The idea here is that policy disagreement can occur without upsetting the stability of the system precisely because there is an underlying agreement on 'fundamentals' which 'contains' the more superficial disagreements.

Consensus in the sense of 'agreement on fundamentals' would, then, seem to be very important. Whether as the basis for substantive consensus, or as that which renders the continued existence of democracy possible in the absence of substantive consensus,[21] this kind of procedural consensus would seem to be an empirically necessary condition for the existence of democracy (or, at least, of a stable democracy). However, as already indicated, not all analysts would agree.[22] Evidence drawn from sample surveys, they argue, shows considerable disagreement, incoherence and ignorance with respect to the 'democratic creed'—the 'fundamental norms' of democracy. And here the argument links up with the democratic theory of apathy and the downgrading of participation—it is contended that relatively stable democratic systems—such as that of the United States—persist in the face of this lack of accord on fundamentals because of the general lack of involvement in politics. The disagreements seldom become 'activated' in the form of political behaviour—and, in any case, they are of no great importance to citizens. Many would accept this argument in part, but most analysts would nonetheless assert that the disagreement must not be too deep. (Incoherence is one thing, profound disagreement quite another.) Thus most analysts would assert that at least some degree of consensus is a necessary condition for democracy (though the question of whether this is an empirical or logical condition is seldom focused upon). 'That democracy requires consensus is probably the formulation that the majority of political scientists now support.'[23] Nonetheless, many would still maintain that some 'dissensus' is also necessary—that a balance between consensus and dissensus is needed.[24] For some, this is a matter of the quality of democratic activity : too much consensus can mean a dull and enervating uniformity. For other analysts, the need for some dissensus connects up with the need for choice and for an opposition. Dahl, for example, in *Political Opposition in Western Democracies*, is somewhat concerned about the *extent* of consensus in many Western democracies. Consensus is also attacked by radical critics of Western democracy—but such criticisms are part of a larger critique which we shall look at in Chapter 9. (For further interconnections between consensus and democracy, see Partridge, *Consent and Consensus*; see also below in the present chapter.)

It is not only with regard to such non-institutional conditions of democracy as the nature of voting behaviour, the extent of participation and the degree of consensus that confusion or uncertainty can arise. There are also a number of constitutional and/or institutional arrangements that are commonly cited as requirements for democracy. One might sometimes expect—especially when it is in the context of 'empirical democratic theory'—that these requirements would be treated as empirically necessary conditions. However, such is not usually the case—and some confusion and obscurity could be avoided if the reasons for this, and the status that the requirements do have, were made explicit.

We have already argued (Chapter 1) that 'freedom of speech' can appear in different relationships to democracy, including that of being a necessary condition. And this is true of a number of other constitutional–institutional features. Their status as necessary conditions—as we have just indicated—is not always made as clear as it might be. However, it would seem that it is as logically necessary conditions that they usually appear. Freedom of speech, for example, has been viewed as 'the prerequisite for the political freedom embodied in the democratic state'[25] (even if not an explicit, this is certainly an implicit, assertion of a logically necessary condition). And it does seem that it is as logically necessary conditions that other features should be viewed. Some of these are intimately connected with freedom of speech, viz. the other 'democratic freedoms', such as freedom of assembly, freedom of association and freedom from arbitrary arrest. 'Free elections'—or, at least, elections at which there is a choice of candidates—are sometimes seen as necessary conditions.[26] Not only free elections as such, but various kinds of electoral systems have been argued to be necessary conditions for the existence of democracy. Both proponents of the British and American single-member, simple plurality system, and of proportional-representation systems,[27] have argued that the existence of democracy depends on the method of election they advocate. Then there are the frequently mentioned governmental institutional requirements, such as representative legislatures and responsible executives. The necessity of opposition is also often mentioned in conjunction both with the requirements concerning elections and with those concerning the central governmental institutions. Party systems sometimes figure here as well. And that this necessity is regarded as a logical one is illustrated, for example, by the following statement in an introduction to a selection of readings on the 'preconditions of democracy': 'The existence of effective opposition parties is frequently regarded as a crucial criterion of democratic government. "Practice and acceptance of opposition" is treated by Edward Shils as a major variable in distinguishing democratic and non-democratic systems.'[28]

These features which, if they are necessary conditions, are best regarded as logically necessary conditions, are sometimes included as defining features of democracy. This is misleading—if not simply incorrect. It is, after all, quite possible to disagree about whether it is necessary for, say, electoral systems of a certain type to exist before it can be said that democracy exists (witness the long-standing controversy about the merits of different electoral systems), while still agreeing that a democracy is a political system in which the people make the basic political decisions. Nonetheless, it does happen that these features become involved in the very definitions of 'democracy'. Sometimes, it is true, it does not quite happen : there are qualifications. One, for example, is Field's statement that 'free expression of opinion and free discussion' 'might almost be called a part of democracy rather than a condition of its working successfully'.[29] And Dahl's statement that 'one is inclined to regard the existence of an opposition party as very nearly the most distinctive characteristic of democracy itself; and we take the absence of an opposition party as evidence, if not always conclusive proof, for the absence of democracy.'[30] However, there are also unequivocal examples of definitions of democracy which list, as defining characteristics, features which should be treated as logically necessary conditions. H. V. Wiseman, for example, wrote that

Political Democracy is the regime of civilian rule through representative institutions and public liberties. Its components are first, a legislative body periodically elected by universal (adult or male) suffrage, empowered to initiate legislation . . . and to enact or repeal legislation initiated by the executive. The latter is subject to review and control. . . . The executive carries out its policies through a hierarchically organized non-political bureaucracy. . . . Candidates for the legislature are normally members of contending political parties. . . . Executive and legislative action is subject to periodic review through free elections, as well as being continually scrutinized by free organs of public opinion. Within the legislature, opposition and minority rights are guaranteed, and governments can be changed by regularized procedures of election. . . .[31]

Besides the institutional, structural and behavioural features already referred to, there is a variety of conditions sometimes said to be necessary for democracy and which might loosely be described as 'cultural'. However, there is a category of these which consist not so much in additional features as in the buttressing of features already mentioned. Thus the existence of widespread beliefs in, or support for, what can be viewed as the components or logically necessary conditions of democracy have sometimes themselves been posited as necessary conditions for democracy. Indeed, this has been generalized to the extent of saying that 'belief in democratic institutions may well be a cultural prerequisite to their survival'.[32] The article from which this quotation is taken also contains examples of the postulation as necessary conditions of 'beliefs' in particular features or principles of liberal-democracy (e.g. 'love of liberty'). It might appear that such conditions would be logically necessary. This may sometimes be the case—for example, it might be argued that 'the necessity for a free acceptance of an overriding public interest'[33] was a logical necessity (i.e. it might be contended that one could not say that the people were choosing communal policies unless such free acceptance occurred). However, in most cases postulated, conditions of this type would seem to be empirical.[34] It may be considered unlikely, but is nonetheless logically possible, that a democracy could exist despite the absence of, say, a 'belief in democratic institutions'. (But here the argument begins to connect up with the previous discussion of consensus, and the suggestion that because of its connections with neo-Idealist ideas, consensus of some kind is a logically necessary condition of democracy.) In fact, it has been argued that investigation shows that beliefs of this kind are not, after all, necessary for the existence of a stable democracy. Prothro and Grigg found that in two American cities there was general agreement on—and therefore general acceptance of—only the most abstract principles. When these principles were 'translated into more specific propositions',[35] the agreement disappeared. Consequently, they came to the conclusion that 'assuming the United States is a democracy, we cannot say without qualification that consensus on fundamental principles is a necessary condition for the existence of democracy'.[36] (Notice the important part played in the argument by what amounts to the definitional fallacy.) One widely accepted explanation of the persistence of democracy in the face of such lack of support for democratic characteristics is that the minority of activists do show greater support—and that it is upon them that the functioning of the democratic system disproportionately rests.[37]

Discussions of necessary conditions for democracy do not always spill over into (empirically unacknowledged) discussions of logically necessary conditions. Indeed, in the above example of the belief in democratic principles this does not always happen. *Provided that* definitional confusion—of the type exemplified by the definitional fallacy—is avoided, empirical investigation obviously has a very important part to play. There is a variety of factors about which one might wonder whether their presence is or is not necessary for the existence of democracy (or of stable, etc., democracy). And empirical investigation is certainly often needed in any attempts to find answers to such questions. Some of these factors can be described as cultural—for example, the incidence and role of religious beliefs.[38] Another very important category is formed by factors relating to the socio-economic environment of the political system. One group of such factors consists in degrees of wealth, industrialization, education and urbanization. And one important hypothesis has been 'that the more socially and economically developed a nation is, the more democratic it is likely to be'.[39] A recent and sophisticated discussion of the relationship between democracy (or 'polyarchy') and level of socioeconomic development is given in Chapter 4 of Dahl's *Polyarchy*—a book which has been described as '. . . the single most important contribution so far toward an empirical theory of the prerequisites for democracy . . .'.[40] Dahl agrees that it is 'pretty much beyond dispute' that

The higher the socioeconomic level of a country, the more likely that its regime is an inclusive or near-polyarchy.

If a regime is a polyarchy, it is more likely to exist in a country at a relatively high level of socioeconomic development than at a lower level.[41]

However, Dahl points out the importance of the 'deviant cases' and concludes that 'the evidence simply does not sustain the hypothesis that a high level of socioeconomic development is either a necessary or a sufficient condition for competitive politics [which he sees as an important component of polyarchy], nor the converse hypothesis . . .'.[42] Nonetheless, Dahl recognizes that there is an important relationship here, and he sums it up in the form of 'a very general hypothesis':

The chances that a country will develop and maintain a competitive political regime (and, even more so, a polyarchy) depend upon the extent to which the country's society and economy

   (a) provide literacy, education and communication,

   (b) create a pluralistic rather than a centrally dominated social order,

   (c) and prevent extreme inequalities among the politically relevant strata of the country.[43]

It is especially in the context of considerations of the prospects for democracy in the 'new' or 'developing' nations that discussion of the socioeconomic prerequisites for democracy occurs. Complications occur since Third World conceptions of democracy often differ from those of liberal-democracy (see Chapter 9), but it is worth drawing attention here to Niebuhr's and Sigmund's study of the fate of democracy in the Third World, in the light of the Western democratic experience.[44] And for the connections with other work on democracy—including the question of its necessary conditions—see the last chapter (and the references there given): 'The Prospects for Democracy: A Review of the Literature'. Of course, as is shown in that last chapter, 'socio-economic conditions' merge into general social conditions (as well as into other categories). And the discussion of the social prerequisites of democracy can often become mixed in with modern analyses of the *nature of* democracy (especially PDT)—exemplifying, yet again, confusion between empirically and logically necessary conditions.[45]

The question of its necessary conditions is one that is of profound importance for all supporters of democracy. And in attempting to provide answers to it, modern, empirical, political science has a crucial contribution to make. However, we should end this chapter with an observation that to many would seem obviously true, but which—owing to the deterministic implications of 'scientific explanation'—modern political science too often overlooks. This is that, whether or not democracy exists—or whether or not it functions satisfactorily—depends not only on 'given' factors but also *at least to a certain extent* upon what decisions people make about the type of political system they want. The importance of this factor in particular cases, and the question of what or how many people have to make the relevant decisions for it to be of any importance, are surely matters regarding which empirical investigation would be appropriate (although it does not follow from this that universally true generalizations could be formulated).

In Chapter 8 we turn to another topic which has not always been clarified by modern political analysis : the question of the justification of democracy.

NOTES AND REFERENCES

1 See p. 66 above.
2 The extent and complexity of the overlap is often underestimated—or even ignored altogether (hence, for example, the 'definitional fallacy' and the confusions regarding necessary conditions that are referred to below). Many complex and fundamental issues are raised here, but that there is an overlap is simply illustrated by considering the extent to which EDT and PDT interweave accounts of what phenomena constitute democracy with explanations of how such phenomena interact in the real world. There is a similar overlap between empirical and traditional democratic theory.
3 By far the longest section of Cnudde and Neubauer's *Empirical Democratic Theory* is devoted to analyses of the necessary conditions of democracy.
4 Vol. 50 (1956), pp. 101–37. John Plamenatz, in his contribution to the symposium, weakens the notion still further—while also bringing in the idea of reciprocity: 'By the cultural prerequisites of democracy we mean the ways of thinking and feeling that go naturally with democratic institutions. This natural association does not mean that, wherever we find the institutions, we find their psychological and moral counterpart, but rather that the two, where they coexist, sustain one another, and that neither is enduring except where it can lean heavily on the other' (ibid., p. 115).
5 It will be remebered that, except where otherwise stated, we are concerned in this book only with liberal-democracy.
6 'Cultural Prerequisites to a Successfully Functioning Democracy . . .', art. cit., p. 115.
7 As we shall mention below, different kinds of argument are found in support of the 'suggestions' (and many would reject the idea that they are putting forward nothing more definite than 'suggestions').
8 In one sense there is an infinite number of necessary conditions—the

existence of oxygen (so that citizens remain alive) is one, for example. Some sort of criterion of relevance is obviously necessary. In fact two such criteria tend to be—although are not always—utilized (explicitly or implicitly): one requires that, in principle, the existence or non-existence of the phenomena in question be determinable by human agency; the other enjoins restriction to phenomena that are deemed necessary for democracy *rather than* for other kinds of political system.

9   See also R. Wollheim, 'Democracy', in *Journal of the History of Ideas*, Vol. 19 (1958), p. 237; and the same writer's 'On the Theory of Democracy', in B. Williams and A. Montefiore (eds.), *British Analytical Philosophy*, London, Routledge & Kegan Paul, 1966, p. 265.

10   This is not the place to go into the complex and controversial issues raised here, but the basic idea referred to in the text is that explanation in political analysis consists to an important extent of conceptual understanding (see pp. 29 and 128 above). See H. Stretton, *The Political Sciences*, for a comprehensive discussion.

11   *The Civic Culture*, p. 230.

12   Pateman, *Participation and Democratic Theory*, p. 5.

13   The *loci classici* are: Berelson, 'Democratic Theory and Public Opinion', art. cit., and Berelson, Lazarsfeld and McPhee, *Voting*, Chapter 14.

14   'Hierarchy, Democracy, and Bargaining in Politics and Economics', in *Research Frontiers in Politics and Government*, Washington, D. C., The Brookings Institution, 1955, p. 59 (reprinted in Eulau, *et al.*, *Political Behaviour*). The italics are added. This passage is also quoted by Duncan and Lukes, who use the same italics to illustrate the point concerning definitional confusion. Although Dahl is not guilty here of the full 'definitional fallacy', it is still arguable that his 'conclusion is an obvious *non sequitur*, involving a slide from "what we call democracy" to "democracy". '(Duncan and Lukes, 'The New Democracy', art. cit., p. 163).

15   The continuing influence of RDT was indicated in Chapter 5. It was suggested that the main reasons for this were its 'greater democraticness' and its historical priority.

16   See, for example, Milbraith, *Political Participation*, p. 142, where the participation requirement is also *logically* linked with an RDT conception of democracy; but the complications this implies for the idea that the requirement is 'merely' a norm are not explored.

17   H. McClosky, 'Consensus and Ideology in American Politics', in Cnudde and Neubauer, *Empirical Democratic Theory*, p. 290 (reprinted from *American Political Science Review*, Vol. 58 (1964), pp. 361–82). See also below.

18   Partridge, *Consent and Consensus*, pp. 78 and 79. This book contains an excellent concise analysis of the concept, and survey of theories, of consensus.

19   See, for example, ibid., p. 124.

20   Of course, when 'procedural consensus' is given an 'ideological' or 'philosophical' content, the distinction between procedural and substantive consensus becomes very blurred indeed.

21   Of course, it has to be explained how a democracy is logically possible in the absence of substantive consensus.

22   See, for example, the influential article by J. W. Prothro and C. M. Grigg:

'Fundamental Principles of Democracy: Bases of Agreement and Disagreement', reprinted in Cnudde and Neubauer, *Empirical Democratic Theory*, from *Journal of Politics*, Vol. 22 (1960), pp. 276–94. See, too, the article by McClosky already cited and the excerpt from Dahl's *Who Governs?* ('Stability, Change and the Democratic Creed'), which are also reprinted in Cnudde and Neubauer. And see Partridge, *Consent and Consensus*.

23 Partridge, *Consent and Consensus*, p. 120. But see, further, below.

24 See, for example, Lipset, *Political Man*, and, more generally, Partridge, *Consent and Consensus*, Chapter 6.

25 L. Lipson, *The Democratic Civilization*, New York, Oxford University Press, 1964, p. 526.

26 For example: '. . . this is not the only condition necessary for a democracy. For an election to do what democracy requires of it, there must be alternatives besides the officially sponsored ones' (Benn and Peters, *Social Principles and the Democratic State*, p. 338). See, however, P. Nettl, *Political Mobilization*, London, Faber & Faber, 1967, pp. 145–7, for the view that elections are not essential for democracy, and that it is only Western conceptualizations and practices that give them this status (see also ibid., pp. 148–61, for further analysis of elections). Nettl's argument can be related to conceptions of liberal-democracy, although such applications are complicated by the fact that, in his analysis of developing societies, he is specifically concerned with drawing attention to non-Western models of development. As a part of this concern, he is more interested in the legitimizing and mobilizing than in the popular decision-making functions of elections.

27 On different kinds of electoral systems and their implications, see, for example, W. J. M. Mackenzie, *Free Elections*; D. W. Rae, *The Political Consequences of Electoral Laws*, New Haven, Yale University Press, 1967; and E. Lakeman, *How Democracies Vote*, London, Faber & Faber, 1970.

28 M. Rejai (ed.), *Democracy: The Contemporary Theories*, New York, Atherton Press, 1967, p. 192. (The work by Shils referred to is *Political Development in the New States*, The Hague, Mouton & Co., 1962, p. 54.) See also, R. A. Dahl, *Polyarchy*, Chapter 1.

29 G. C. Field, *Political Theory*, London, Methuen (University Paperback), 1963, p. 132 (first published 1956).

30 *Political Oppositions in Western Democracies*, p. xvi.

31 H. V. Wiseman, *Political Systems*, London, Routledge & Kegan Paul, 1966, p. 72. For similar, even if not always such clear-cut, examples see, for instance, Pickles, *Democracy*, p. 13; Mayo, *An Introduction to Democratic Theory*, p. 70; G. A. Jacobsen and M. H. Lipman, *Political Science*, New York, Barnes & Noble, 1965, pp. 25–6; Lipson, *The Democratic Civilization*, p. 275; M. Shaw, *Anglo-American Democracy*, London, Routledge & Kegan Paul, 1968, p. 3; and Elliott and Sumerskill, *A Dictionary of Politics*, p. 89.

32 E. S. Griffith, in 'Cultural Prerequisites to a Successfully Functioning Democracy . . .', art. cit., p. 102. With a slightly different emphasis, the question of the extent of belief in democratic institutions becomes an instance of the question, often at the centre of modern political inquiry, of the extent of legitimacy enjoyed by the political institutions within a system.

33 ibid., p. 111.
34 cf. the statement about logically and empirically necessary beliefs in Prothro and Grigg, 'Fundamental Principles of Democracy . . .', art. cit., p. 239 (of the reprint in Cnudde and Neubauer).
35 ibid., p. 242.
36 ibid., p. 250.
37 See, for example, H. McClosky, 'Consensus and Idealogy in American Politics', art. cit.; I. Budge, *Agreement and the Stability of Democracy*, Chicago, Markham Publishing Co., 1970; and I. Budge, *et al.*, *Political Stratification and Democracy*, London, Macmillan, 1972.
38 See, for example, 'Cultural Prerequisites to a Successfully Functioning Democracy . . .', art. cit.
39 D. E. Neubauer, 'Some Conditions of Democracy', in Cnudde and Neubauer, *Empirical Democratic Theory*, p. 227 (reprinted from *American Political Science Review*, Vol. 61, No. 4 (December 1967), pp. 1002–9). See also the articles by Lipset, Cutright, and McCrone and Cnudde which immediately precede Neubauer's; and Cnudde and Neubauer's introduction to this section of the book (in which they describe these four articles as a series which ' "fit together" and emphasize the cumulative and integrative possibilities of empirical theorizing in this area'—p. 143). See, further, Lipset, *Political Man*, Chapter 2. It should be pointed out, however, that these discussions, good as they are in many ways, are marred by definitional confusions. But see the reference to Dahl's *Polyarchy* that follows in the text.

   It should be noted that focusing upon the socioeconomic conditions for democracy can, of course, take a Marxist direction. For a Marxist analysis of necessary conditions for bourgeois democracy, see Barrington Moore, *Social Origins of Dictatorship and Democracy*, London, Allen Lane, The Penguin Press, 1967. For an outline and critique of Moore's book, see J. V. Femia, 'Barrington Moore and the Preconditions for Democracy', in *British Journal for Political Science*, Vol. 2, Part 1 (January 1972), pp. 21–46.
40 A. Lijphart, 'Towards Empirical Democratic Theory' (a review article), in *Comparative Politics*, Vol. 4, No. 3 (April 1972), p. 427.
41 *Polyarchy*, p. 65.
42 ibid., p. 71.
43 ibid., p. 74.
44 R. Neibuhr and P. E. Sigmund, *The Democratic Experience*, London, Pall Mall, 1969.
45 However, *Polyarchy*, Chapter 4, includes some discussion of pluralism as an *empirically* necessary condition for democracy. See also pp. 76–80.

CHAPTER 8

The Justification of Democracy

The question we are concerned with in this chapter is 'How, if at all, is democracy to be justified?' Or, to put the emphasis slightly differently : 'Is democracy a good system of government—and, if so, why? In fact, the latter question is usually put in a 'stronger' form : 'Is democracy the *best* system of government—and, if so, why?' Our consideration of this question will be divided into two parts. First we shall look at some modern attitudes to questions of this sort, and discuss some of the issues they raise; and then we will consider some possible anwers to the question itself.

First of all, then, an assessment of some modern ways of regarding this question of the justification of democracy. The issues raised concern the nature of the justification of any political system rather than of democracy in particular. It will be remembered that, in the Introduction, some of the implications of modern political analysis for the justification of political systems were pointed out. And, shortly, it will be with an expansion of these remarks that we shall be concerned. First, however, a brief indication of the nature of another, to some extent complementary, modern current of thought.

This other stream of thought derives from the movement or approach within Anglo-Saxon philosophy sometimes known as 'linguistic analysis'. In so far as there is anything as definite as a common theme running through the work of philosophers said to be exponents of this approach, it is the view that the analysis of the problems and issues of philosophy is to be carried out by means of the analysis of ordinary language. T. D. Weldon, in the best-known application of this approach to the problems and issues of political philosophy, characterized its development in these words :

What has happened is that philosophers have become extremely self-conscious about language. They have come to realize that many of the problems which their predecessors have found insuperable arose not from anything mysterious or inexplicable in the world but from the eccentricities of the language in which we try to describe the world.[1]

Now, it is true that the youthful excesses of this 'movement' have become outmoded. Moreover, the distinctiveness of the approach has been very considerably blurred as the guiding ideas have been ever more widely accepted, and have become considerably 'diluted' in the process.[2] Nonetheless, linguistic analysis has left an enduring mark on political analysis, and some of the more important contentions formulated in the earlier crusading days are still widely accepted—or, at least, are not widely and explicitly challenged. The effect on political analysis has largely complemented that of positivism[3] (for the meaning of 'positivism' here, see Introduction, p. vii). For example, as usually interpreted linguistic analysis implied that the philosopher's concern was not with the analysis of the empirical world, which was the business of science. However, at times the ideas and practice of the kind of conceptual analysis that linguistic philosophy could be said to involve were themselves used to critically analyse positivist ideas.[4] In the main, though, linguistic philosophy tended to reinforce the view that the actual analysis of politics is, or ought to be, a scientific enterprise. Political philosophy, on this view, was left merely with the task of clearing up conceptual confusions.[5] And the evaluation of political system was thus not deemed to fall within the province of either political science or political philosophy. Again, this meant that the citizen was left with no guidance when considering the question of the justification of democracy. But, worse than this, linguistic philosophy's confirmation of the primacy of scientific investigation left the justification of democracy exposed, as we saw in the Introduction, to the implications of scientific value relativism (see further below).

However, it is not only in this general way that linguistic philosophy has caused difficulties for the justification of democracy. It is also the case that the techniques of linguistic analysis have been trained specifically on what were seen as the traditional forms of justification—with the result that justifications of this type were declared to be of no use. Democracy suffered no less from the undermining of its traditional forms of justification than did other types of political system.

This specific type of 'attack' on justification by linguistic philosophy can be referred to as the undermining of foundations, or the rejection of the notion that the worth of a political system can be 'proved'. Thus Weldon in *The Vocabulary of Politics* attacks the idea that the worth of democracy (or, indeed, of any type of political system) can be deduced from 'basic principles'. Or, to put it another way, the argument is that justification cannot—as was often supposed—take the form of discerning metaphysical foundations for that which is to be justified. Apart from the linguistic philosopher's dislike—if not downright rejection—of metaphysics, such foundations are said to be so general and vague as to be useless as premises from which to deduce anything. Weldon's view is that propositions such as 'All men are created free and equal', and 'Men are always to be treated as ends and never as means', are so vague as to imply nothing in particular (and this is in addition to difficulties concerning the verification of the truth of such statements). 'Nothing follows from these high abstractions, or if you like anything does.'[6] It has also been contended that such premises are often confused. In particular, references to natural rights and/or natural law attract condemnation as mixing fact and value in a wholly confusing way. They are viewed, at best, as having a meaning that is unclear, and at worst as amounting to metaphysical nonsense. It may be that the kind of view of natural rights and natural law involved in such contentions should itself be questioned.[7] Nonetheless, it is true that serious confusions very often occur, and that statements concerning natural rights and natural law that are found in justifications of democracy can be insufficiently meaningful to be of much use (see, for example, the quotation from Bryce given below).

However, it is not merely that it is difficult to formulate 'foundations' in a sufficiently precise way. The problem goes deeper than this. The fundamental reason for the inability to derive justifications by deductions from foundations lies in the inappropriateness of deduction for this purpose. As T. L. Thorson reminds us in a lucid survey of the issues here involved, one must pay attention to the implications of the logical rule that 'any deductively valid conclusion, including an imperative one [and many would maintain that moral judgements incorporated imperatives], must be implicit in the premises'. It follows, therefore, that one cannot proceed from foundations to justifications that were not already contained in the premises.[8] But, if premises do contain justifications, this seems to mean that the problem of justification is merely pushed one stage further back : the question now becomes one of justifying the premises. In fact, as we have just seen, the so-called 'premises' are so vague that they cannot be regarded as the only source of the particular conclusions forming the justifications. As Thorson points out, implicit supplementary premises are inserted in the course of the justificatory argument. But, again, the problem merely re-forms itself into the question of how to justify these surreptitious premises (see *The Logic of Democracy*, Chapter 4, for a fuller development of this argument).

Not only did linguistic philosophy attack the notion of justifications based upon 'foundations', but also the whole idea of general justifications. This type of argument was applied most particularly to the justification of political obligation—when it was argued that there can be no single answer to a question such as 'When ought I to obey the state?' Any attempt to cater in one formula for the multifarious circumstances covered by such a general question was held to lead either to tautology or to vacuity. The only way to avoid this was to formulate answers that would not cover all cases. Hence, according to this argument, there is no general justification of political obligation, and all that one can ask is whether, and why, particular states on particular occasions ought to be obeyed.[9] But this argument also has implications for the justification of types of political system. It could similarly be contended that any attempted general answer to the question of whether democracy is a good system of government would result in tautologies or uselessly vague generalities—and that all that is possible is particular answers to particular questions like 'Is this particular democratic political system, functioning in this particular way, a good one?'

Linguistic philosophy, then, apparently showed the absurdity of attempting to provide proofs of the value of democracy, or of any rational justifications of democracy as such. But linguistic philosophy also provided the philosophical basis for the modern political scientist's rejection of a concern with justification, which is a hallmark of the positivist doctrine of 'value freedom'.

The notion of value freedom was referred to in the Introduction. A brief reference cannot adequately convey its character since it consists in a somewhat variable cluster of ideas rather than a single conception. However, it is primarily with but one aspect of this cluster that we are here concerned. As was indicated earlier, this is the doctrine called by Arnold Brecht 'scientific value relativism' (see Introduction, n. 5, p. xiii). This doctrine asserts that scientific analysis cannot provide answers to questions of value—it cannot tell us what is right and wrong, good and bad.[10] There is a good deal that scientific analysis can do in the sphere of moral judgements—such as investigating the consequences of attempting to realize cherished values[11]—but it cannot provide the final answer to the questions of what values to hold, and therefore of what moral judgements to make.

The philosophical basis of scientific value relativism is usually held to be the logical principle that an 'ought statement' cannot be deduced from an 'is statement'—that value judgements cannot be deduced from statements of fact.[12] This is labelled by Brecht the 'gulf doctrine'[13] —since the idea is that there is an unbridgeable logical gulf between 'is' and 'ought'. The 'gulf doctrine' has come under some attack recently,[14] nonetheless it is still very much the orthodoxy in the philosophy of the social sciences. It is held to underpin scientific value relativism since it shows that factual analysis cannot logically entail moral judgements. As Strauss has pointed out, however, scientific value relativism basically asserts something different from—or, at least, more than—what is involved in the gulf doctrine : it contends that there 'cannot be any genuine knowledge of the ought'.[15] In short, since there cannot be any genuine, or at least any scientific, knowledge of the 'ought', scientific investigation cannot provide answers to moral questions. But modern, positivist, political science takes scientific knowledge as the only true form of knowledge. Therefore it follows that valid political analysis cannot answer questions of value. And, despite a rejection of important aspects of the early form of the doctrine of value freedom, and despite an increasing tendency to question this central argument itself,[16] the argument from scientific value relativism is still very much the orthodoxy in political science.

The import of this for the justifying of democracy is clear and devastating : valid academic political analysis has been pronounced irrelevant for this purpose. Political science does not, allegedly, attempt to answer questions about the worth of democracy; but political philosophy is no more capable of answering such questions, since they are said to be incapable of being answered (and, as we saw just now, modern philosophy has in any case tended to outlaw such questions on other grounds as well). According to scientific value relativism, moral judgements are irrational (or, at least, non-rational) choices. Arbitrary 'choice', not factual analysis, is what 'settles' moral questions. Moral judgements may be seen as reducible 'to emotional responses conditioned by the individual's total life-experiences'. Or the conception of them may be that outlined by R. M. Hare in his influential book *The Language of Morals* : imperative utterances derived from 'principles for the advisory guidance . . . of one's own and other people's actions'.[17] Either way it would seem that the basis of a moral judgement is arbitrary : although derivation from universal principles is rational and non-arbitrary, the choice of the principles themselves seems ultimately as arbitrary as the expression of emotional responses (although this is not a view that Hare himself would necessarily accept). And either of these still widely accepted views of value judgements supports scientific value relativism's thesis that scientific knowledge is irrelevant for the making of moral judgements (at least, ultimate ones).

The enterprise of justifying democracy has, then, apparently been invalidated by positivism. Brecht himself insists that scientific value relativism does not imply relativism as such ('philosophical relativism').[18] However, as we have just seen, the sort of account of the nature of value judgements with which it is—and, it would seem, must be—associated, does not seem to leave room for anything but relativism in some important sense. If moral judgements are arbitrary, then there is no way—whether scientific or otherwise—of demonstrating the greater moral worth of one judgement as against another. This, of course, includes judgements concerning democracy. Hence there is no way of demonstrating that democracy is better than other forms of government. Positivists sometimes seem uneasily aware of these implications. Brecht, for example, talks of scientific value relativism being the 'seamy side of Scientific Method',[19] and in the Introductory to *Political Theory* he graphically portrays the sorry state in which positivism left the intellectual defence of democracy against the rise of totalitarianism. And although they are often pushed aside, it seems to the present writer that such doubts are entirely justified. The intellectual defence of democracy *would* be in a sorry state—indeed it would be non-existent— if the positivist account of evaluation had to be accepted. It is necessary, then, to see whether this account—and the arguments of the 'Weldonite' philosophers—do have to be accepted.

Let us look first at the arguments from linguistic philosophy. The attack on 'foundations' or proofs has been subjected to a powerful critique by Thorson. His central point is that although linguistic philosophy was right in showing there could be no deductive (or inductive) *proof* of the worth of democracy, it is wrong to suggest that this implies relativism or the impossibility of rational justification. 'I suggest that this is the crux of the problem. We shall have to show that justification is not always the same thing as proof.'[20] In a stimulating and lucid discussion, Thorson then goes on to outline a view of what justification does consist in. It is not possible to summarize his argument here: it must be read in full. However, we can point out that his central contention is that there can, after all, be rational justification—including rational justification of democracy—even though this does not consist in proof. (We shall be saying a little more about Thorson's book in a moment.)

Thorson's argument does not, however, really touch the other objection which we also saw as derived from linguistic philosophy. This was the idea that there cannot be justifications which are general— including justifications of democracy as such. However, this objection is surely misconceived. The argument that there can be no one formula which will always yield an acceptable answer to the question 'Ought I to obey this state now?' seems correct. However, it does not follow from this that no general reasons can be given for obeying the state. It is true that, in particular cases, it *can be* that there are individual moral decisions to be made; but these take the form of weighing the general reasons for obeying the state (reasons usually derived from the analyses of traditional political philosophy) against any particular reasons for disobeying the state on the occasion in question.[21] Similarly, with regard to the justification of democracy, there can be general reasons for commending it as a type of system of government while acknowledging that there may be particular reasons why a particular democracy is not to be commended. Thus general justifications of democracy as such can sensibly be proposed.

The difficulties for the justification of democracy which stem from linguistic philosophy can, then, be overcome. But what of scientific value relativism and its implications?

Scientific value relativism can be challenged. One type of challenge is exemplified by Thorson. In *The Logic of Democracy* he uses the argument that scientific analysis is not simply factual, and that it requires theorizing. Such theorizing consists not so much in simplified pictures of the world as it is, as in *recommendations* to look at the world in a certain way. Even the physical sciences are recommendatory in this way. Referring with approval to N. R. Hanson,[22] Thorson says that the great physicists '. . . are seeking to understand physical reality, and in doing so they are above all making recommendations about the way in which the world should be viewed'. For example, 'the physicist recommends that electrons be regarded as absolutely identical. This is not something which can be tested; it is accepted because it helps in understanding physical reality.'[23] Thus, if the 'archetype of science' is recommendatory, there is no reason to suppose that political science is not also recommendatory. Moral recommendations may be of a different kind; nonetheless the great divide between evaluation and scientific analysis is broken down by this argument.

The argument that scientific analysis actually *incorporates* recommendation is to be distinguished from the idea that evaluations merely influence such analysis. Even the doctrine of value freedom now acknowledges this latter idea: the influence of analysts' values is recognized, but it is held that this can and ought to be counteracted by a prefaratory declaration of what these values are.[24] The point is that to accept the influence of value judgements upon academic analysis is not the same as to accept that such analysis can itself play a part in the making of value judgements. As Taylor put this way of looking at the role of values: even if ' "values" steer, as it were, the process of discovery, they do not gain or lose plausibility by it'.[25] In other words, the acknowledgement that values steer analysis does nothing to touch scientific value relativism, whereas the Thorson argument is a direct challenge to it.

Thorson's argument, however, does not take us much beyond the contention that scientific analysis is in part recommendatory. It is true that he gives us an account of how the making of moral judgements is analogous to the recommendatory aspects of scientific analysis—and hence that justification, including the justification of democracy, is a rational process. However, this account is unconvincing. Apart from anything else, it leaves out a crucial component of moral judgements: the expression of approval or disapproval.[26]

What, then, are we left with? Is the thesis of scientific value relativism correct in the important sense that evaluation, of the kind which includes moral evaluation, is beyond the province of academic analysis?

The present writer would insist that this is not the case. Part of the reason for this is the view that not all academic analysis is scientific analysis (in an important sense of that term). And political analysis would be an example of non-scientific analysis. There is not the space to defend this view here; however, the more important part of the rejection of the thesis of scientific value relativism consists in the rejection of the view that moral judgements are arbitrary. (As we saw earlier, scientific value relativism in fact implies more than simply the contention that science is not relevant to the making of ultimate moral judgements.) As we have already seen, the idea of the exclusive concern of 'valid' analysis with facts uninfluenced by values has already largely been dropped. And some have taken this argument further and insisted that values inevitably become incorporated into the whole fabric of the analysis—including the very concepts themselves.[27] Another argument is that there is a need to engage in moral evaluation in order to organize 'factual' analysis properly.[28]

Views such as these are, however, still compatible with scientific value relativism—with the idea that academic analysis is irrelevant to the *choice* of values. But there has also been some challenge to this orthodoxy itself. There is a growing number of analysts who reject the idea that factual analysis can or ought to have no relevance to the making of basic evaluations. One argument is simply that anything more than the most superficial and trivial of factual analyses of politics imply corresponding evaluations.[29] But others have argued that the academic analysis of society can and should specifically concern itself with moral guidance—with the question of deciding which are the values to pursue and to hold.[30] And some never did accept the positivist contention that academic analysis of society should not be concerned with questions such as the form which society ought to take. Leo Strauss, for example, sees social analysis as properly continuing the tradition of classical political philosophy and having as its central concern this kind of question.[31] The present writer would agree that academic political analysis can be relevant to the making of moral judgements—basic as well as instrumental—about political systems. Indeed, it would seem absurd to presume otherwise. Even if a logical gulf between 'is' and 'ought' does exist, this does not imply that 'factual' investigation and analysis are irrelevant to the making of moral judgements. Even if moral judgements cannot be *deduced* from statements of fact, it does not follow that they are in no other way based upon facts. Whatever else they are, moral judgements are surely decisions based upon and related to facts in at least one important sense : the judgements one makes depend upon what is involved in acting upon them. Scientific value relativism is wrong in thinking that this point does not apply to the ultimate moral choices.

Thus, ultimate values are postulated and defended by means of demonstrating what holding them would involve.[32] But this presumes knowledge of what would be involved. And such knowledge is not always easy to come by. Indeed, it may well be that sophisticated analysis is required to obtain it. Thus academic political analysis is not only *relevant* to the evaluation of political systems; it may well be essential—especially since political systems are complex phenomena.

If our rejection of the implications of linguistic analysis and positivism for the nature of justification is accepted, it follows that the justification of democracy is a matter that is open to rational analysis. Indeed, the whole analysis of democracy of the type exemplified in the preceding chapters is relevant here. Our task, however, will be to sketch in some types of justification of democracy that have been put forward rather than to attempt a comprehensive one of our own.

As we have just argued, the general form of these examples of justifications does not consist in attempts at 'proofs', in emotional utterances, or in arbitrarily held principles of advisory guidance. Rather, it consists in argument designed to evoke moral approval by demonstrating and highlighting certain features of democracy. Now, it might be objected that this is simply to dodge central issues. What is to be said, it might be asked, when moral approval is not evoked by such argument? Is not the evocation of moral approval as arbitrary as the expression of emotion? At this point we are entering upon complex and controversial issues of moral philosophy which cannot be dealt with here. All we can do is to suggest that the concept of moral approval differs from (though it may overlap with) that of emotion; and that such approval is generated by the belief that its object contributes in some way to meeting human needs and aspirations (see, for example, Taylor's use of Mrs Foot's arguments, already cited). Obviously, there is a vast area for disagreement and argument regarding what is good, etc., even if an account such as this is correct, and the objective of such argument is to demonstrate a connection with human needs and aspirations. However, this is to acknowledge that it *is* argument and not simply conflicting expressions of emotion or statements of conflicting principles.

If the above argument were anything like correct, justifications of democracy would take the form of attempts to show how democracy meets people's needs and aspirations. This would involve giving an account of democracy and/or some of its features[33] as well as of human needs and aspirations. And, indeed, this is the general form that justifications of democracy have taken, although sometimes the needs and aspirations receive more attention than the nature of democracy, and sometimes it is the other way round. We shall now glance briefly at some of the more important of these justifications.

Justifications of democracy are sometimes divided into those that point to the benefits of the democratic process itself and those that point to the beneficial results of the process. It would seem necessary, however, to have a threefold classification—in order to take account of justifications which do not point to benefits, whether of the results or of the nature of the democratic process, so much as to the consistency of the idea of democracy with basic moral principles. (The distinctions between these categories are, however, very blurred and will only partially organize the discussion that follows.)

This third type of justification might be seen as the type which has been attacked for purporting to take the form of deductive proof. Such justifications need not, however, be seen in this way. It is true that they are argued out in a highly general and abstract way. This consists, however, in exploring the linkages between ideas rather than in attempts at deduction from first principles. This is similar to the kind of reasoning concerning the links between democracy and liberty referred to in the Appendix to Chapter 2 of this book. (Indeed, as we shall see, some would justify democracy by linking it with the preservation or expression of individual liberty). And such explorations of the connections between ideas are not completely insulated from the empirical world—they are not merely exercises in *a priori* reasoning. Some very basic and complex issues are here raised, but the essential point is that, in a sense, this kind of analysis of general ideas involves a testing of their validity. In other words, the extent to which the analysis is acceptable turns—in part, at least—on the extent to which it incorporates a view of reality which can be accepted. And here we are back to our suggestions concerning the nature of moral reasoning : that is to say, suggestions to the effect that making or supporting a moral judgement involves analysis of the nature of the world, and especially of the nature of human aspirations and needs. This 'abstract' type of justification of democracy, then, is not to be ruled out as constituting a defective form of moral argument (which does not deny that particular examples of it may be defective).

A typical form of the 'abstract' type of justification is one which connects democracy with the ideal of equality. As we have already seen (Chapter 1), there is often held to be a strong conceptual link between democracy and equality. This, indeed, illustrates a point already alluded to : some of the features—perhaps the defining features—of democracy itself are often the characteristics that are picked out as being the desirable concomitants of democracy. (It will also be remembered that, in Chapter 1, we saw that the questions about democracy's defining features could become complicated by a failure to distinguish these from the questions about its desirable features. This is not to deny that the same features can be both defining and desirable; rather, it is to point out that they need not be, and that the question 'What are the defining features of democracy?' is different from the question 'What are the desirable features of democracy?')

A justification of democracy in terms of equality has recently been argued in a lucid article in the philosophical journal *The Monist*: 'The Justification of Democracy' by Carl Cohen.[34] Cohen argues that if a community is a community of equals, 'all having an essentially equal stake in its affairs', then 'we are likely to insist upon an equal voice for each in the making of its directive decisions'[35]—that is to say, a democratic decision-making procedure. In order to justify democracy in the state, then, it is necessary to contend that the state is, in an important sense, a community of equals. 'What is the sense of the principle of human equality upon which the justification of democracy in the body politic depends? It is, simply, that beneath all the undeniable differences among men there is in every human being an element, or aspect, or essential quality which justifies our treating him as the equal of every other in the largest sphere of human life.'[36] The point is that the all-inclusive community which is the state or body politic has as its members men as such. The contrast is with 'functional organizations'—for example, trades unions or chess clubs—the purpose of which is only to cater for certain aspects of a man's life; aspects that are determined by the category within which the members fall or the characteristic or activity that they have in common. 'One's membership in his polity has no ground other than that he is a man. The origin and foundation of his membership is—equally with all others— the simple fact that he was born or lives there, just as the others do.'[37]

The contention that men are in an important and basic sense equal is one which Cohen regards as ultimately undemonstrable, although in fact he provides us with persuasive argumentation in its support. In an earlier idiom, this basic equality of man would have been said to be self-evident.[38] The idea of 'self-evidence' can be connected with the idea of natural law (see, for example, the quotation from Bryce below). That is to say, the 'self-evidence' of a proposition can be conceived of as due to the discovery by reason that it is a postulate or natural law. Equality may itself be said to be a postulate of natural law; or the idea of the equality of men may be combined with that of natural law in a justification of democracy—as in the case of J. H. Hallowell's *The Moral Foundations of Democracy*.[39] Ideas such as 'self-evidence' and 'natural law' were—as we have seen—targets for attack by linguistic philosophy. And it does seem that they bring obscurity rather than extra cogency to the justification of democracy in terms of equality. (Hallowell's book is also explicitly attacked by Thorson as exemplifying the purportedly deductive—and thereby defective—form of justification.)[40]

The idea of natural law can be closely connected with that of natural rights. And a justification of democracy in terms of equality can be closely connected with one in terms of natural rights (or 'human rights'). In the latter, the idea is that all men have certain basic rights[41] simply by virtue of the fact that they are all human beings. As in the argument from equality, the focus is upon the 'essential human qualities'—those that are possessed by all human beings and which can be discerned beneath 'all the undeniable differences among men'.

The idea of natural rights often becomes part of a justification of democracy in terms of individual liberty. Thus, according to some conceptions, democracy is a necessary condition for (or, at least, helps to maintain) the existence of individual liberty (see Appendix to Chapter 2). And many would argue that the preservation of individual liberty is one of the highest—if not the supreme—political good : the classic expression of this viewpoint was, of course, John Stuart Mill's essay *On Liberty*. Mill did not argue in terms of natural rights, but there is an important tradition of thought—stemming from Locke and including Paine—in which areas of individual liberty are sanctified as an individual's natural rights. Indeed, liberty itself is frequently posited as a natural right.[42] In this tradition of thought, then, democracy is justified as the system of government which preserves natural rights. It is held that, in a democracy, the people collectively control the government, and will see to it that the government sticks to the task for which it was instituted—the maintenance of individuals' rights. But also, since control by the people is held to involve an equal share of such control by each individual, it can be conceived that each person contributes individually to the securing of the governmental main-tenance of his rights.

Arguments such as these from equality and natural rights are some-times combined. The result can be a rather woolly form of justification of the type attacked by linguistic philosophy—both the form of the argument and the nature of the premises being dismissed as too vague or confused to be what they purport to be. An example is provided by Lord Bryce in a chapter on 'The Theoretical Foundations of Democ-racy'. He gives the following statement of the 'truths' on which democ-racy claims to rest (such a statement is derived from the American Declaration of Independence, 1776, and the Declaration of the Rights of Man made by the National Assembly of France, August 1791) :

... All men are born Equal, with an equal right to the pursuit of happiness. That each man may secure this right and preserve his liberty as a member of a community, he must have an equal share in its government, that government being created and maintained by the consent of the community. Equality is the guarantee of independence.

These axioms, being delivered as self-evident truths, antecedent to and independent of experience, require no proof. They are propounded as parts of the universal Law of Nature, written on men's hearts, and therefore true always and everywhere.[43]

This kind of argument can perhaps be improved by more rigorous phrasing. But it also requires a response to the fact/value problem, and to the difficulties involved in a conception of democracy that equates the power of the people with the autonomy of individuals (see Chapter 2 and its Appendix). Nonetheless, if carefully developed, there is an important justificatory argument in terms of individual liberty : it can reasonably be contended that individuals are less liable to suffer from undesirable actions by the government in a liberal-democracy than they are in other kinds of political system. This is basically because first, the people as a whole are not normally likely to sanction certain kinds of action by the government (such as arrests without trial); and secondly, it can be argued that the absence of certain kinds of action by the government (notably those excluded by the 'freedoms' implied by the idea of 'free elections') is a logically necessary condition for the existence of democracy.

Natural-rights justifications of democracy can lead off in another direction, if it is asserted that everyone has a natural right to govern—or share in the government of—themselves. Here the rationale is not that individuals are protected from government in a democracy, but that they partake in it. The participatory justification of democracy is discussed below, but the notion of a natural right to govern need not be developed into ideas about the virtues of the process of partici-pation : there is another argument here as well; although, as before, the effect of the 'natural rights' terminology may be to obscure it. One might perhaps call this the 'common sense' justification of democracy, and it could be summarized colloquially in the form of a rhetorical question : 'Why on earth shouldn't people govern themselves?' It is true that, put as simply as this, the tricky and important questions about the relationship of the individual to the whole people are obscured. Nonetheless, a carefully formulated argument would still have as its basis the contention that individuals ought themselves to decide what they should do. The argument would seek to show that self-government by the people involved all individuals themselves deciding what they should do[44]—or, at least, that there was an even smaller component of such individual decision-making in any other system of government. (One of the assumptions would be that govern-ment was necessary : without this assumption a justification of anarchy, rather than of democracy, would result.)[45]

Let us now turn to our other two categories of justifications of democracy. In the category referred to in terms of the benefits of the democratic process itself, there is basically one type of argument : that which seeks to demonstrate the virtues of participation. The idea here is that there is value in the very activity of popular participation in the process of government, rather than—or as well as—in the results of such participation (i.e. decisions that reflect the wishes of the people). Originally stemming from a view of the nature of civic life in the ancient Greek *polis*, this idea has, in more modern times, had much to do with Rousseau, and has recently been taken up again in 'new democratic theory'. John Stuart Mill was also an important exponent of this viewpoint.

The virtues of participation are not seen as arising at the individual level only. Individuals are conceived to benefit from participation, but, besides—or interconnected with—this, there are benefits which accrue to the community. Indeed, the two kinds of benefit tend to merge, since an important aspect of both is the role conceived as being played by participation in linking the individual with the community. The basic idea here is that because of his involvement in the governing of the community the individual identifies with it and comes to appreciate the claims of other individuals and of the community as a whole. The neo-Idealist conception of the role of discussion has obvious affinities with this kind of view : appreciation by individuals of the viewpoints of other individuals and of the community as a whole—and the integration of these—was seen as an important part of the purpose of discussion.

In more particular terms the main aspect of the value of participation has been seen as its educative function—educative both in a narrower sense of leading to the acquiring of information, and in a broader sense of developing a responsible and moral personality. Both Rousseau and Mill emphasized this. Other aspects can be summarized as the part held to be played by participation in securing the acceptance by individuals of communal decisions, and the general integration of the collectivity and enhancement of its sense of community.[46]

In one important sense, extolling participation is not the same as justifying democracy as such. Rather, it amounts to justifying one kind of democracy. Indeed, as we have seen, in another model of democracy—that derived from EDT—extensive participation is seen as harmful to, rather than as a desirable feature of, democracy. And, in some contexts today, the justification of liberal-democracy becomes a matter very different from that of extolling participation—it can become, in fact, a matter of challenging the critique of liberal-democracy (or 'bourgeois democracy', as some critics would have it) frequently developed by participatory theorists. However, as a feature of such a critique, advocates of participatory democracy would normally consider that they *were* justifying democracy *as such*. That is to say, they would contend that what they advocated was the only form of system that could properly be called democracy. Aspects of these themes will be touched upon again in Chapter 9.

We come now to the category of arguments for democracy that we called justification in terms of the beneficial results of the democratic process. That is to say, arguments that focus upon the benefits that result from having a democracy, other than the virtues which might be said to inhere in the process of self-government itself.

The key point in some of the most commonly cited of these arguments is that a democracy allows the opinions of the common man to prevail. From the Greeks onwards, one of the reasons traditionally given for regarding this as a good thing is the contention that 'true opinion on political and moral matters is the privilege of the common man. Accordingly, power in a community should reside with him : and this it does only in a democracy. Hence the superiority of democracy.'[47] Variations on this theme have included the idea that 'true opinion' is the possession of a majority of men, even if not of every man, and therefore the majority should rule.[48] If majority rule is taken as synonymous with democracy (which it often, if mistakenly, is), then this becomes an instance of a kind of argument mentioned in Chapter 4 : a justification of majority rule which is at one and the same time a justification of democracy. Another variant is the argument that wisdom is scattered throughout the community, and hence that wise policies can only be obtained by tapping as much of it as possible in the decision-making process. This can only be done (or, at least, it is only practicable to do this) by involving everyone in the decision-making process. A stronger form of this argument is the one developed by Aristotle to the effect that, although each individual may be deficient in the qualities necessary for political decision-making, the people collectively are not deficient in this way—are, indeed, better endowed than any 'experts', since the *combined* qualities of all the individuals add up to a far from deficient totality.[49]

Whether or not such contentions about the 'true opinion' or the wisdom of (many or all) common men are valid is a matter about which there has been dispute down the ages, and it has been one of the main issues dividing those who support democracy from those who do not. And, it will be remembered, this was the issue behind much of the discussion in Chapters 5 and 6. It can be argued that the conclusions reached in Chapter 6 support the pro-democratic contention.

It might be objected that it is one thing to accept that the common man has a certain amount of wisdom—or common sense—but quite another to accept that he has greater wisdom than those who might be specially trained or otherwise specially qualified to rule. Or, to put it another way, it might be said that our conclusions in Chapter 6 support the idea that the common man is not devoid of wisdom, but not that he possesses 'true opinion'. From Plato onwards, a powerful stream of thought has asserted that the common man is insufficiently qualified to rule.[50] But here we must bring in the main argument that has been adduced in support of the view that the opinion of the common man should prevail.

In its 'strongest form', this additional argument is the one especially associated with Utilitarian democratic theory. This is the idea that whether or not common men—or all individuals—are wiser than the select few (or one) in some absolute sense, it is at least the case that each individual knows his own interest better than anyone else. And a specifically Utilitarian justification of democracy builds on this conception to reach the conclusion that a democracy is the best system of government since it secures the greatest happiness of the greatest number. (Individuals achieve happiness by pursuing their interests; democracy is the system of government in which it is assured that the interests of all, or a majority of individuals—'the people'—will be pursued; therefore democracy secures the greatest happiness of the greatest number.) Now, as we have seen before, there are great difficulties that stand in the way of a theory of democracy in terms of self-interest alone. And this greatly complicates—if not entirely frustrates —any attempt at a straightforward Utilitarian justification of democracy. Nonetheless, there is an important core to the argument from the idea of individuals being the best judges of their own interests that survives these difficulties. This is simply the notion that whatever else goes into the making of communal decisions, in the end such decisions are only justifiable if the mass of the people judge their experiences of them to be acceptable. And a democracy provides the means whereby the mass of the people can effectively overturn policies that they find unacceptable.

This type of argument has been stated in terms of a 'shoe-pinching' analogy : only the wearer (the people) knows where the shoe pinches (the effect of governmental policies).[51]

As Lindsay points out, this idea is quite compatible with fairly 'elitist conceptions' (although this is not his terminology) of democracy. The 'expert' could be said to propose and the mass dispose : the shoemaker makes the shoes and the people decide whether to accept them or call for others (and perhaps other shoemakers), according to whether they pinch or not. Stated in this way, this constitutes a powerful argument for democracy.

Another type of argument for democracy to be found in our third category of justifications is to the effect that conflict tends to be minimized in a liberal democracy (if, at least, it is not one that is in the process of breaking down). The argument is that such things as freedom of discussion, freedom of association and the opportunity to attempt to convert people to one's own point of view tend to lessen frustration and thereby to minimize violent conflict. They also facilitate peaceful change. But, above all, the electoral mechanism provides a peaceful solution to one of the key problems of modern political systems : the problem of succession. A significant justification of democracy, then, is that it provides for an orderly succession of rulers.

A further type of justification is that called by Wollheim the completely sceptical argument for democracy :

According to this argument, it is impossible for anyone to discover what is the right course of action for the community, or where the true interests of its inhabitants reside. From this it follows that everyone in the community should be allowed to do what he wants to do as far as is socially possible. The only society in which this can happen is the one in which everyone has some control in the government: therefore Democracy is favored.[52]

A variation of this kind of justification is one to the effect that relativism implies democracy. The argument is that if it is the case that there are no absolute standards of right and wrong, then it follows that all viewpoints are equally valid and ought to have an equal chance to compete and to be adopted as public policy. That is to say, in the absence of absolute standards the only criterion left by which to decide which policy ought to be chosen is popularity : that policy should be adopted which can attract the most votes.

Superficially, this form of justification may seem convincing. However, it is fundamentally misconceived. The absence of absolute standards would not imply the non-existence of moral judgements, as the very judgement asserted by the argument itself shows. Indeed, the whole argument is self-contradictory : a moral judgement asserting that democracy ought to obtain is derived from what amounts to a contention that no moral judgements can be made.[53] And in any case, we have already argued that the idea of the arbitrariness of moral judgements is mistaken.[54]

Another argument in favour of democracy that we should mention is, to an extent, a combination of the previous two. Even if the relativism argument is mistaken, it can still be acknowledged that democracy might be said to cope well with the existence of a diversity of values. Within certain limits, it allows for the expression of, and influence upon policy by, many different viewpoints. In this way, it could be argued, dangerous frustrations are avoided. And here we come back to the justification indicated earlier : the argument that liberal democracy minimizes conflict. If it is presumed that, in modern societies, there is likely to be a substantial diversity of values and

interests—and there is much to support such a view—then a justification could be formulated to the effect that democracy is the only
system of government likely to be viable in modern society. Wollheim
includes another dimension when he writes of the argument that

. . . under modern conditions [democracy] is the only working possibility. No
member of an emancipated industrial society will put up with political tutelage.
He insists on having a fair chance of influencing the government in accordance
with his own desires and ideas; and by a 'fair' chance he means a chance 'as
good as the next man's'. This argument was succinctly summarized in the
nineteenth century by the conservative James Fitzjames Stephen who said
that in Democracy we count heads to avoid breaking them; and it remains
today one of the best arguments in favor of democracy on account of its
extreme economy.[55]

The present writer would simply maintain that it is one of the best
arguments for democracy—quite apart from its possible additional
virtue of economy. And it complements the final justification to be
mentioned. The argument just indicated is of the form : (even) if
democracy has nothing else to commend it, it is at least likely to work.
The justification that it complements adds that democracy is at least
better than other systems of government. This was exemplified in
Winston Churchill's remark in the House of Commons in 1947 that 'It
has been said that democracy is the worst form of government except
all those other forms that have been tried from time to time.'
    The foregoing, then, are some of the main justifications that have
been proposed for democracy—or, more precisely in many cases, for
liberal-democracy. There is a good deal to be said for many of them,
but some stand out—for the present writer at least—as especially
convincing. In particular, we can point to the equality argument (when
carefully developed), the 'shoe-pinching' argument, and the argument
that in Western society democracy is likely to be the only workable
system of government. The individual liberty and the 'why on earth
not' arguments can be converted into convincing justifications provided that some important difficulties are faced and not by-passed or
drastically oversimplified.
    Finally, we should point out that the justifications with which we
have here been concerned have taken the form of justifications of
democracy as against systems of government by the few (oligarchy) or
by one man (autocracy). We have not focused upon the matter of the
justification of liberal-democracy—or, at least, of the kind of liberal
democracy which we have argued Britain and the United States to be
—as against arguments to the effect that it is not sufficiently democratic.
We shall touch on this issue in Chapter 9.[56]

NOTES AND REFERENCES

1 *The Vocabulary of Politics*, p. 9. For a brief introduction to this kind of philosophy, and some of its implications for political philosophy, see W. T. Deininger, *Problems in Social and Political Philosophy*, New York, Macmillan , 1965, Chapter 15: 'Language Analysis and Politics'.

2 See the changes of attitudes manifested in the three introductions to the first three series of *Philosophy, Politics and Society*. The fourth series' introduction suggests a complete reaction against 'Weldonism'.

3 Indeed, the precursor of linguistic analysis was logical positivism—a philosophical movement that was, in a sense, the extreme statement of positivism. For a brief and clear description and assessment of logical positivism, see G. J. Warnock, *English Philosophy since 1900*, London, Oxford University Press, 1958, Chapters 4 and 5.

4 The most extreme example of this is to be found in P. Winch, *The Idea of a Social Science*. This book is a sustained attack on the whole idea that the study of social phenomena is, or can be, a science. It is also, in part, an explicit attack on Weldon's linguistic analysis. This apparent paradox is due to the fact that Weldon sees the analysis of language as quite different from (though liable to be confused with) the analysis of reality; whereas Winch argues that the analysis of language (conceptual analysis) and of reality—at least, social reality—are not separate in this way. According to the type of thinking exemplified by Winch, to analyse the concepts operative within a society *is* to analyse that society. Both Weldon and Winch agree that philosophy consists in linguistic, or conceptual, analysis; what they disagree on—and this is fundamental—is the 'meaning' and significance of such analysis.

5 However, as already indicated, a 'less extreme' form of linguistic philosophy later emerged. One aspect of this was the idea that philosophical analysis had a slightly larger role to play in political analysis. A very good example of this, and one that is specifically concerned with democracy, is R. Wollheim's article already cited 'On the Theory of Democracy'. This article is well worth reading apart from its specific relevance here. (Some of the points Wollheim covers are ones that have been discussed elsewhere in this book.)

6 *The Vocabulary of Politics*, p. 97.

7 It is not universally accepted today that the whole idea of natural law should be dispensed with because it rests upon a confusion between fact and value. See A. Brecht, *Political Theory*, esp. Chapter 4, section 2, and Chapter 8, sections 4 and 5, for the historical background to, and modern thinking about, natural law in relation to various objections and counter-conceptions. For a reinterpretation of natural law that takes cognisance of (indeed, actually utilizes) the approach of linguistic analysis, see H. L. A. Hart, *The Concept of Law*, Oxford, Oxford University Press, 1961, Chapter 9.

8 T. L. Thorson, *The Logic of Democracy*, New York, Holt, Rinehart & Winston, 1962, pp. 43–4. Although in some important ways this is a disappointing book, it does contain an excellent survey and analysis of important aspects of the problem of justification in the modern world of

the linguistic philosopher and the positivist. The views of Weldon, among others, are analysed and assessed. See also the text below.

9 See M. Macdonald, 'The Language of Political Theory', in A. G. N. Flew (ed.), *Logic and Language* (First Series), Oxford, Basil Blackwell, 1955 (reprinted from *Proceedings of the Aristotelian Society*, Vol. 41 (1940–1)). For a general description of the nature and background of this kind of approach, see J. C. Rees, 'The Limitations of Political Theory', in *Political Studies*, Vol. 2 (1954), pp. 242–57.

10 Moral judgements are a special category within the more general one of value judgements. It may well be that discussions of value judgements are sometimes vitiated by a failure to attend to this point and a consequent tendency to treat all value judgements as having the same logic as moral judgements. However, an examination of this complex issue is well outside the scope of this book.

11 Brecht follows Weber in making this dual point about the relationship of scientific analysis to moral evaluation—i.e. that such analysis is relevant in subsidiary ways, but that in the end it is irrelevant. See Brecht, *Political Theory* (1967 edition), pp. xii-xiii, 121ff. and 223ff. For Weber's own statement see his ' "Objectivity" in Social Science and Social Policy', in *Max Weber on the Methodology of the Social Sciences*, edited and translated by E. A. Shils and H. A. Finch. Weber's essay, together with a powerful critique of it by L. Strauss (Chapter 2 of his *Natural Right and History*), is reprinted, with some introductory remarks, in M. Natanson (ed.), *Philosophy of the Social Sciences: A Reader*, New York, Random House, 1963.

12 A good introduction to the modern philosophical background to this issue— and to other aspects of the doctrine of value freedom—is provided by an article by A. Montefiore, 'Fact, Value and Ideology', in Williams and Montefiore (eds.), *British Analytical Philosophy*.

13 See *Political Theory*, pp. 126ff.

14 See, for example, C. Taylor's use of Mrs P. Foot's arguments in his 'Neutrality in Political Science', in Laslett and Runciman (eds.), *Philosophy, Politics and Society* (Third Series).

15 'Natural Right and the Distinction Between Facts and Values', in Natanson (ed.), *The Philosophy of the Social Sciences*, p. 425.

16 See below.

17 The first quotation is from D. Easton, *The Political System*, New York, Knopf, 1971 (first edition, 1953), p. 221. The view of value judgements exemplified by Easton's statement has been called the emotive theory of ethics (associated particularly with A. J. Ayer and C. L. Stevenson), and is still widely accepted by social scientists. The second quotation is a statement of Montefiore's characterizing Hare's conception of value judgements ('Fact, Value and Ideology', art. cit., p. 184), as set out in *The Language of Morals*.

18 *Political Theory*, pp. 262ff.

19 ibid., p. 118.

20 Thorson, *The Logic of Democracy*, p. 32.

21 It is quite possible that there will also be *particular* reasons for obeying the state. And, of course, according to some viewpoints, there are *general* reasons for *not obeying* the state.

22 *Patterns of Discovery: An Inquiry into the Conceptual Foundations of Science*, Cambridge, Cambridge University Press, 1959.

23 Thorson, *The Logic of Democracy*, pp. 108–9.

24 This was an aspect of Weber's view. For a more recent as well as a lucid statement of a similar viewpoint, see Easton, *The Political System* (Easton, however, argues that a 'declaration of values' would have to be lengthy and complex). Taylor, in 'Neutrality in Political Science', art. cit., briefly indicates the nature of this viewpoint.

25 Taylor, 'Neutrality in Political Science', art cit., p. 27.

26 See, for example, A. Montefiore, *A Modern Introduction to Moral Philosophy*, London, Routledge & Kegan Paul, 1958, particularly Chapters 9, 10 and 11.

27 G. Myrdal, *Value in Social Theory*, London, Routledge & Kegan Paul, 1958.

28 This is one of the central arguments in H. Stretton's *The Political Sciences*. This book contains perhaps the most thorough critique of the whole idea of value freedom.

29 Taylor, 'Neutrality in Political Science', art. cit.

30 See, for example, T. S. Simey, *Social Science and Social Purpose*, London, Constable, 1968.

31 See, for example, 'Natural Right and the Distinction Between Facts and Values', art. cit. For a recent discussion of (among other things) Strauss's approach, see T. H. Greene, 'Values and Methodology in Political Science', in *Canadian Journal of Political Science*, Vol. 3, No. 2 (June 1970), pp. 275–98; and B. Cooper, 'Values and the Methodology of Political Science: A Comment', in *Canadian Journal of Political Science*, Vol. 4, No. 1 (March 1971), pp. 119–22.

32 Thus Mill postulates liberty as an ultimate rather than as an instrumental value, and his defence of liberty as an end consists of an analysis of what is involved in the pursuit of such an end. It might be argued that Mill sees liberty as the means to some other end—such as the promotion of individuality. But in this case, the essay *On Liberty* would be viewed as portraying what is involved in the pursuit of individuality. The general point here is that justification consists in displaying a whole moral viewpoint rather than in arguing that the whole viewpoint is derived from one particular value or principle. For a broadly similar argument, see J. R. Pennock, 'Political Philosophy and Political Science', in O. Garceau (ed.), *Political Research and Political Theory*, Cambridge, Mass., Harvard University Press, 1968. See also the references cited therein.

33 Sometimes the concern is with democracy in a general sense, but often it is with a particular model of democracy. In a sense, examples of the latter are not general justifications of democracy as such. However, it must be remembered that proponents of such models usually see them as the only form democracy can properly take.

34 *The Monist*, Vol. 55, No. 1 (January 1971), pp. 1–28. This issue of *The Monist* is devoted to the general topic of 'Foundations of Democracy', and also contains the article referred to in Chapter 4—'On the Justification of Democracy' by N. M. L. Nathan. The article by Cohen has since appeared as a chapter in a book by the same author: *Democracy*, Athens, Georgia, University of Georgia Press, 1971.

35 ibid., p. 8.

36 ibid., p. 12.

37 ibid., p. 18.

38 'We hold these truths to be self-evident, that all men are created equal. . .' —American Declaration of Independence, 1776.

39 Chicago, University of Chicago Press, 1954.

40 Thorson, *The Logic of Democracy*, pp. 44–50.

41 As we have seen, the concept of 'a natural' or 'a human right' poses some difficulties, and such concepts have not infrequently been dismissed as too confused (particularly in respect of failing to distinguish between fact and value); as postulating purely metaphysical qualities; and/or as simply meaningless. However it would seem that the assertion of a natural right can without undue difficulty be understood as an assertion of an entitlement to (do) something, which every human being ought to have, and which ought to be universally recognized, respected and upheld (especially by governments). On concepts of rights, including natural and human rights, see, for example, D. D. Raphael (ed.), *Political Theory and the Rights of Man*, London, Macmillan, 1967; and A. J. Milne, *Freedom and Rights*, London, Allen & Unwin, 1968.

42 'We hold these truths to be self-evident, that all men are created equal, that they are endowed by their Creator, with certain inalienable Rights that among these are Life, Liberty and the pursuit of Happiness . . .'— American Declaration of Independence.

43 J. Bryce, *Modern Democracies*, Vol. I, p. 49.

44 Of course, Rousseau's theory of individual and collective self-government is often a strong influence here. However, it should be realized that 'self-government' is not, in individualist thought, connected into the kind of moral theory associated with the idea of the general will. For the liberal democrat, 'self-government' does not imply a theory of control of the 'lower self' by the 'higher self'. And, partly because of this, liberal thought has a hard time avoiding paradoxes and contradictions.

45 It is worth noting here that there is often a tendency for democratic theory to spill over into anarchism. Anarchism emphasizes individual autonomy like many theories of democracy; but, unlike the latter, it focuses clearly on the tension between individual autonomy and the power of the people as a whole—and, if necessary, rejects the power of the people. (When democrats emphasize the individual at the expense of the people there is, then, an affinity with anarchism.) Anarchism completely rejects the power of the state, even if such power is exercised by the people. Some varieties of anarchism concentrate on small groups—and their autonomy—rather than on individuals. Such versions have some apparent affinities with pluralism, but the closest connections are with varieties of the 'new democratic theory' discussed in Chapter 9. On anarchism, see, for example, G. Woodcock, *Anarchism*, Harmondsworth, Penguin Books, 1963 (first published by The World Publishing Company, Cleveland, Ohio, 1962); and April Carter, *The Political Theory of Anarchism*, London, Routledge & Kegan Paul, 1971 (see, for example, pp. 72–3 for some relationships between anarchism and democracy).

46 See Pateman, *Participation and Democratic Theory*, esp. Chapter 2, for

references to Rousseau and Mill and for a fuller discussion of these themes. Pateman also analyses the connections between the ideas of participation and freedom in Rousseau's thought.

47 Wollheim, 'Democracy', art. cit., p. 240.

48 Of course, this formulation leaves out discussion of the assumption that the majority—or majorities—by which decisions are made, will be the same as the majority possessing 'true opinion'.

49 *The Politics*, III: 11.

50 See, for example, D. Spitz, *Patterns of Anti-Democratic Thought*, New York, Free Press, 1965.

51 This is developed by Lindsay from an argument of Aristotle's. See *The Modern Democratic State*, pp. 269ff.

52 Wollheim, 'Democracy', art. cit., p. 241.

53 As Strauss argued in respect of Weber's scientific value relativism, the contention that the validity of moral judgements cannot be demonstrated in fact amounts to moral nihilism—that is to say, to the view that it is impossible to make judgements to the effect that one thing is better than another ('Natural Right and the Distinction Between Facts and Values', art. cit., p. 425). All that would remain would be the expression of preferences.

54 In Thorson, *The Logic of Democracy*, there is, in effect, a double contra-diction. Thorson ends up with a justification of democracy which is a form of the relativism-implies-democracy argument (see esp. pp. 138–9). But besides the contradiction which is, as we have just seen, involved in this argument, Thorson is contradicting the whole thrust of the argument of the previous part of the book—where he is concerned to show that the non-existence of proof of the validity of moral judgements does not imply relativism; i.e. he is contradicting himself when, despite his earlier arguments, he constructs a justification of democracy from what amounts in effect to an assertion of relativism (p. 139, first paragraph). Having argued that rational justification is possible after all, he ignores this argument at the critical point.

55 Wollheim, 'Democracy', p. 242.

56 Arguments to the effect that the liberal democracies are not sufficiently democratic merge into those to the effect that these so-called 'democracies' are not actually democracies.

CHAPTER 9

The Radical Critique of Liberal-Democracy

In this final chapter we shall refer to some problems and issues that hitherto we have neglected : mainly those involved in, or raised by, a critique of the sorts of accounts of democracy that were discussed in Chapter 6. This is to put the matter very broadly, since not only is there more than one critique, but such critiques are directed at more than one object. Different models of democracy were discussed in Chapter 6; and also it is not just the models that are attacked. Sometimes it is actual 'democratic' political systems (usually that of the United States) that form the object of the attacks;[1] sometimes it is the models of democracy offered by LDT, PDT or EDT as portrayals of such systems, and sometimes it is both. Despite this diversity, however, there is a broad connecting theme. Thus the various critiques could all be characterized as radical analyses of the lack of democracy—whether total or partial—in the orthodox or 'establishment' ideas and structures of Western (especially United States) democracy. It should also be noted here that some see an intermeshing between orthodox democratic theory and orthodox political science—and hence there is sometimes an interpenetration of the critiques of each.[2]

Very broadly speaking, we can divide our references to these analyses into two parts. First, there is the 'negative' aspect : lines of criticism of the orthodox view of Western democracies. Secondly, we have the positive aspect : the ideas for the remodelling of the structure and theory of modern Western democracy.

Many of the arguments under the first heading are linked to a general view of modern Western democracy as being so vast and complex that, as presently organized at least, the ordinary person is unable to relate to the system and to have—or to feel that he has—any influence upon its government. In other words, this is to focus upon some of the factors that led to the rejection of RDT, but to refuse to accept that we simply have to live with them and/or to accept that modern democratic theory has adequately compensated for the loss of

220

RDT. For example, R. J. Pranger has pointed to what he sees as 'the eclipse of citizenship'.[3] He argues that the ordinary citizen does not, and sees that he does not, have the resources to play any part in decision-making in the vast and complex politics of modern democracies —and he refers particularly to the United States. Apathy is thus not part of a healthy democracy, but is a manifestation of the people's lack of power. Decision-making is by the few, and even indirect influence is discounted : '. . . if indirect influence exists, it is so intangible that its effects cannot be precisely measured and Pranger contended that most Americans are actually convinced that voting bears no necessary relationship to many policies formulated in the people's name and affecting everyone'.[4] Such arguments connect up with the factors referred to in Chapter 5 as leading to the downfall of RDT. But there are necessary as well as contingent factors. The simple fact of there being vast numbers of voters makes the influence exerted by any particular individual's vote infinitesimal. As Dahl has so ably pointed out, one of the great problems of 'the Democratic Leviathan' is, indeed, sheer numbers. 'Severe upper limits are set on effective participation in "democratic" decisions by the sheer number of persons involved.' Dahl illustrates the inexorable logic involved and concludes by pointing out that some things are not possible

. . . because the requirements of time exceed the time available in any circumstances. Just as there is quite literally no conceivable way by which every citizen of New York can be guaranteed an opportunity to speak at a meeting where every other citizen also speaks, so there is literally no way by which every citizen of New York or Sweden (let alone the United States) can be guaranteed the right to participate in decisions at every stage of the process.[5]

Besides the refusal to accept that the political sphere as such has been cleansed of the undemocratic aspects of elitist structure, there are also arguments that focus upon the economic structure and its undemocratic ramifications. Traditional arguments about the power of big business and the fundamental importance of the economic arrangements of society are re-emphasized. These vary from Dahl's discussion of 'The Corporate Leviathan'—'the appropriation of public authority by private rulers that is the essence of the giant firm'[6]—to reassertions of Marxist and neo-Marxist critiques of the capitalist state. The latter include both traditional Marxist analyses of the structure of capitalist society—and the associated arguments concerning the undemocratic character of the polity—and Marcuse's 'embourgeoisement' argument : his analysis of the cultural domination and consequent depoliticization of the masses by the ruling class and the affluent society.

Arguments concerning the undemocratic and elitist structure of society are paralleled by denunciations of bureaucracy. Bureaucracy is viewed as undemocratic, and the belief that the organizational imperatives of modern society make the development of large and powerful bureaucracies inevitable is argued to be false.[7]

Other arguments are also used in radical critiques of modern democracy. One of these is that the quality of life in modern democracies has not improved, but deteriorated.[8] The specific aspects focused upon range from pollution and the quality of the physical environment, through the imbalance between the dearth of public goods and excess of private goods,[9] to the dehumanization of the work process and the quality of the cultural environment. Again, the attack is on the whole structure of society with which modern 'democracy' is closely associated —and which, therefore, is conceived to be incapable of being restructured by such a 'democracy'. This line of argument tends to be associated with another, which is more directly related to the general charge that modern 'democracy' is insufficiently democratic. The latter type of argument is based on the contention that the pluralist analysis of democracy is inadequate because it ignores (or fails to show how a system can be democratic in which there exist) permanently 'excluded' or underprivileged minorities.[10] Again, the primary focus is upon America. This is largely due to the problem of the position of the large black minority, but other groups are also frequently regarded as 'excluded minorities'—for example, Mexican-Americans, American Indians and migrant farm workers. Of course, a general principle underlying this line of argument is that democracy requires a measure of equality, and not just of formal political equality. And it is not always just the inequalities suffered by specifiable minorities that is at issue. Indeed, one of the commonest lines of criticism is to the effect that the inequalities in Western 'democracies' are too widespread, and too profound, for it to be said that they are properly democracies. Dahl, for example, considers that the prevailing inequalities of political resources—the resources (including wealth) that are needed to influence people—is one of the most serious faults in Western democracies.[11]

What ideas are generated by critical analyses of the kind we have just been indicating? Or, to put the point another way, what are the positive aspects of these critiques? Although there are a number of sometimes very different ideas, there are also some interconnections and common features. One such feature is, of course, the view that the present structure of society and politics is not a given reality, and that it can change and be changed. (It is important to notice that one of the key differences between a radical critique and a belief in piecemeal reform is a difference of view concerning the nature and extent of change that is possible. The radical believes in change in what the piecemeal reformer would see as basic and permanent features of society and human nature.) As Ricci puts it :

It . . . is a major contention of antipluralist scholars that we cannot accept the present behaviour of men as final proof that they are capable of no better; apathy, on this score, is *not* an indication that limited participation is all men can collectively achieve. To accept only the observable facts virtually pre-determines the conclusion that what is, ought to be, or, as Peter Bachrach put the same proposition in social science language, reliance on 'explanatory theory' alone would lead us 'to accept as unalterable the configuration of society as shaped by impersonal forces'. . . . We must therefore go beyond the evidence [presented by the limited patterns of society that have shaped men] in order to plan in terms of what men *ought* to do, *ought* to want, *ought* to receive, *ought* to pay for.[12]

Positive aspects of the critiques, then, share the view that the kind of reasoning that led to our earlier dismissal of RDT is faulty. This is not to say that there is a movement simply to re-establish RDT, although it is the case that many of the suggested changes and theories have important similarities with, and/or take their inspiration from, RDT. We shall now turn to a brief indication of the nature of some of these proposed changes and theories.

One of the guiding themes behind all the ideas concerning the greater democratization of Western 'democracy' is that of the extension of *participation*.[12] 'Participation' has, indeed, become one of the great rallying-cries of reformers and revolutionaries of all descriptions. Very roughly, we can divide these ideas into two categories—although they obviously merge into one another. First, the suggested changes in the structure of the political system; and, secondly, the theories that parallel such suggestions and which are advocated as replacements for modern (and often, indeed, traditional liberal) democratic theory.

In the first category there are two main types of restructuring that tend to be focused upon. The first of these is a reassertion of the need for some form of industrial democracy. Thus a possible answer to the dehumanization of work and the illegitimate power of big industrial corporations is seen as being provided by the participation of the workers in the running of the industry in which they work. Such participation, it is argued, would give the worker more interest in his work. At the very least, it would lead to an increase in 'job satis-faction';[13] and at best, it would completely alter the worker's view of society and his relationship to it—alienation would be replaced by the feeling that he was helping to shape his own destiny. It is also argued that such participation would bring industry under popular control. Not only is it held to be important in itself that industry should be controlled by someone other than—or, at least, as well as—'the bosses', it is also seen as being of profound importance for the establishment (or re-establishment) of democracy in the political system as a whole. This is the argument of, for example, Bachrach in *The Theory of*

Democratic Elitism (Chapter 7), but it is obviously closely connected with a central element within the socialist tradition of thought. Whatever the larger theoretical perspective, however, the central idea is that the people should gain power within the political system by gaining control—via workers' control—of a key element within (or affecting) that system, viz. the economic power structure. It should be noticed that, as the argument has proceeded, we have moved from workers' 'participation' to workers' 'control'. And, indeed, as Pateman points out, 'participation' as used in the context of industry has rather a wide range of meaning—varying, in effect, from mere 'consultation' to 'full sharing in decision-making'[14] (and this breadth of meaning is not, in fact, confined to the context of industry).

Assessment of the validity of these arguments is difficult. Part of the problem is that such assessment inevitably moves off in the direction of a full-scale discussion of the validity of fundamental theories of society. But, at a more superficial level, one can play around with such empirical evidence as is available. And there is a fascination with Yugoslavia as a real-life example of fairly thorough-going workers' self-management.[15] It should be remembered, however, that, basic to this whole style of thought, is the idea that one must also move beyond the empirical evidence—beyond the given.

The second type of approach to restructuring—and one that has been attracting considerable support of late—can be loosely referred to as the advocacy of 'community politics'.[16] Again, the guiding theme is increased participation, but in this case the basic idea is that an increase in participation should be obtained by means of devolving power to communities small enough to allow something approaching direct democracy.[17] The conceptions are, in a sense, wider than those involved in ideas of industrial democracy (except in so far as the latter are involved with a Marxist analysis of power in society (see below)). It is not restructuring of just one aspect of the polity or society—albeit one that is argued to be of peculiar importance—that is advocated, but a restructuring of whole political systems. And, indeed, it is with this kind of demand for a change in the political system itself that 'a belief in participation' is usually associated : 'participation' or 'participatory democracy' usually has this general implication.[18] There are numerous variations within this general mode of thought, but as just indicated, they share the idea that the political system should be broken down into smaller units. Within these smaller units, democracy, at least on the RDT model—and preferably direct democracy—should be practised. It is also argued that the conventional institutions and structures of modern democracy, such as national representative assemblies and large political parties, should be abolished or that their nature and functions should be drastically changed. The transfer of functions from these national structures to local communities will, it is hoped, 'bring government back to the people'. The nature of the community political units will contribute to this in two ways. First, because of their relative smallness they will overcome the obstacles to participatory democracy constituted by largeness of scale. Secondly, by being based on genuine communities—'neighbourhoods' are much favoured—they will evoke the genuine involvement necessary for a meaningful degree of participation.

In their emphasis on extensive and positive power being exercised by the people—and, indeed, simply in their emphasis on participation—such ideas as these have clear affinities with RDT. In fact, they are often a part of what can, to a significant extent, be regarded as a reassertion of RDT. There is, however, a difference : the explicit attempt to combat those features of society that were factors in the undermining of RDT. And one of the main specific differences flowing from this is the solution to the problem of scale. But the solution involves a crucial difficulty. Anarchism aside,[19] there is not really a demand for complete autonomy for the small communities. There *is* a general recognition of the inevitability of some overall political organization for large-scale modern society. The difficulty, then, is one of combining this with the idea of small political units. The solutions offered vary from loose federal (and usually multi-stage) combinations of political units, to the development of important, but subordinate, roles for the community political organizations within the existing type of national institutional framework. In so far as these solutions involve interplay between 'groups'—the communities—there is a similarity with PDT. But, of course, the difference is in the nature of the 'groups' : not only are the communities necessarily characterized by extensive rank-and-file participation, but they are fully political and multi-functional in contrast to the 'one-dimensional' unifunctional groups mainly focused upon by PDT. And the implications of this with regard to the differences in the kinds of decisions that would emerge from the total national process of interaction are important : the 'self-interest-cannot-generate-communal-decisions' critique of PDT (see Chapter 6) is no longer applicable in the same way.

It is, then, not with PDT but, as already suggested, with RDT that there are basic similarities. And this brings us to our other perspective on the positive aspects of the radical analysis : the kinds of theory with which the proposals for restructuring are associated. In fact there is little in the way of explicit systematic theory. This is in part because there is frequently an opposition to theory. As Cook and Morgan put it :

For several reasons, the advocates of participatory democracy have developed little in the way of systematic theory. For one thing, many of them are hostile to elaborate theorizing at an abstract level, regarding abstractness as one of the chief features of today's 'irrelevant' academic communities. Others fall into the anarchist tradition of asserting that the proper forms and patterns of human interaction cannot be ascertained but will emerge after the old order has been destroyed.[20]

Nonetheless, there is, in a sense, some kind of theory or theories— even if, as Megill says, they are 'implicit in the actions of democratic movements in many countries today'.[21] Much of the substance of such theories has already been indicated in the preceding outline of ideas on structural changes, and it is now just a question of bringing the threads together.

The theories tend to have been associated with the 'New Left', and, in an important sense, they are necessarily 'left wing'. However, there are significant differences in the 'degrees of leftness' involved. Very roughly, in fact, there is a division of theories into Marxist and non-Marxist varieties (although even those that are not explicitly Marxist are often influenced by Marxism). It is the non-Marxist varieties that come closest to being reassertions of RDT. However, even apart from the fact that 'New Radical Democratic Theory' ('NRDT') contains responses to the 'anti-RDT factors' outlined in Chapter 5, there is usually a significant difference—at least of emphasis—between NRDT and RDT. RDT was individualist, whereas NRDT has important collectivist features. Even when it does not come from Marx, the inspiration tends to come from Rousseau as much as from Paine. A manifestation of this is Colin Crouch's view that 'participatory democracy [is seen as an] answer to the problem of maintaining individualism while returning to the warmth of belonging to an intimate community'.[22] Cook and Morgan (whose characterization of Crouch's analysis this is) go on : 'Thus participatory democracy may gratify man's need for community in an age of massive bureaucratic institutions.'[23] This connects up with the whole theme of the need to overcome alienation by a greater identification of the individual with a community. Thus NRDT consists in the application of RDT ideas on the positive role of the people, but with the difference that such a role is conceived of as being performed via popular involvement in small-scale political communities.

The Marxist type of New Democratic Theory is outlined in Megill's *The New Democratic Theory* (which is quite a useful summary, but which is somewhat superficial and doctrinaire rather than profound). Like NRDT, Marxist New Democratic Theory emphasizes the importance of meaningful participation and the importance of community (indeed, as befits the Hegelian roots of Marxism, there is almost an Idealist conception of the importance of community).[24] It differs, of course, from NRDT in that it is explicitly Marxist theory. As such it contains the thoroughgoing Marxist critique of the whole structure of capitalist society, with which it holds modern 'democracy' to be indissolubly connected. And the corollary of this is that 'liberal-democracy' is a sham since economic power, and real political power, is held by the bourgeoisie. It also follows from this that genuine democratization must be (or must, at least, include) democratization of economic structures. Hence the focus is upon industrial democracy :

The extent to which the worker is in control of his working situation is the most essential criterion for determining whether or not a society is democratic. The new democratic theory, by focusing on the working situation rather than on the formal governmental structure, has correctly identified where the problem of establishing democracy lies. Democracy means that the worker has the power to control the decisions which affect him.[25]

But, being a Marxist analysis, there is also another dimension. This is the idea that by understanding and working with historical forces, man can control his own fate.[26] Full democracy entails the government of man by man rather than by a hostile system. Finally, we should note that the New Democratic Theory is held to be the authentic democratic Marxism, rather than the bureaucratic perversion of it that is manifested in the U.S.S.R.[27] The so-called communist régimes that exist today are not democracies. True democracy will only exist in the truly communist society, discerned by Marx as the end of the historical process, in which alienation has actually been overcome.[28] Thus, according to Marxist New Democratic Theory, it would seem that so-called 'people's democracy', as well as so-called 'liberal-democracy', fails to be democratic.

What are we to make of these radical analyses of modern democracy? We shall now indicate the more important directions of argument that arise in answer to this large and complex question. One of these is represented by the argument by Dahl, to which we have already referred. This was to the effect that sheer numbers make impossible the kind of straightforward direct or primary democracy that some radicals advocate. Or, to put the point another way, either the state has to be so small as to be ineffective in coping with modern problems such as pollution, public health, control of economic enterprises, monetary and fiscal policies, poverty, military aggression . . . etc.;[29] or else it is so large that direct participation—of the kind often desired at least—is literally impossible. As Dahl concludes : 'To insist upon primary democracy as the exclusive form of democracy is to condemn "the people" to impotence.'[30] The radical answer to this is, of course, the combination of 'community politics' and the large-scale state. But one of the problems here is that stemming from what Dahl calls the Principle of Affected Interests, which limits the autonomy of small units

*; Valueless ;
my yield...*

and their range of activities because the varying and sometimes widely dispersed interests that are directly affected by the relevant decisions all have to be taken into account.[31] And then there is the problem faced by all federal or quasi-federal systems : that of the division of functions between national and local political units; and the associated difficulty of what often appears as the inexorable growth in the power of the national government—which brings us back to square one with the problem of the remoteness of government from the people.

The Principle of Affected Interests also complicates the advocacy of a system of industrial democracy. However, in this case the idea is, usually, that industry will be organized within the overall framework of the state. Hence, the problem becomes one concerning the organization of the state, and the issue of the democratization of the power structure *within* industry emerges in a relatively 'pure' form (at least, in so far as it can be considered apart from the general socialist and Marxist analyses with which it is often associated[32]). Now, although empirical evidence here is not held to be conclusive, it is relevant. The Yugoslav experience seems to indicate that there are genuine difficulties in the way of attempting to democratize industry. Extensive 'low-level' and partial participation (that which amounts to 'having a say' rather than fully entering into the making of the crucial decisions) is considerably easier to bring about than complete democratization. The main problem is the old one of the lack of expertise of the rank-and-file participant, and the consequent guidance by the professional experts. Nonetheless, Pateman considers these to be difficulties in the way of, rather than conclusive objections to, industrial democracy. After examining the evidence, she concludes that 'the Yugoslav experience gives us no good reason to suppose that the democratization of industrial authority structures is impossible, difficult and complicated though it may be'.[33] Dahl, also, believes in the possibility of some form of industrial democracy, although he is less sanguine about the desire of blue-collar workers to participate; and he recognizes that such 'participation' must include the employment of experts in a key role.[34]

If there is, then, something to be said for at least some approach towards industrial democracy by means of rank-and-file participation, does it not follow that similar ideas with regard to the wider political system itself also have some validity? Or, to put the point another way, if it is possible to come to grips with the problems posed for 'community politics' by the Principle of Affected Interests—and there are, of course, various ways of at least partially overcoming the difficulties[35]—does it not follow that the new radical democracy is feasible? Now, it is true that radical analyses claim that new structures would so alter empirical reality that the kind of evidence concerning the nature of political behaviour with which we were concerned in Chapters

5 and 6 would be irrelevant. However, it is not really possible to dismiss this kind of evidence as totally irrelevant. Nor it is possible to ignore the *increasing* complexity of the technology that comes within the purview of political discussion. It may be true that behaviour would be altered by new structures. But it is also true that, to say anything about the nature of the altered behaviour, one must have *some* idea—which can only be based on present knowledge of human nature—of what that behaviour would be like. And one does not have to be excessively anti-utopian to believe that such alterations in behaviour would not amount to complete transformations of human nature. Thus, our knowledge of how men do behave and think at present is not totally irrelevant. And not only is there all the evidence about the lack of detailed knowledge (and the increasing technological complexity makes knowledge ever more important), but, as Barker points out, there is no evidence of any general demand for more participation.[36]

It is not, however, just the strictly empirical evidence that is at issue here. The 'logic of the situation' also has to be appraised. And one conclusion to be drawn from such appraisal, with which the present writer would agree, is that differences between participation in industry and in politics proper are very significant in this context. There are, of course, important similarities; but the crucial difference is that participation in industry involves an area in which there is already a deep, direct and personal involvement on the part of the participants. This is not to deny that politics or political activity are important, or that the mass of people have no interest in them at all. Of course, there is a real sense in which the most important dimensions of people's existence are determined by politics. And it is for reasons such as this that people do wish to—and in Western democracy do—exercise the final decision-making power. But, to some extent, the 'theorists of apathy' are right. For all the reasons already indicated, most people simply do not have the time, energy and knowledge necessary for a detailed and continuous concern with politics. And it is unreasonable to suppose that they should have. People have to work, and therefore they are necessarily involved in a detailed and personal way with their work situation. But when they are not working they need time for relaxation. It is perfectly reasonable, indeed essential, that they should be able to leave the detailed stuff of politics to those who choose to organize their lives in a different way— provided always that they retain an overall control. There is also, of course, the argument that intensive participation—with all that it would involve in the way of volatile opinion and/or ardent attention to everything—would lead to an undesirable instability. The present writer judges this to be an important argument; but it is a difficult one to introduce here since a part, or at least a concomitant, of much of the new democratic theory—especially the Marxist varieties—is the

Greece 523/2/(?)

idea that the breakdown of presently existing political systems is to be desired. However, apart from challenging the idea that such breakdowns are desirable, we must point out that this is to miss the essential point of the argument—which is that postulated radical *alternatives* to the present type of system would, after all, be undesirable because of the instability generated by the intensive participation.

It does not follow from this that there is nothing to agree with in the participationists' case. It could well be that there should be more provision for small-scale partial participation, for consultation, and for institutionalized means of protest. (It is also arguable that decision-making should be 'opened up' more, and that mass education—on the lines of the Open University—should be further emphasized.) The greater development of neighbourhood councils may be an important way of providing for this greater involvement. The provision of such opportunities for those who wish their voices to be heard, and who wish to be directly involved in some aspects of community work, would allow some measure of direct participation while avoiding the dangers of excessive opportunities for it. And for those who wish to become more fully involved there are, after all, the traditional opportunities— made more meaningful by the organizational support available from mass political parties—to stand for political office. And here it should be remembered that the traditional system of defined governmental functions being performed by those who are appointed and made accountable by popular election provides for a combination of popular and responsible and deliberate decision-making that is structured by certain limitations. It avoids another undesirable feature of directly participatory systems: the constant need for attendance at meetings by those who do not wish to attend, in case undesirable decisions— perhaps contrary to their interests—are made. And the likelihood that there will not be constant attendance by a majority of those concerned means that directly participatory systems run the danger of becoming systems of unrestrained minority government.

A defence of liberal-democracy against the specifically Marxist varieties of New Democratic Theory would lead us too far afield. It would, of course, involve a rebuttal of the whole Marxist analysis of 'bourgeois democracy'. All that we can do here is to point to the conclusions that have already been reached in this book to the effect that the opinions of the mass of the people do affect policy in Western democracy and the electoral process does allow for such further influence as might in fact be desired.[37] To the further argument that the opinions of the mass are only reflections of indoctrination by the ideology of the ruling class—and that therefore they do not express the 'true wishes' of the people—three types of reply could be developed. First, it is exceedingly difficult to show that such an argument is correct

—and the present writer would contend that it is shot through with absurdities. Secondly, even if it is true that the mass of the people's wishes are derived from the ideology of the ruling class, this does not —in an important sense—mean that they are not the people's wishes. To explain the existence of something is not to explain it away. Which leads us to the third type of reply: once it is asserted that it is not necessary to pay attention to people's declared wishes in arriving at a judgement about their real wants, then one has started on—indeed one is half-way down—a slippery slope to the justification of pernicious forms of tyranny.

This brings us back to the notion that was outlined in Chapter 2— that of the single-party state in which the party rather than the people decides what the people's wishes are. But democratic theory containing ideas of this kind is not confined to communist countries. It is also characteristic of much of the democratic theory to be found in the 'Third World'. Such theory is different from that of 'people's democracy', but it does share the idea of the single party divining, expressing and implementing the unified 'general will' of the people. The difference is that, in the case of 'Third World democracy'—or, as C. B. Macpherson calls it, 'non-liberal democracy : the underdeveloped variant'[38]—the entity whose unity is to be expressed (or reinforced) through the 'general will' is a nation rather than a class. As in the contrast with 'people's democracy', the present writer would argue the superiority of liberal-democracy, and for the same sorts of reasons. It must be acknowledged, however, that there are problems posed by the need to develop the economy and to create a reasonably unified nation out of often stubbornly tribal or parochial constituent units. And it can well be argued that one of the implications of this is that there is a need for the creation or maintenance of governmental authority and for political mobilization that does not exist in Western systems, and which demands something other than a political system on the liberal-democratic model.[39] This argument requires very careful scrutiny, but even if it is to be accepted, the conclusion to be drawn from it is not that another kind of democracy is suitable for the 'Third World'—or some of the 'Third World' nations—but that democracy is not (or not yet) suitable. What is called 'Third World democracy' may, in certain circumstances, be necessary,[40] but it is not democracy.

The present writer would argue, then, that the logically necessary conditions of democracy are (or include many of) those features that differentiate liberal from other so-called forms of democracy (indeed, this is one way of arguing the superiority of liberal-democracy). These features are those traditionally held to be of crucial importance and often referred to in terms of freedoms : free elections, freedom of speech, freedom of association, and so on. The key point is that which has been made more than once already : genuine decision-making by the people entails genuine choice, which in turn entails the existence of opportunities for the advocacy and effective presentation of different viewpoints.

Our conclusion, then, must be that a belief in liberal-democracy is thoroughly justified. In particular, all arguments stressing the 'real' views or needs of the masses, but which ignore their declared views, must be rejected. Not only are such arguments extremely dangerous, but they rest upon an astonishing intellectual arrogance : 'We—the "theorists"—know much better than you—the masses—what is good for you.'

The theory and practice of liberal-democracy, it is true, pose many significant difficulties. But, in the course of this book, we have examined many of the more important of these, and have found that they can be surmounted. Thus it can, after all, be confidently reiterated that liberal-democracy is the best form of government.

NOTES AND REFERENCES

1 It is not always the case that such attacks are derived from criteria outside modern democratic theory. As we said in Chapter 6, sometimes the argument is that the reality is undemocratic even according to the criteria supplied by modern democratic theory (although such arguments can sometimes merge into critiques of those criteria themselves).

2 The argument seeks to establish more than that some findings of modern political science—such as those relating to voting behaviour—suggest or support modern theories of democracy. See, for example, H. S. Kariel, *The Decline of American Pluralism*, Stanford, California, Stanford University Press, 1961, Chapter 9 (reprinted as 'The Pluralist Norm', in Kariel (ed.), *Frontiers of Democratic Theory*). Kariel's contention is that modern social science gives a bogus validity—and therefore moral worth (despite its alleged value freedom)—to the pluralist model that is implied or revealed by its 'scientific' analysis.

3 *The Eclipse of Citizenship : Power and Participation in Contemporary Politics*, New York, Holt, Rinehart & Winston, 1968. Pranger's views are outlined in Ricci, *Community Power and Democratic Theory*, which, more generally, contains a convenient summary of some of the main lines of argument within this general viewpoint.

4 Ricci, *Community Power and Democratic Theory*, p. 186.

5 R. A. Dahl, *After the Revolution?*, New Haven and London, Yale University Press, 1970, pp. 143 and 145. Dahl uses this as an argument *against* 'radical solutions' such as a return to primary democracy (pp. 146–7). The book gives a sympathetic account of many of the problems that have provoked radical analyses, but it also deflates some of the more absurd radical responses with common sense and some brisk and lucid reasoning. *After the Revolution?* is, indeed, a superb little book and should be read by everyone with any interest in this whole area of discussion.

6 ibid., p. 115.

7 See, for example, A. W. Gouldner, 'Metaphysical Pathos and the Theory of Bureaucracy', in *American Political Science Review*, Vol. 49 (1955), pp. 496–507 (reprinted in *Frontiers of Democratic Theory* as 'The Denial of Options'); and Chapter 7 of Megill, *The New Democratic Theory*: 'What is to be Done with Bureaucrats?'

8 In *Usual Politics* (New York, Holt, Rinehart & Winston, 1970) George D. Beam argues against what he calls 'usual politics', which 'defines the good society by its procedures rather than by its attainment of certain goals or values' (p. v).

9 J. K. Galbraith, *The Affluent Society*, Boston, Houghton Mifflin, 1958; Ricci, *Community Power and Democratic Theory*, pp. 191–3.

10 See, for example, Ricci, *Community Power and Democratic Theory*, pp. 188–90.

11 Dahl, *After the Revolution?*, pp. 105ff. and *passim*.

12 Ricci, *Community Power and Democratic Theory*, pp. 210–11. The quotation from Bachrach is from *The Theory of Democratic Elitism*, p. 99. Bachrach advances a critique as well as an outline of EDT.

12a For a comprehensive and recent discussion of participation, see G. Parry (ed.), *Participation in Politics*, Manchester, Manchester University Press, 1972.

13 In *Participation and Democratic Theory*, Carole Pateman reviews the empirical evidence concerning the effects of participation upon workers.

14 ibid., pp. 67ff.

15 On the Yugoslav system, see ibid., Chapter 5; and, for example, J. Kolaja, *Workers' Councils. The Yugoslav Experience*, New York, Praeger, 1966. On this, and other aspects of worker's control, see also Cook and Morgan (eds.), *Participatory Democracy*, Chapter 6.

16 For a recent discussion of some of the themes involved, see *Government and Opposition*, Vol. 7, No. 2 (Spring 1972): J. Grimond, 'Community Politics', pp. 135–44; G. Parry, 'The Revolt against "Normal Politics": a Comment on Mr Grimond's Paper', pp. 145–52; A. Barker, ' "Communities" and "Normal Politics": a Further Comment,' pp. 153–65.

17 This kind of idea shades off into a belief simply in greater participation in the political system more or less as it stands—piecemeal reform (such as the introduction or greater use of referenda) rather than basic restructuring.

18 This is the substance of Anthony Wedgwood Benn's belief in participatory democracy. It also forms the main theme in Cook and Morgan's *Participatory Democracy* (although the comprehensive collection of readings contained in this book covers other topics as well).

19 See Chapter 8, n. 45, for a reference to the relationship of anarchism to democratic theory.

20 Cook and Morgan, *Participatory Democracy*, p. 21. The authors then go on to 'focus on the elements that would be critical in the formulation of a sound theory of participatory democracy' (pp. 22ff.).

21 Megill, *The New Democratic Theory*, p. ix. Megill goes on to remark: 'As Marx once said of another process, "They do not know it, but they *do it*." '

22 Cook and Morgan, *Participatory Democracy*, p. 10. The reference is to Crouch's 'The Chiliastic Urge', in *Survey*, No. 69 (October 1968), p. 57. He is here referring to New Left views.

32 Cook and Morgan, *Participatory Democracy*, p. 10.

24 See, for example, Megill, *The New Democratic Theory*, p. 101.

25 ibid.

26 ibid., p. 58.

27 ibid., Chapter 3.

28 ibid., p. 132.

29 Dahl, *After the Revolution?*, p. 86.

30 ibid., p. 88.

31 ibid., pp. 64 and 160.

32 It should be remembered that the connections are with 'guild socialism' as well as with Marxism. On guild socialism in general, see, for example, S. T. Glass, *The Responsible Society: The Ideas of Guild Socialism*, London, Longmans, 1966; and on G. D. H. Cole's theory of participation in particular, see Pateman, *Participation and Democratic Theory*, Chapter 2.

33 Pateman, *Participation and Democratic Theory*, p. 102.

34 Dahl, *After the Revolution?*, pp. 130ff.

35 For Dahl's discussion of this, see ibid., pp. 88–103.

36 ' "Communities" and "Normal Politics": a Further Comment', art. cit., p. 158.

37 And if mass opinions are influencing—and, in the final instance, controlling—the actions of the state, then it cannot be said that the economic structure, or the ruling class, are determining those actions.

38 *The Real World of Democracy*, Chapter 3. On Third World conceptions of democracy, see also, for example, R. Niebuhr and P. E. Sigmund, *The Democratic Experience*, and P. E. Sigmund (ed.), *The Ideologies of the Developing Nations*, New York and London, Praeger, 1963.

39 For a development of the argument that it is mistaken to apply the liberal-democratic model to the developing nations, see, for example, J. P. Nettl, *Political Mobilisation*.

40 This is not to deny the validity of the arguments of Chapter 8 to the effect that democracy is the best system of government; rather, it is to accept the argument that conditions are not always such as to make desirable that which is best. cf. J. S. Mill's argument that while representative government is the ideally best form of government, it is not always applicable (it is to the form rather than the substance of the argument that reference is here being made).

Index

Pressure groups, x, 129, 130, 131, 159, 163, 165, 166; seen as threat to democracy, 133–6; and pressure-group theory of democracy, 161–2

Presthus, Robert, 140

Price, Richard, 52, 70

Principle of affected interests, Dahl's concept of, 227–8

Proletariat, 25 n, 43, 44, 62 n

Proportional representation, 83, 86, 129, 189

Prothro, J. W., 191

Quality of life, in modern democracies, 222

Radical democratic theory (RDT), 35, 40–41, 66, 68, 69, 70–71, 72, 74 m, 76 m, 77, 83, 86–8, 100, 127–30, 132, 133, 134, 135, 136 m, 137, 138, 139–40, 141, 145, 146, 154, 163, 164, 167, 171–2, 173, 185, 220, 221, 223, 224, 225, 226; see also New radical democratic theory

Rank-order method, of voting, 111

Rationality, assumption of in traditional theory, 85–8, 95–6 n; and problems of in reality, 143–5, 170; and rational justification for democracy, 202, 205

RDT, see Radical democratic theory

Realities, political, v. application of democratic theory, viii, 127, 128, 139–40, 143–4, 171, 185; see also Empirical democratic theory

Reflections on the Revolution in France (Burke), 70

Relativism, 213, 219 n

Representation, theories of, 30–34, 45, 72–3, 74, 81–3, 85, 178 n; and role of representatives, 72, 76–7, 78–81, 130–31

Representative democracy, see Indirect democracy

Representative Government (J. S. Mill), 75

Revolt, ultimate right to, 67–8

Ricci, D. M., 222

Rights of Man (Paine), 61 n, 76

Riker, W. H., 109

Robespierre, Maximilian, 45, 63 n

Rose, R., 143

Rousseau, Jean-Jacques, 28, 29, 32, 37, 38, 40, 41, 42, 44, 45, 47, 48, 49, 54, 55, 56 n, 59 n, 61 n, 63 n, 70, 71, 88, 90, 93 n, 116, 119 n, 127, 128, 129, 135, 165, 210, 218 n, 226

Rousseauist theory, see Rousseau

Sartori, G., 27, 140, 155, 156, 167

Scientific value relativism, in political theory, 198, 200–201, 202, 203, 204, 219 n

Schattschneider, E. E., 6

Schumpeter, Joseph, 14, 15, 128, 157

Second Treatise on Government (Locke), 67, 127

Self-interest, see Utilitarianism

Self-government, by the people, idea of, 209, 211; see also Direct democracy

Seliger, M., 68

Shils, Edward, 189

'Shoe-pinching' argument, 91, 212, 214

Sigmund, P. E., 192

Single-party government, see People's democracy

Smith, Adam, 84

Social choice, theory of, 109, 110

Social Choice and Individual Values (Arrow), 109

'Social contract', idea of, 39, 60 n

Social democracy, 19–20, 47

Socio-economic factors in democracy, 191–2; and dubious 'scientific' value of social science, 215 n

Socrates, 145

Sovereignty, idea of, 10, 11; of the people, 67; and 'popular', 68

Stalin, Joseph, 44, 62 n, 63 n

State, complexity of the modern, 129, 136, 156, 160, 164, 171, 220, 221

State and Revolution (Lenin), 43

Strauss, Leo, 200, 204

Talmon, J. L., 54

Tawney, R. H., 175 n

Taylor, C., 203

Nelson's Political Science Library

Nelson's Political Science Library is under the general editorship of **Dr K. W. Watkins** of the Department of Political Theory and Institutions at Sheffield University.

MAURICE DUVERGER
Party Politics and Pressure Groups

MAURICE DUVERGER
The Study of Politics

BARRY HOLDEN
The Nature of Democracy

L. J. MACFARLANE
Modern Political Theory

L. J. MACFARLANE
Violence and the State

MICHAEL RUSH
The Selection of Parliamentary Candidates

MICHAEL RUSH AND PHILLIP ALTHOFF
An Introduction to Political Sociology

JOHN W. SPANIER
American Foreign Policy Since World War II

JOHN W. SPANIER
Games Nations Play : Analyzing International Politics

W. THORNHILL
The Nationalized Industries